LOW FAT
Baking

LOW FAT
Baking

CAROLE HANDSLIP

Photography by Amanda Heywood

southwater

This edition is published by Southwater

Distributed in the UK by
The Manning Partnership
251–253 London Road East
Batheaston
Bath BA1 7RL
UK
tel. (0044) 01225 852 727
fax. (0044) 01225 852 852

Distributed in the USA by
Ottenheimer Publishing
5 Park Center Court
Suite 300
Owing Mills MD 2117-5001
USA
tel. (001) 410 902 9100
fax. (001) 410 902 7210

Distributed in Australia by
Sandstone Publishing
Unit 1, 360 Norton Street
Leichhardt
New South Wales 2040
Australia
tel. (0061) 2 9560 7888
fax. (0061) 2 9560 7488

Distributed in New Zealand by
Five Mile Press NZ
PO Box 33-1071
Takapuna
Auckland 9
New Zealand
tel. (0064) 9 4444 144
fax. (0064) 9 4444 518

Southwater is an imprint of Anness Publishing Limited
© 1996, 2000 Anness Publishing Limited

1 3 5 7 9 10 8 6 4 2

Publisher: Joanna Lorenz
Senior Cookery Editor: Linda Fraser
Assistant Editor: Emma Brown
Designer: Alan Marshall
Photographer: Amanda Heywood

Previously published as *Step-by-step Low Fat Baking*

Printed and bound in China

For all recipes, quantities are given in both metric and imperial
measures, and, where appropriate, measures are also given in standard
cups and spoons. Follow one set, but not a mixture, because they are
not interchangeable.

CONTENTS

INTRODUCTION

It is generally agreed that a high fat diet is bad for us, especially if the fats are of the saturated variety. Unless you are making meringues or angel cakes, it is rarely possible to do entirely without fat in baking. However, it is possible to cut down considerably on the amount used and equally good results can be achieved using unsaturated oils instead of saturated fats.

Polyunsaturated oils such as sunflower oil, corn oil and safflower oil are excellent for most baking purposes, but choose olive oil, which is mono-unsaturated, for recipes that require a good, strong flavour. When an oil is not suitable, a soft margarine which is high in polyunsaturates is the fat to choose. Low fat spreads are ideal for spreading but not good for baking as they contain a high proportion of water.

Although cheese is high in saturated fat, its flavour makes it invaluable in many recipes. Choose either reduced-fat or half-fat varieties with a mature flavour, or much less of a highly flavoured cheese such as Parmesan. When using less fat you can add extra moisture to cakes and teabreads in the form of fresh or dried fruits. There is no need to use full cream milk – try skimmed milk or fruit juice instead. Buttermilk (the liquid left over from churning butter) is, surprisingly, virtually fat free and is perfect for soda bread and scones. Cream undoubtedly adds a touch of luxury to special occasion cakes, however, fromage frais, thick yogurt or curd cheese sweetened with honey make delicious, low fat fillings and toppings for even the most elaborate cakes.

So you will see that using less fat doesn't prevent you from making scrumptious cakes and bakes that look and taste every bit as good as those made traditionally with butter and cream. The recipes in this book are sure to inspire, impress and amaze everyone who believed low fat baking to be an idea too good to be true.

Store Cupboard

Many of the most useful and important baking ingredients are found in the store cupboard. The following guide highlights a few of the most essential items.

FLOURS

Mass-produced, highly refined flours are fine for most baking purposes, but for the very best results choose organic stone-ground flours because they will add flavour as well as texture to your baking.

Strong flour

Made from hard wheat which contains a high proportion of gluten, this flour is the one to use for bread-making.

Soft flour

This flour, sometimes called sponge flour, contains less gluten than plain flour and is ideal for light cakes and biscuits.

Wholemeal flour

Because this flour contains the complete wheat kernel, it gives a coarser texture and a good wholesome flavour to bread.

Rye flour

This dark-coloured flour has a low gluten content and gives a dense loaf with a good flavour. It is best mixed with strong wheat flour to give a lighter loaf.

NUTS

Most nuts are low in saturated fats and high in polyunsaturated fats. Use them sparingly as their total fat content is high.

HERBS AND SPICES

Chopped fresh herbs add a great deal of interest to baking. They add flavour to breads, scones and soda breads. In the absence of fresh herbs, dried herbs can be used: less is needed but the flavour is generally not as good.

Spices can add either strong or subtle flavours depending on the amount and variety used. Ground cinnamon, nutmeg and mixed spice are most useful for baking, but more exotic spices, such as saffron or cardomom, can also be used to great effect.

SWEETENERS

Unrefined sugars

Most baking recipes call for sugar; choose unrefined sugar, rather than refined sugars, as they have more flavour and contain some minerals.

Honey

Good honey has a strong flavour so you can use rather less of it than the equivalent amount of sugar. It also contains traces of minerals and vitamins.

Malt extract

This is a sugary by-product of barley. It has a strong flavour and is good to use in bread, cakes and teabreads as it adds a moistness of its own.

Molasses

This is the residue left after the first stage of refining sugar cane. It has a strong, smoky and slightly bitter taste which gives a good flavour to bakes and cakes. Black treacle can often be used as a substitute for molasses.

Fruit juice

Concentrated fruit juices are very useful for baking. They have no added sweeteners or preservatives and can be diluted as required. Use them in their concentrated form for baking or for sweetening fillings.

Pear and apple spread

This is a very concentrated fruit juice with no added sugar. It has a sweet-sour taste and can be used as a spread or blended with a little fruit juice and added to baking recipes as a sweetener.

Dried fruits

These are a traditional addition to cakes and teabreads and there is a very wide range available, including more unusual varieties such as peach, pineapple, banana, mango and pawpaw. The natural sugars add sweetness to baked goods and keep them moist, making it possible to use less fat.

cracked wheat *olives* *flour*

bottled apricots

dried pineapple *dried yeast*

eggs

light muscovado sugar

currants poppy seeds honey herbs

fresh fruit oatmeal cinnamon sticks dried apricots sesame seeds

chestnuts physalis linseed

raisins glacé cherries sunflower seeds olive oil pear and apple spread apricot compôte dates

garlic extra virgin olive oil fresh fruit red onions

rolled oats orange juice semolina

Oils, Fats and Dairy Produce

OILS AND FATS

Low fat spreads are ideal for spreading on breads and teabreads, but are unfortunately not suitable for baking because they have a high water content.

When you are baking, try to avoid saturated fats such as butter and hard margarine and use oils high in polyunsaturates such as sunflower, corn or safflower oil. When margarine is essential, choose a variety which is high in polyunsaturates.

Reduced-fat butter

This contains about 40% fat; the rest is water and milk solids emulsified together. It is not suitable for baking.

Low fat spread, rich buttermilk blend

Made with a high proportion of buttermilk, which is naturally low in fat. Unsuitable for baking.

Sunflower light

Not suitable for baking as it contains only 40% fat, plus emulsified water and milk solids.

Olive oil reduced-fat spread

Based on olive oil, this spread has a better flavour than some other low fat spreads, but is not suitable for baking.

Very low fat spread

Contains only 20–30% fat and so is not suitable for baking.

Olive oil

Use this mono-unsaturated oil when a recipe requires a good strong flavour. It is best to use extra virgin olive oil.

Sunflower oil

High in polyunsaturates, this is the oil used most frequently in this book as it has a pleasant but not too dominant flavour.

LOW FAT CHEESES

There are a lot of low fat cheeses that can be used in baking. Generally, harder cheeses have a higher fat content than soft cheeses. Choose mature cheese whenever possible as you need less of it to give a good flavour.

Cottage cheese

A low fat soft cheese which is also available in a half-fat form.

Quark

Made from fermented skimmed milk, this soft, white cheese is virtually free of fat.

Curd cheese

This is a low fat soft cheese made with either skimmed or semi-skimmed milk and can be used instead of cream cheese.

Feta cheese

This is a medium fat cheese with a firm, crumbly texture. It has a slightly sour, salty flavour which can range from bland to strong.

olive oil · sunflower oil · buttermilk blend · sunflower light · very low fat spread · olive oil reduced-fat spread · reduced-fat butter

cottage cheese · curd cheese · Mozzarella · Edam · feta · Maasdam · Cheddar · Red Leicester · soft cheese · quark

Mozzarella light
This is a medium-fat version of an Italian soft cheese.

Edam and Maasdam
Two medium fat hard cheeses well suited to baking.

Half-fat Cheddar and Red Leicester
These contain about 14% fat.

CREAM ALTERNATIVES
Yogurt and fromage frais make excellent alternatives to cream, and when combined with honey, liqueurs or other flavourings they make delicious fillings or toppings for cakes and bakes.

Fromage frais
This is a fresh soft cheese available in two grades: virtually fat free (0.4% fat), and a more creamy variety (7.9% fat).

Crème fraîche
This thick soured cream has a mild, lemony taste. Look out for half-fat crème fraîche which has a fat content of 15%.

Yogurt
Natural and flavoured yogurts can be used in place of cream. Low fat yogurt has a fat content of about 1%.

Bio yogurt
This contains bacterial cultures that aid digestion. Bio yogurt has a mild, sweet taste.

Greek yogurt
This thick, creamy yogurt is made from whole milk with a fat content of 10%. A low fat version is also available.

semi-skimmed milk

buttermilk

low fat yogurt

half-fat crème fraîche

bio yogurt

light fromage frais

eggs

LOW FAT MILKS

Skimmed milk
This milk has had virtually all fat removed leaving 0.1–0.3%. It is ideal for those wishing to cut down their fat intake.

Semi-skimmed milk
With a fat content of only 1.5–1.8%, this milk tastes less rich than full-cream milk. It is favoured by many people for everyday use for precisely this reason.

Powdered skimmed milk
A useful, low fat standby.

Buttermilk
Made from skimmed milk with a bacterial culture added, it is very low in fat.

Equipment

Baking sheet
Choose a large, heavy baking sheet that will not warp at high temperatures.

Balloon whisk
Perfect for whisking egg whites and incorporating air into other light mixtures.

Box grater
This multi-purpose grater can be used for citrus rind, fruit and vegetables, and cheese.

Brown paper
Used for wrapping around the outside of cake tins to protect the cake mixture from the full heat of the oven.

Cake tester
A simple implement which, when inserted into a cooked cake, will come out clean if the cake is ready.

Cook's knife
This has a heavy, wide blade and is ideal for chopping.

Deep round cake tin
This deep tin is ideal for baking fruit cakes.

Electric whisk
Ideal for creaming cake mixtures, whipping cream and whisking egg whites.

Honey twirl
For spooning honey without making a mess!

Juicer
Made from porcelain, glass or plastic – used for squeezing the juice from citrus fruits.

Loaf tin
Available in various sizes and used for making loaf-shaped breads and teabreads.

Measuring jug
Essential for measuring any kind of liquid accurately.

Measuring spoons
Standard measuring spoons are essential for measuring small quantities of ingredients.

Metal spoons
Large metal spoons are perfect for folding as they minimize the amount of air that escapes.

Mixing bowls
A set of different sized bowls is essential in any kitchen for whisking, mixing and so on.

Muffin tin
Shaped into individual cups, this tin is much simpler to use than individual paper cases. It can also be used for baking small pies and tarts.

Non-stick baking paper
For lining tins and baking sheets to ensure cakes, meringues and biscuits do not stick.

Nutmeg grater
This miniature grater is used for grating whole nutmegs.

Nylon sieve
Suitable for most baking purposes, and particularly for sieving foods which react adversely with metal.

Palette knife
This implement is needed for loosening pies, tarts and breads from baking sheets and for smoothing icing over cakes.

Pastry brush
Useful for brushing excess flour from pastry and brushing glazes over pastries, breads and tarts.

Pastry cutters
A variety of shapes and sizes of cutter are useful when stamping out pastry, biscuits and scones.

Rectangular cake tin
For making tray bakes and cakes, served cut into slices.

Ring mould
Perfect for making angel cakes and other ring-shaped cakes.

Sandwich cake tin
Ideal for sponge cakes; make sure you have two of them!

Scissors
Vital for cutting paper and snipping doughs and pastry.

Square cake tin
Used for making square cakes or cakes served cut into squares.

Swiss roll tin
This shallow tin is designed especially for Swiss rolls.

Vegetable knife
A useful knife for preparing the fruit and vegetables which you may add to your bakes.

Wire rack
Ideal for cooling cakes and bakes, allowing circulation of air to prevent sogginess.

Wire sieve
A large wire sieve is ideal for most baking purposes.

Wooden spoon
Essential for mixing ingredients and creaming mixtures.

rectangular cake tin

square cake tin

loaf tin

baking sheet

balloon whisk

large metal spoon

wooden spoon

electric whisk

mixing bowls

parchment paper

brown paper

scissors

spongecake pan

ring mold

pastry brush

measuring cup

cake tester

wire rack

deep round cake pan

pastry cutters

vegetable knife

honey twirl

wire rack

juicer

jelly roll tin

wire mesh strainer

nutmeg grater

cook's knife

spatulas

box grater

nylon sifter

measuring spoons

muffin pan

Facts about Fats

Most of us eat far more fat every day than the 10 g/¼ oz that our bodies need; on average we each consume about 115 g/4 oz fat each day.

Current nutritional advice isn't quite that strict on fat intake though, and it suggests that we should limit our daily intake to no more than 30% of total calories. In real terms, this means that for an average intake of 2,000 calories a day, 30% of energy would come from about 600 calories. Since each gram of fat provides 9 calories, your total daily intake should be no more than 67 g fat.

It's easy to cut down on obvious sources of fat such as butter, margarine, cream, whole milk and high fat cheeses, but watch out for "hidden" fats. Although we may think of cakes and biscuits as sweet foods, more calories come from their fat than from their sugar. Indeed, of the quarter of our fat intake that comes from non-meat sources, a fifth comes from dairy products and margarine and the rest from cakes, biscuits, pastries and other foods. The merits of low fat baking are enormous, as you are able not only to cut down on your fat intake in general, but you also

have control over exactly how much fat you and your family consume and the type of fat it is.

Fats can be divided into two main categories – saturated and unsaturated. We are all well aware of the dangers of saturated fats in relation to blocking arteries and causing coronary heart disease. Much of the saturated fat we eat comes from animal sources – meat and dairy products such as suet, lard and butter – which are solid at room temperature. However, there are also some saturated fats of vegetable origin, notably coconut and palm oils. In addition, a number of margarines are "hydrogenated", a process which increases the proportion of saturated fat they contain. Such margarines should be avoided.

Unsaturated fats can be divided into two main types: mono-unsaturated and polyunsaturated. Mono-unsaturated fats are found in various foods including olive oil, rapeseed oil and some nuts. These fats may actually help

lower blood cholesterol and this could explain why in Mediterranean countries, where olive oil is widely consumed, there is such a low incidence of heart disease.

The most familiar poly-unsaturated fats are of vegetable or plant origin and include sunflower oil, corn oil, soya oil, walnut oil and many soft margarines. It was believed at one time that it was beneficial to switch to polyunsaturated fats as they may also help lower cholesterol. Today, however, most experts believe that it is more important to reduce the total intake of all kinds of fat.

Above: *Animal products such as lard, suet, butter and some margarines are major sources of saturated fats.*

Left: *Some oils, such as olive and rapeseed, are thought to help lower blood cholesterol.*

Right: *Vegetable and plant oils and some margarines are high in polyunsaturated fat.*

The Fat and Calorie Contents of Food

This chart shows the weight of fat and the energy content of 115 g/4 oz of various foods.

FRUIT AND NUTS	Fat	Energy
Apples, eating	0.1 g	47 Kcals/197 kJ
Avocados	19.5 g	190 Kcals/795 kJ
Bananas	0.3 g	95 Kcals/397 kJ
Dried mixed fruit	1.6 g	227 Kcals/950 kJ
Grapefruit	0.1 g	30 Kcals/125 kJ
Oranges	0.1 g	37 Kcals/155 kJ
Peaches	0.1 g	33 Kcals/138 kJ
Almonds	55.8 g	612 Kcals/2560 kJ
Brazil nuts	68.2 g	682 Kcals/2853 kJ
Peanut butter, smooth	53.7 g	623 Kcals/2606 kJ
Pine nuts	68.6 g	688 Kcals/2878 kJ

DAIRY PRODUCE, FATS AND OILS	Fat	Energy
Cream, double	48.0 g	449 Kcals/1897 kJ
Cream, single	19.1 g	198 Kcals/828 kJ
Cream, whipping	39.3 g	373 Kcals/1560 kJ
Milk, skimmed	0.1 g	33 Kcals/130 kJ
Milk, whole	3.9 g	66 Kcals/276 kJ
Cheddar cheese	34.4 g	412 Kcals/1724 kJ
Cheddar-type, reduced-fat	15.0 g	261 Kcals/1092 kJ
Cream cheese	47.4 g	439 Kcals/1837 kJ
Brie	26.9 g	319 Kcals/1335kJ
Edam cheese	25.4 g	333 Kcals/1393 kJ
Feta cheese	20.2 g	250 Kcals/1046 kJ
Parmesan cheese	32.7 g	452 Kcals/1891 kJ
Greek yogurt	9.1 g	115 Kcals/481 kJ
Low fat yogurt, natural	0.8 g	56 Kcals/234 kJ
Butter	81.7 g	737 Kcals/308 kJ
Lard	99.0 g	891 Kcals/3730 kJ
Low fat spread	40.5 g	390 Kcals/1632 kJ
Margarine	81.6 g	739 Kcals/3092 kJ
Coconut oil	99.9 g	899 Kcals/3761 kJ
Corn oil	99.9 g	899 Kcals/3761 kJ
Olive oil	99.9 g	899 Kcals/3761 kJ
Safflower oil	99.9 g	899 Kcals/3761 kJ
Eggs (2, size 4)	10.9 g	147 Kcals/615 kJ
Egg white	Trace	36 Kcals/150 kJ
Egg yolk	30.5 g	339 Kcals/1418 kJ

OTHER FOODS	Fat	Energy
Sugar	0	94 Kcals/648 kJ
Chocolate, milk	30.3 g	529 Kcals/2213 kJ
Honey	0	88 Kcals/1205 kJ
Jam	0	61 Kcals/1092 kJ
Marmalade	0	61 Kcals/1092 kJ
Lemon curd	5.1 g	283 Kcals/1184 kJ

Using Yeast

There are three main types of yeast currently available – dried, easy-blend and fresh. Easy-blend is added directly to the dry ingredients, whereas dried and fresh yeast must first be mixed with warm liquid and a little sugar to activate them.

USING DRIED YEAST

1 Measure dried yeast, then sprinkle it into the warm liquid in a jug or small bowl with a pinch of sugar. Stir well and set aside in a warm place for about 10–15 minutes.

2 When the yeast liquid becomes frothy, stir into the dry ingredients.

COOK'S TIP
Dried yeast doesn't dissolve well in milk. You must either leave it for about 30 minutes to froth, or if you are in a hurry, dissolve it in a little water first.

USING EASY-BLEND YEAST

1 Add easy-blend yeast to the dry ingredients directly from the packet. Do not dissolve it in liquid first.

COOK'S TIP
Easy-blend yeast is a special kind of dried yeast with a fine grain – it raises bread in as little as half the normal time. Bread made with this kind of yeast can be shaped after mixing and given only one rising.

USING FRESH YEAST

1 Place fresh yeast in a small bowl with a pinch of sugar and a little lukewarm water. Cream together until smooth, then leave for 5–10 minutes until frothy, before adding to the dry ingredients.

Shaping Rolls

Bread rolls can be made in all sorts of interesting shapes and sizes. Begin by dividing the dough into even-size portions.

1 To make cottage rolls, divide each portion of dough into two, making one piece about twice the size of the other. Shape both pieces into smooth balls. Dampen the top of the large ball and place the small ball on top. Push a lightly floured index finger through the middle of the dough.

2 To make clover leaf rolls, divide each portion of dough into three equal pieces. Shape each piece into a smooth ball, lightly dampen, and arrange in a clover leaf formation. Lightly press together.

3 To make knots, roll each dough portion into a fairly long sausage shape. Carefully knot the dough sausage, as you would a piece of string.

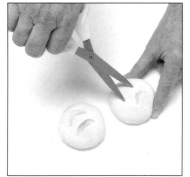

4 To make plaits, divide each dough portion into three equal pieces. Roll each piece into an even sausage shape. Dampen the three sausages at one end and pinch together. Plait the sausages loosely and pinch together at the other end, dampening lightly first.

5 To make snipped-top rolls, roll each dough portion into a smooth ball. Using a pair of kitchen scissors, make two or three snips in the top of each ball.

6 To make twists, divide each dough portion into two equal pieces. Roll each piece into an even sausage shape then twist the two pieces together, dampening at each end and pressing together firmly.

Lining Baking Tins

Ensure that your cakes and teabreads don't stick to the tin by lining the tins with greaseproof or non-stick baking paper.

LINING A ROUND TIN

1 To line a round tin, place the tin on greaseproof or non-stick baking paper and draw around the edge. Cut out two rounds that size, then cut a strip, a little longer than the tin's circumference and one and a half times its depth. Lightly grease the tin and place one paper round on the base. Make small diagonal cuts along the edge of the paper strip.

2 Put the paper strip inside the tin, with the snipped fringe along the base. Place the second paper circle in the base of the tin, covering the fringe. Grease once more.

LINING A SWISS ROLL TIN

1 To line a Swiss roll tin, cut a piece of non-stick baking paper or greaseproof paper large enough to line the base and sides of the tin. Lay the paper over the tin and make four diagonal cuts, one from each corner of the paper to the nearest corner of the tin.

2 Lightly grease the tin. Place the paper in the tin and smooth into the sides, overlapping the paper corners to fit neatly.

LINING A LOAF TIN

1 To line a loaf tin, cut a strip of greaseproof or non-stick baking paper three times as long as the depth of the tin and as wide as the length of the base.

2 Lightly grease the tin. Place the strip of paper in the tin so that the paper covers the base and comes up over both long sides.

Testing Cakes

It is very important to check that cakes and bakes are properly cooked, otherwise they can be soggy and cakes may sink in the middle.

TESTING A FRUIT CAKE

1 To test if a fruit cake is ready, push a skewer or cake tester into it: the cake is cooked if the skewer or cake tester comes out clean.

2 Fruit cakes are generally left to cool in the tin for 30 minutes. Then turn the cake out carefully, peel away the paper and place on a wire rack or board.

TESTING A SPONGE CAKE

1 To test if a sponge cake is ready, press down lightly in the centre of the cake with your fingertips – if the cake springs back, it is cooked.

2 To remove the cooked sponge cake from the tin, loosen around the edge by carefully scraping round the inside of the tin with a palette knife. Invert the cake on to a wire rack, cover with a second rack, then invert again. Remove the top rack and leave to cool.

TESTING BREAD

1 To test if a loaf of bread is ready, first loosen the edges of the loaf with a palette knife, then tip out the loaf.

2 Hold the loaf upside-down and tap it gently on the base. If it sounds hollow, the bread is cooked.

Making an Icing Bag

Being able to make your own piping bag is a very handy skill, particularly if you are dealing with small amounts of icing or several colours.

Icing a Cake

Confident icing of a cake makes all the difference to its appearance. With just a little practice, your cakes will look completely professional!

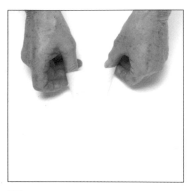 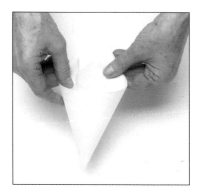  

1 Fold a 25 cm/10 in square of grease-proof paper in half to form a triangle. Using the centre of the long side as the central tip, roll half the paper into a cone.

2 Holding the paper in position, continue to roll the other half of the triangle around the first, to form a complete cone.

1 To create a simple zig-zag effect, ice the cake all over, then pipe lines in a different colour backwards and forwards over the top.

2 To create a feathered effect, follow step 1, then drag a knife through the icing at regular intervals in opposite directions, perpendicular to the lines.

3 To make a figure-of-eight, or a similar effect, ice the cake all over, then, using a different coloured icing, pipe figures of eight around the edge of the cake, in a steady stream.

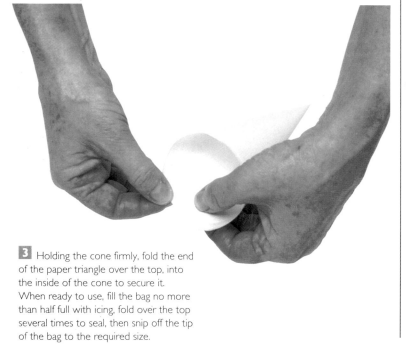 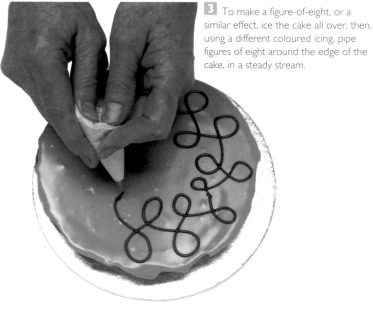

3 Holding the cone firmly, fold the end of the paper triangle over the top, into the inside of the cone to secure it. When ready to use, fill the bag no more than half full with icing, fold over the top several times to seal, then snip off the tip of the bag to the required size.

Citrus Fruits

Oranges, lemons and other citrus fruits are widely used in baking, both as flavourings and as decoration.

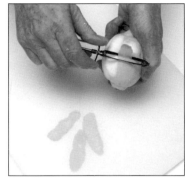

1 To grate the rind from a citrus fruit, use the finest side of a grater. Don't remove any of the white pith and brush off any rind which remains in the grater.

2 To pare the rind from a citrus fruit, use a swivel vegetable peeler. Remove the rind in strips as if peeling a potato and don't remove any of the white pith.

3 To make citrus rind shreds, or juliennes, cut strips of pared rind into very fine shreds using a sharp knife. Boil the shreds for a couple of minutes in water or sugar syrup to soften them.

Making Apricot Glaze

Apricot glaze is extremely useful for brushing over any kind of fresh fruit topping or filling to give it a lovely shiny appearance.

1 Place a few spoonfuls of apricot jam in a small pan along with a squeeze of lemon juice. Heat the jam, stirring until it is melted and runny.

2 Pour the melted jam into a wire sieve set over a bowl. Stir the jam with a wooden spoon to help it go through.

3 Return the strained jam from the bowl to the pan. Keep the glaze warm and brush it generously over the fresh fruit until evenly coated.

Banana Gingerbread Slices

Bananas make this spicy bake delightfully moist. The flavour develops on keeping, so store the gingerbread for a few days before cutting into slices, if possible.

Makes 20 slices

INGREDIENTS
275 g/10 oz/2½ cups plain flour
5 ml/1 tsp bicarbonate of soda
20 ml/4 tsp ground ginger
10 ml/2 tsp mixed spice
115 g/4 oz/²⁄₃ cup soft light
   brown sugar
60 ml/4 tbsp sunflower oil
30 ml/2 tbsp molasses or
   black treacle
30 ml/2 tbsp malt extract
2 eggs
60 ml/4 tbsp orange juice
3 ripe bananas
115 g/4 oz/²⁄₃ cup raisins or sultanas

orange juice

plain flour

malt extract

raisins

mixed spice

soft light brown sugar

eggs

sunflower oil

bicarbonate of soda

ground ginger

bananas

molasses

1 Preheat the oven to 180°C/350°F/ Gas 4. Lightly grease and line a 28 × 18 cm/11 × 7 in shallow baking tin.

2 Sift the flour, bicarbonate of soda and spices into a mixing bowl. Place the sugar in the sieve over the bowl, add some of the flour mixture and rub through the sieve with a wooden spoon.

3 Make a well in the centre of the dry ingredients and add the oil, molasses or treacle, malt extract, eggs and orange juice. Mix thoroughly.

4 Mash the bananas on a plate. Add the raisins or sultanas to the gingerbread mixture then mix in the mashed bananas.

5 Scrape the mixture into the prepared baking tin. Bake for about 35–40 minutes or until the centre of the gingerbread springs back when lightly pressed.

6 Leave the gingerbread in the tin to cool for 5 minutes, then turn out on to a wire rack to cool completely. Transfer to a board and cut into 20 slices to serve.

NUTRITIONAL NOTES
PER PORTION:

ENERGY 148 Kcals/621 KJ
FAT 3.07 g **SATURATED FAT** 0.53 g
CHOLESTEROL 19.30 mg **FIBRE** 0.79 g

COOK'S TIP
If your brown sugar is lumpy, mix it with a little flour and it will be easier to sift.

Lemon Sponge Fingers

These sponge fingers are perfect for serving with fruit salads or light, creamy desserts.

Makes about 20

INGREDIENTS
2 eggs
75 g/3 oz/6 tbsp caster sugar
grated rind of 1 lemon
50 g/2 oz/½ cup plain flour, sifted
caster sugar, for sprinkling

eggs

plain flour

caster sugar

lemon

VARIATION

To make Spicy Orange Fingers, substitute grated orange rind for the lemon rind and add 5 ml/1 tsp ground cinnamon with the flour.

1 Preheat the oven to 190°C/375°F/ Gas 5. Line two baking sheets with non-stick baking paper. Whisk the eggs, sugar and lemon rind together with a hand-held electric whisk until thick and mousse-like (when the whisk is lifted, a trail should remain on the surface of the mixture for at least 15 seconds). Gently fold in the flour with a large metal spoon using a figure-of-eight action.

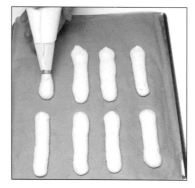

2 Place the mixture in a large piping bag fitted with a 1 cm/½ in plain nozzle. Pipe the mixture into finger lengths on the prepared baking sheets.

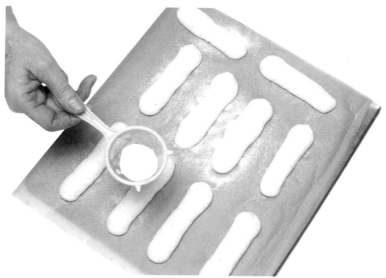

3 Sprinkle the fingers with caster sugar. Bake for about 6–8 minutes until golden brown, then transfer the sponge fingers to a wire rack to cool.

Snowballs

These light, almost fat-free morsels make an excellent accompaniment to yogurt ice cream.

Makes about 20

INGREDIENTS
2 egg whites
115 g/4 oz/¹/₂ cup caster sugar
15 ml/1 tbsp cornflour, sifted
5 ml/1 tsp white wine vinegar
1.5 ml/¹/₄ tsp vanilla essence

caster sugar

vanilla essence

cornflour

eggs

white wine vinegar

1 Preheat the oven to 150°C/300°F/Gas 2 and line two baking sheets with non-stick baking paper. Whisk the egg whites in a grease-free bowl using a hand-held electric whisk until very stiff.

2 Add the caster sugar, a little at a time, whisking until the meringue is very stiff. Whisk in the cornflour, vinegar and vanilla essence.

VARIATION
Make Pineapple Snowballs by folding about 50 g/2 oz/¹/₄ cup finely chopped semi-dried pineapple into the meringue.

3 Using a teaspoon, mound the mixture into balls on the prepared baking sheets. Bake for 30 minutes.

4 Cool slightly on the baking sheets, then transfer the snowballs to a wire rack to cool completely.

Filo and Apricot Purses

Filo pastry is very easy to use and is low in fat. Keep a packet in the freezer ready for rustling up a speedy tea-time treat.

Makes 12

INGREDIENTS
115 g/4 oz/³/₄ cup ready-to-eat
  dried apricots
45 ml/3 tbsp apricot compôte
  or conserve
3 amaretti biscuits, crushed
3 filo pastry sheets
20 ml/4 tsp soft margarine, melted
icing sugar, for dusting

filo pastry

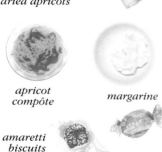

*ready-to-eat
dried apricots*

*apricot
compôte*   *margarine*

*amaretti
biscuits*

COOK'S TIP

The easiest way to crush amaretti biscuits is to put them in a plastic bag and roll with a rolling pin.

NUTRITIONAL NOTES
PER PORTION:

ENERGY 58 Kcals/245 KJ
FAT 1.85 g **SATURATED FAT** 0.40 g
CHOLESTEROL 0.12 mg **FIBRE** 0.74 g

1 Preheat the oven to 180°C/350°F/ Gas 4. Grease two baking sheets. Chop the apricots, put them in a bowl and stir in the apricot compôte. Add the crushed amaretti biscuits and mix well.

2 Cut the filo pastry into twenty-four 13 cm/5 in squares, pile the squares on top of each other and cover with a clean dish towel to prevent the pastry from drying out and becoming brittle.

3 Lay one pastry square on a flat surface, brush lightly with melted margarine and lay another square diagonally on top. Brush the top square with melted margarine. Spoon a small mound of apricot mixture in the centre of the pastry, bring up the edges and pinch together in a money-bag shape. Repeat with the remaining filo squares and filling to make 12 purses in all.

4 Arrange the purses on the prepared baking sheets and bake for 5–8 minutes until golden brown. Transfer to a wire rack and dust lightly with icing sugar. Serve warm.

Filo Scrunchies

Quick and easy to make, these pastries are ideal to serve at tea-time. Eat them warm or they will lose their crispness.

Makes 6

INGREDIENTS
5 apricots or plums
4 filo pastry sheets
20 ml/4 tsp soft margarine, melted
50 g/2 oz/¹/₃ cup demerara sugar
30 ml/2 tbsp flaked almonds
icing sugar, for dusting

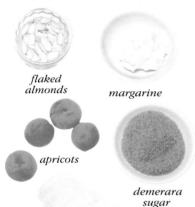

flaked almonds

margarine

apricots

demerara sugar

filo pastry

COOK'S TIP

Filo pastry dries out very quickly. Keep it covered as much as possible with a dry cloth or clear film to limit exposure to the air, or it will become too brittle to use.

NUTRITIONAL NOTES
PER PORTION:

ENERGY 132 Kcals/555 KJ
FAT 4.19 g **SATURATED FAT** 0.63 g
CHOLESTEROL 0 **FIBRE** 0.67 g

1 Preheat the oven to 190°C/375°F/ Gas 5. Halve the apricots or plums, remove the stones and slice the fruit. Cut the filo pastry into twelve 18 cm/7 in squares. Pile the squares on top of each other and cover with a clean dish towel to prevent the pastry from drying out.

2 Remove one square of filo and brush it with melted margarine. Lay a second filo square on top, then, using your fingers, mould the pastry into folds. Make five more scrunchies in the same way, working quickly so that the pastry does not dry out.

3 Arrange a few slices of fruit in the folds of each scrunchie, then sprinkle generously with the demerara sugar and flaked almonds.

4 Place the scrunchies on a baking sheet. Bake for 8–10 minutes until golden brown, then loosen the scrunchies from the baking sheet with a palette knife and transfer to a wire rack. Dust with icing sugar and serve at once.

Banana and Apricot Chelsea Buns

Old favourites are given a low fat twist with a delectable fruit filling.

Serves 9

INGREDIENTS
90 ml/6 tbsp warm skimmed milk
5 ml/1 tsp dried yeast
pinch of sugar
225 g/8 oz/2 cups strong plain flour
10 ml/2 tsp mixed spice
2.5 ml/½ tsp salt
25 g/1 oz/2 tbsp soft margarine
50 g/2 oz/¼ cup caster sugar
1 egg

FOR THE FILLING
1 large ripe banana
175 g/6 oz/1 cup ready-to-eat
    dried apricots
30 ml/2 tbsp light muscovado sugar

FOR THE GLAZE
30 ml/2 tbsp caster sugar
30 ml/2 tbsp water

dried
yeast

egg

ready-to-eat
dried apricots

soft
margarine

muscovado
sugar

mixed
spice

banana

caster
sugar

strong
plain
flour

salt

skimmed
milk

COOK'S TIP
Do not leave the buns in the tin for too long or the glaze will stick to the sides, making them very difficult to remove.

1 Grease an 18 cm/7 in square cake tin. Put the warm milk in a jug. Sprinkle the yeast on top. Add a pinch of sugar to help activate the yeast, mix well and leave for 30 minutes.

2 Sift the flour, spice and salt into a mixing bowl. Rub in the margarine, then stir in the sugar. Make a central well, pour in the yeast mixture and the egg. Gradually mix in the flour to make a soft dough, adding extra milk if needed.

3 Turn the dough out on to a floured surface and knead for 5 minutes until smooth and elastic. Return to the clean bowl, cover with a damp dish towel and leave in a warm place to rise for about 2 hours until doubled in bulk.

4 Meanwhile prepare the filling. Mash the banana in a bowl. Using kitchen scissors, snip the apricots, then stir them into the mashed banana with the sugar.

5 Knead the risen dough on a floured surface for 2 minutes, then roll out to a 30 x 23 cm/12 x 9 in rectangle. Spread the banana and apricot filling over the dough and roll up lengthways like a Swiss roll, with the join underneath.

NUTRITIONAL NOTES

PER PORTION:

ENERGY 214 Kcals/901 KJ
FAT 3.18 g **SATURATED FAT** 0.63 g
CHOLESTEROL 21.59 mg **FIBRE** 2.18 g

6 Cut the roll into 9 pieces and place, cut side down, in the prepared tin. Cover and leave to rise in a warm place for about 30 minutes. Preheat the oven to 200°C/400°F/Gas 6.

7 Bake the buns for 20–25 minutes until golden brown and cooked in the centre. Meanwhile make the glaze. Mix the caster sugar and water in a small saucepan. Heat, stirring, until dissolved, then boil for 2 minutes. Brush the glaze over the buns while still hot, then remove the buns from the tin and leave them to cool on a wire rack.

Raspberry Muffins

These American muffins are made using baking powder and low fat buttermilk, giving them a light and spongy texture. They are delicious to eat at any time of day.

Makes 10–12

INGREDIENTS
275 g/10 oz/2½ cups plain flour
15 ml/1 tbsp baking powder
115 g/4 oz/½ cup caster sugar
1 egg
250 ml/8 fl oz/1 cup buttermilk
60 ml/4 tbsp sunflower oil
150 g/5 oz/1 cup raspberries

egg

buttermilk

sunflower oil

caster sugar

plain flour

baking powder

raspberries

NUTRITIONAL NOTES
PER PORTION:

ENERGY 171 Kcals/719 KJ
FAT 4.55 g **SATURATED FAT** 0.71 g
CHOLESTEROL 16.50 mg **FIBRE** 1.02 g

1 Preheat the oven to 200°C/400°F/ Gas 6. Arrange 12 paper cases in a deep muffin tin. Sift the flour and baking powder into a mixing bowl, stir in the sugar, then make a well in the centre.

2 Mix the egg, buttermilk and sunflower oil together in a bowl, pour into the flour mixture and mix quickly until just combined.

3 Add the raspberries and lightly fold in with a metal spoon. Spoon the mixture into the paper cases to within a third of the top.

4 Bake the muffins for 20–25 minutes until golden brown and firm in the middle. Transfer to a wire rack and serve warm or cold.

Date and Apple Muffins

You will only need one or two of these wholesome muffins per person as they are very filling.

Makes 12

INGREDIENTS
150 g/5 oz/1¼ cups self-raising
  wholemeal flour
150 g/5 oz/1¼ cups self-raising
  white flour
5 ml/1 tsp ground cinnamon
5 ml/1 tsp baking powder
25 g/1 oz/2 tbsp soft margarine
75 g/3 oz/½ cup light muscovado
  sugar
1 eating apple
250 ml/8 fl oz/1 cup apple juice
30 ml/2 tbsp pear and apple spread
1 egg, lightly beaten
75 g/3 oz/½ cup chopped dates
15 ml/1 tbsp chopped pecan nuts

chopped dates *egg* *pecan nuts* *self-raising wholemeal flour* *ground cinnamon* *muscovado sugar* *self-raising white flour* *apple juice* *soft margarine* *pear and apple spread* *eating apple* *baking powder*

1 Preheat the oven to 200°C/400°F/ Gas 6. Arrange 12 paper cases in a deep muffin tin. Put the wholemeal flour in a mixing bowl. Sift in the white flour with the cinnamon and baking powder. Rub in the margarine until the mixture resembles breadcrumbs, then stir in the muscovado sugar.

2 Quarter and core the apple, chop the flesh finely and set aside. Stir a little of the apple juice with the pear and apple spread until smooth. Mix in the remaining juice, then add to the rubbed-in mixture with the egg. Add the chopped apple to the bowl with the dates. Mix quickly until just combined.

3 Divide the mixture among the muffin cases.

4 Sprinkle with the chopped pecan nuts. Bake the muffins for 20–25 minutes until golden brown and firm in the middle. Remove to a wire rack and serve while still warm.

NUTRITIONAL NOTES
PER PORTION:

ENERGY 163 Kcals/686 KJ
FAT 2.98 g **SATURATED FAT** 0.47 g
CHOLESTEROL 16.04 mg **FIBRE** 1.97 g

Muscovado Meringues

These light brown meringues are extremely low in fat and are delicious served on their own or sandwiched together with a fresh fruit and soft cheese filling.

Makes about 20

INGREDIENTS
115 g/4 oz/²⁄₃ cup light muscovado
  sugar
2 egg whites
5 ml/1 tsp finely chopped walnuts

eggs

*light
muscovado
sugar*

walnuts

NUTRITIONAL NOTES
PER PORTION:

ENERGY 30 Kcals/124 KJ
FAT 0.34 g **SATURATED FAT** 0.04 g
CHOLESTEROL 0 **FIBRE** 0.02 g

COOK'S TIP

For a sophisticated filling, mix 115 g/4 oz/¹⁄₂ cup low-fat soft cheese with 15 ml/1 tbsp icing sugar. Chop 2 slices of fresh pineapple and add to the mixture. Use to sandwich the meringues together in pairs.

1 Preheat the oven to 160°C/325°F/Gas 3. Line two baking sheets with non-stick baking paper. Press the sugar through a metal sieve into a bowl.

2 Whisk the egg whites in a grease-free bowl until very stiff and dry, then whisk in the sugar, about 15 ml/1 tbsp at a time, until the meringue is very thick and glossy.

3 Spoon small mounds of the mixture on to the prepared baking sheets.

4 Sprinkle the meringues with the chopped walnuts. Bake for 30 minutes. Cool for 5 minutes on the baking sheets, then leave to cool on a wire rack.

Apricot and Almond Fingers

These apricot and almond fingers will stay moist for several days.

Makes 18

INGREDIENTS
225 g/8 oz/2 cups self-raising flour
115 g/4 oz/²/₃ cup light muscovado
  sugar
50 g/2 oz/¹/₃ cup semolina
175 g/6 oz/1 cup ready-to-use dried
  apricots, chopped
2 eggs
30 ml/2 tbsp malt extract
30 ml/2 tbsp clear honey
60 ml/4 tbsp skimmed milk
60 ml/4 tbsp sunflower oil
few drops of almond essence
30 ml/2 tbsp flaked almonds

clear honey

skimmed milk

sunflower oil

eggs

ready-to-use dried apricots

light muscovado sugar

semolina

self-raising flour

malt extract

flaked almonds

1 Preheat the oven to 160°C/325°F/ Gas 3. Lightly grease and line a 28 × 18 cm/11 × 7 in shallow baking tin. Sift the flour into a bowl and add the muscovado sugar, semolina, dried apricots and eggs. Add the malt extract, clear honey, milk, sunflower oil and almond essence. Mix well until smooth.

2 Turn the mixture into the prepared tin, spread to the edges and sprinkle with the flaked almonds.

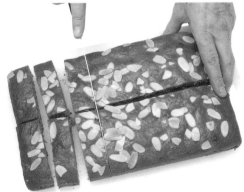

3 Bake for 30–35 minutes or until the centre of the cake springs back when lightly pressed. Transfer to a wire rack to cool. Remove the paper, place the cake on a board and cut it into 18 slices with a sharp knife.

NUTRITIONAL NOTES
PER PORTION:
ENERGY 153 Kcals/641 KJ
FAT 4.56 g **SATURATED FAT** 0.61 g
CHOLESTEROL 21.50 mg **FIBRE** 1.27 g

Coffee Sponge Drops

These are delicious on their own, but taste even better with a filling made by mixing low fat soft cheese with drained and chopped stem ginger.

Makes 12

INGREDIENTS
50 g/2 oz/$\frac{1}{2}$ cup plain flour
15 ml/1 tbsp instant coffee powder
2 eggs
75 g/3 oz/6 tbsp caster sugar

FOR THE FILLING
115 g/4 oz/$\frac{1}{2}$ cup low fat soft cheese
40 g/1$\frac{1}{2}$ oz/$\frac{1}{4}$ cup chopped
    stem ginger

eggs

instant coffee powder

plain flour

caster sugar

low fat soft cheese

stem ginger

NUTRITIONAL NOTES
PER PORTION:

ENERGY 69 Kcals/290 KJ
FAT 1.36 g **SATURATED FAT** 0.50 g
CHOLESTEROL 33.33 mg **FIBRE** 0.29 g

1 Preheat the oven to 190°C/375°F/ Gas 5. Line two baking sheets with non-stick baking paper. Make the filling by beating together the soft cheese and stem ginger. Chill until required. Sift the flour and instant coffee powder together.

2 Combine the eggs and caster sugar in a bowl. Beat with a hand-held electric whisk until thick and mousse-like (when the whisk is lifted a trail should remain on the surface of the mixture for at least 15 seconds).

3 Carefully add the sifted flour and coffee mixture and gently fold in with a metal spoon, being careful not to knock out any air.

4 Spoon the mixture into a piping bag fitted with a 1 cm/$\frac{1}{2}$ in plain nozzle. Pipe 4 cm/1$\frac{1}{2}$ in rounds on the baking sheets. Bake for 12 minutes. Cool on a wire rack. Sandwich together with the filling.

Oaty Crisps

These biscuits are very crisp and crunchy – ideal to serve with morning coffee.

Makes 18

INGREDIENTS
175 g/6 oz/1¾ cups rolled oats
75 g/3 oz/½ cup light muscovado
   sugar
1 egg
60 ml/4 tbsp sunflower oil
30 ml/2 tbsp malt extract

malt extract   *sunflower oil*

*rolled
oats*

egg

*light muscovado
sugar*

NUTRITIONAL NOTES
PER PORTION:

ENERGY 86 Kcals/360 KJ
FAT 3.59 g **SATURATED FAT** 0.57 g
CHOLESTEROL 10.70 mg **FIBRE** 0.66 g

VARIATION
To give these crisp biscuits a coarser texture, substitute jumbo oats for some or all of the rolled oats.

1 Preheat the oven to 190°C/375°F/ Gas 5. Lightly grease two baking sheets. Mix the rolled oats and brown sugar in a bowl, breaking up any lumps in the sugar. Add the egg, sunflower oil and malt extract, mix well, then leave to soak for 15 minutes.

2 Using a teaspoon, place small heaps of the mixture well apart on the prepared baking sheets. Press the heaps into 7.5 cm/3 in rounds with the back of a dampened fork.

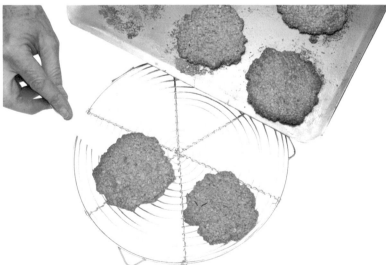

3 Bake the biscuits for 10–15 minutes until golden brown. Leave them to cool for 1 minute, then remove with a palette knife and cool on a wire rack.

Irish Whiskey Cake

This moist rich fruit cake is drizzled with whiskey as soon as it comes out of the oven.

Serves 12

INGREDIENTS

115 g/4 oz/²/₃ cup glacé cherries
175 g/6 oz/1 cup dark muscovado
   sugar
115 g/4 oz/²/₃ cup sultanas
115 g/4 oz/²/₃ cup raisins
115 g/4 oz/¹/₂ cup currants
300 ml/¹/₂ pint/1¹/₄ cups cold tea
300 g/10 oz/2¹/₂ cups self-raising
   flour, sifted
1 egg
45 ml/3 tbsp Irish whiskey

raisins

currants

sultanas

muscovado sugar

glacé cherries

cold tea

Irish whiskey

self-raising flour

egg

COOK'S TIP

If time is short use hot tea and soak the fruit for just 2 hours.

1 Mix the cherries, sugar, dried fruit and tea in a large bowl. Leave to soak overnight until all the tea has been absorbed into the fruit.

2 Preheat the oven to 180°C/350°F/ Gas 4. Grease and line a 1 kg/2¹/₄ lb loaf tin. Add the flour, then the egg to the fruit mixture and beat thoroughly until well mixed.

NUTRITIONAL NOTES
PER PORTION:

ENERGY 265 Kcals/1115 KJ
FAT 0.88 g SATURATED FAT 0.25 g
CHOLESTEROL 16.00 mg FIBRE 1.48 g

3 Pour the mixture into the prepared tin and bake for 1¹/₂ hours or until a skewer inserted into the centre of the cake comes out clean.

4 Prick the top of the cake with a skewer and drizzle over the whiskey while the cake is still hot. Allow to stand for about 5 minutes, then remove from the tin and cool on a wire rack.

Fruit and Nut Cake

A rich fruit cake that improves with keeping.

Serves 12–14

INGREDIENTS
175 g/6 oz/1½ cups self-raising
    wholemeal flour
175 g/6 oz/1½ cups self-raising
    white flour
10 ml/2 tsp mixed spice
15 ml/1 tbsp apple and
    apricot spread
45 ml/3 tbsp clear honey
15 ml/1 tbsp molasses or black
    treacle
90 ml/6 tbsp sunflower oil
175 ml/6 fl oz/³⁄₄ cup orange juice
2 eggs, beaten
675 g/1½ lb/4 cups luxury mixed
    dried fruit
45 ml/3 tbsp split almonds
50 g/2 oz/½ cup glacé
    cherries, halved

*luxury mixed
dried fruit*

*clear
honey*

molasses

mixed spice

eggs

*apple and
apricot spread*

*orange
juice*

*split
almonds*

*sunflower
oil*

*self-raising
white flour*

*glacé
cherries*

*self-raising
wholemeal flour*

1 Preheat the oven to 160°C/325°F/
Gas 3. Grease and line a deep round
20 cm/8 in cake tin. Secure a band of
brown paper around the outside.

2 Sift the flours into a mixing bowl
with the mixed spice and make a well in
the centre.

NUTRITIONAL NOTES

PER PORTION:

ENERGY 333 Kcals/1400 KJ
FAT 8.54 g **SATURATED FAT** 1.12 g
CHOLESTEROL 29.62 mg **FIBRE** 3.08 g

3 Put the apple and apricot spread in a
small bowl. Gradually stir in the honey
and molasses or treacle. Add to the dry
ingredients with the oil, orange juice,
eggs and mixed fruit. Mix thoroughly.

4 Turn the mixture into the prepared
tin and smooth the surface. Arrange the
almonds and cherries in a pattern over
the top. Stand the tin on newspaper and
bake for 2 hours or until a skewer
inserted into the centre comes out clean.
Transfer to a wire rack until cold, then lift
out of the tin and remove the paper.

Chocolate Banana Cake

A chocolate cake that's deliciously low fat – it is moist enough to eat without the icing if you want to cut down on calories.

NUTRITIONAL NOTES

PER PORTION:

ENERGY 411 Kcals/1727 KJ
FAT 8.79 g **SATURATED FAT** 2.06 g
CHOLESTEROL 48.27 mg **FIBRE** 2.06 g

Serves 8

INGREDIENTS

225 g/8 oz/2 cups self-raising flour
45 ml/3 tbsp fat-reduced
  cocoa powder
115 g/4 oz/²⁄₃ cup light muscovado
  sugar
30 ml/2 tbsp malt extract
30 ml/2 tbsp golden syrup
2 eggs
60 ml/4 tbsp skimmed milk
2 large ripe bananas
60 ml/4 tbsp sunflower oil

FOR THE ICINGS

225 g/8 oz/2 cups icing
  sugar, sifted
35 ml/7 tsp fat-reduced cocoa
  powder, sifted
15–30 ml/1–2 tbsp warm water

golden syrup  *eggs*

skimmed milk

icing sugar
self-raising flour

fat-reduced cocoa powder

sunflower oil

bananas *malt extract* *light muscovado sugar*

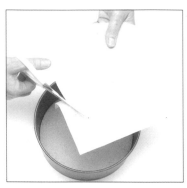

1 Preheat the oven to 160°C/325°F/ Gas 3. Grease and line a deep round 20 cm/8 in cake tin.

2 Sift the flour into a mixing bowl with the cocoa powder. Stir in the sugar.

3 Make a well in the centre and add the malt extract, golden syrup, eggs, milk and oil. Mash the bananas thoroughly and stir them into the mixture until thoroughly combined.

4 Pour the cake mixture into the prepared tin and bake for 1–1¼ hours or until the centre of the cake springs back when lightly pressed.

5 Remove the cake from the tin and leave on a wire rack to cool.

COOK'S TIP

This cake also makes a delicious dessert if heated in the microwave. The icing melts to a puddle of sauce. Serve a slice topped with a large dollop of fromage frais for a really special treat.

6 Reserve 50 g/2 oz icing sugar and 5 ml/1 tsp cocoa powder. Make a darker icing by beating the remaining sugar and cocoa powder with enough of the warm water to make a thick icing. Pour it over the top of the cake and spread evenly to the edges. Make a thinner, lighter icing by mixing the remaining icing sugar and cocoa powder with a few drops of water. Drizzle or pipe this icing across the top of the cake to decorate.

Mango and Amaretti Strudel

Fresh mango and crushed amaretti wrapped in wafer-thin filo pastry make a special treat that is equally delicious made with apricots or plums.

NUTRITIONAL NOTES

PER PORTION:

ENERGY 239 Kcals/1006 KJ
FAT 8.45 g SATURATED FAT 4.43 g
CHOLESTEROL 17.25 mg FIBRE 3.30 g

Serves 4

INGREDIENTS
1 large mango
grated rind of 1 lemon
2 amaretti biscuits
25 g/1 oz/3 tbsp demerara sugar
60 ml/4 tbsp wholemeal
   breadcrumbs
2 sheets of filo pastry, each 48 x
   28 cm/19 x 11 in
20 g/³/₄ oz/4 tsp soft margarine,
   melted
15 ml/1 tbsp chopped almonds
icing sugar, for dusting

filo pastry

mango

wholemeal breadcrumbs

lemon rind

amaretti biscuits

demerara sugar

chopped almonds

soft margarine

1 Preheat the oven to 190°C/375°F/Gas 5. Lightly grease a large baking sheet. Halve, stone and peel the mango. Cut the flesh into cubes, then place them in a bowl and sprinkle with the grated lemon rind.

2 Crush the amaretti biscuits and mix them with the demerara sugar and the wholemeal breadcrumbs.

3 Lay one sheet of filo on a flat surface and brush with a quarter of the melted margarine. Top with the second sheet, brush with one-third of the remaining margarine, then fold both sheets over, if necessary, to make a rectangle measuring 28 x 24 cm/11 x 9¹/₂ in. Brush with half the remaining margarine.

4 Sprinkle the filo with the amaretti mixture, leaving a 5 cm/2 in border on each long side. Arrange the mango cubes over the top.

5 Roll up the filo from one of the long sides, Swiss roll fashion. Lift the strudel on to the baking sheet with the join underneath. Brush with the remaining melted margarine and sprinkle with the chopped almonds.

6 Bake for 20–25 minutes until golden brown, then transfer to a board. Dust with the icing sugar, slice diagonally and serve warm.

COOK'S TIP

The easiest way to prepare a mango is to cut horizontally through the fruit, keeping the knife blade close to the stone. Repeat on the other side of the stone and peel off the skin. Remove the remaining skin and flesh from around the stone.

Angel Cake

Serve this light-as-air cake with low fat fromage frais – it makes a perfect dessert.

Serves 10

INGREDIENTS
40 g/1¹/₂ oz/¹/₃ cup cornflour
40 g/1¹/₂ oz/¹/₄ cup plain flour
8 egg whites
225 g/8 oz/1 cup caster sugar, plus
   extra for sprinkling
5 ml/1 tsp vanilla essence
icing sugar, for dusting

cornflour

vanilla essence

*plain
flour*

*caster
sugar*

eggs

NUTRITIONAL NOTES
PER PORTION:

ENERGY 139 Kcals/582 KJ
FAT 0.08 g SATURATED FAT 0.01 g
CHOLESTEROL 0 FIBRE 0.13 g

1 Preheat the oven to 180°C/350°F/Gas 4. Sift both flours on to a sheet of greaseproof paper.

2 Whisk the egg whites in a large grease-free bowl until very stiff, then gradually add the sugar and vanilla essence, whisking until the mixture is thick and glossy.

COOK'S TIP

Make a lemony icing by mixing 175 g/6 oz/1¹/₂ cups icing sugar with 15–30 ml/1–2 tbsp lemon juice. Drizzle the icing over the cake and decorate with physalis or lemon slices and mint sprigs.

3 Gently fold in the flour mixture with a large metal spoon. Spoon into an ungreased 25 cm/10 in angel cake tin, smooth the surface and bake for about 45–50 minutes, until the cake springs back when lightly pressed.

4 Sprinkle a piece of greaseproof paper with caster sugar and set an egg cup in the centre. Invert the cake tin over the paper, balancing it carefully on the egg cup. When cold, the cake will drop out of the tin. Transfer it to a plate, decorate if liked (see Cook's Tip), then dust with icing sugar and serve.

Pear and Sultana Teabread

This is an ideal teabread to make when pears are plentiful – an excellent use for windfalls.

Serves 6–8

INGREDIENTS

25 g/1 oz/scant ⅓ cup rolled oats
50 g/2 oz/⅓ cup light muscovado
 sugar
30 ml/2 tbsp pear or apple juice
30 ml/2 tbsp sunflower oil
1 large or 2 small pears
115 g/4 oz/1 cup self-raising flour
115 g/4 oz/⅔ cup sultanas
2.5 ml/½ tsp baking powder
10 ml/2 tsp mixed spice
1 egg

small pears

egg

baking powder

sunflower oil

self-raising flour

rolled oats

sultanas

mixed spice

light muscovado sugar

pear juice

NUTRITIONAL NOTES

PER PORTION:

ENERGY 200 Kcals/841 KJ
FAT 4.61 g **SATURATED FAT** 0.79 g
CHOLESTEROL 27.50 mg **FIBRE** 1.39 g

1 Preheat the oven to 180°C/350°F/ Gas 4. Grease and line a 450 g/1 lb loaf tin with non-stick baking paper. Put the oats in a bowl with the sugar, pour over the pear or apple juice and oil, mix well and leave to stand for 15 minutes.

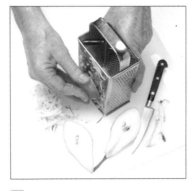

2 Quarter, core and grate the pear(s). Add to the oat mixture with the flour, sultanas, baking powder, mixed spice and egg, then mix together thoroughly.

3 Spoon the mixture into the prepared loaf tin and level the top. Bake for 50–60 minutes or until a skewer inserted into the centre comes out clean.

4 Transfer the teabread on to a wire rack and peel off the lining paper. Leave to cool completely.

COOK'S TIP

Health food shops sell concentrated pear and apple juice, ready for diluting as required.

Peach Swiss Roll

A feather-light sponge enclosing peach jam –
delicious at tea time.

Serves 6–8

INGREDIENTS
3 eggs
115 g/4 oz/¹/₂ cup caster sugar
75 g/3 oz/³/₄ cup plain flour, sifted
15 ml/1 tbsp boiling water
90 ml/6 tbsp peach jam
icing sugar, for dusting (optional)

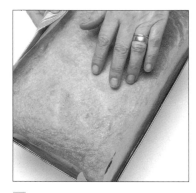

eggs

plain flour

*caster
sugar*

peach jam

NUTRITIONAL NOTES
PER PORTION:

ENERGY 178 Kcals/746 KJ
FAT 2.45 g **SATURATED FAT** 0.67 g
CHOLESTEROL 82.50 mg **FIBRE** 0.33 g

COOK'S TIP

Decorate the Swiss roll with glacé
icing. Put 115 g/4 oz glacé icing in a
piping bag fitted with a small
writing nozzle and pipe lines over
the top of the Swiss roll.

1 Preheat the oven to 200°C/400°F/
Gas 6. Grease a 30 x 20 cm/12 x 8 in
Swiss roll tin and line with non-stick
baking paper. Combine the eggs and
sugar in a bowl. Beat with a hand-held
electric whisk until thick and mousse-like
(when the whisk is lifted a trail should
remain on the surface of the mixture for
at least 15 seconds).

2 Carefully fold in the flour with a
large metal spoon, then add the boiling
water in the same way.

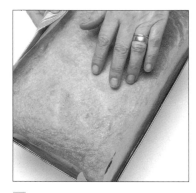

3 Spoon into the prepared tin, spread
evenly to the edges and bake for about
10–12 minutes until the cake springs
back when lightly pressed.

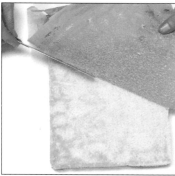

4 Spread a sheet of greaseproof paper
on a flat surface, sprinkle it with caster
sugar, then invert the cake on top. Peel
off the lining paper.

5 Neatly trim the edges of the cake.
Make a neat cut two-thirds of the way
through the cake, about 1 cm/¹/₂ in from
the short edge nearest you.

6 Spread the cake with the peach jam
and roll up quickly from the partially cut
end. Hold in position for a minute,
making sure the join is underneath. Cool
on a wire rack. Decorate with glacé icing
(see Cook's Tip) or simply dust with
icing sugar before serving.

Banana and Ginger Teabread

Serve this teabread in slices with low fat spread. The stem ginger adds an interesting flavour.

Serves 6–8

INGREDIENTS
175 g/6 oz/1½ cups self-raising flour
5 ml/1 tsp baking powder
40 g/1½ oz/3 tbsp soft margarine
50 g/2 oz/⅓ cup dark muscovado sugar
50 g/2 oz/⅓ cup drained stem ginger, chopped
60 ml/4 tbsp skimmed milk
2 ripe bananas, mashed

baking powder

stem ginger

muscovado sugar

bananas

self-raising flour

skimmed milk

soft margarine

NUTRITIONAL NOTES
PER PORTION:

ENERGY 214 Kcals/899 KJ
FAT 5.16 g SATURATED FAT 0.96 g
CHOLESTEROL 0.57 mg FIBRE 1.59 g

1 Preheat the oven to 180°C/350°F/ Gas 4. Grease and line a 450 g/1 lb loaf tin. Sift the flour and baking powder into a mixing bowl.

2 Rub in the margarine until the mixture resembles breadcrumbs.

VARIATION

To make Banana and Sultana Teabread, add 5 ml/1 tsp mixed spice and omit the stem ginger. Stir in 115 g/4 oz/⅔ cup sultanas.

3 Stir in the sugar. Add the ginger, milk and bananas and mix to a soft dough.

4 Spoon into the prepared tin and bake for 40–45 minutes. Run a palette knife around the edges to loosen them, turn the teabread on to a wire rack and leave to cool.

Spiced Apple Cake

Grated apple and chopped dates give this cake a natural sweetness – omit 25 g/1 oz of the sugar if the fruit is very sweet.

Serves 8

INGREDIENTS

225 g/8 oz/2 cups self-raising
   wholemeal flour
5 ml/1 tsp baking powder
10 ml/2 tsp ground cinnamon
175 g/6 oz/1 cup chopped dates
75 g/3 oz/½ cup light muscovado
   sugar
15 ml/1 tbsp pear and apple spread
120 ml/4 fl oz/½ cup apple juice
2 eggs
90 ml/6 tbsp sunflower oil
2 eating apples, cored and grated
15 ml/1 tbsp chopped walnuts

ground cinnamon

apple juice

sunflower oil

self-raising wholemeal flour

chopped walnuts

chopped dates

baking powder

muscovado sugar

pear and apple spread

eating apples

eggs

1 Preheat the oven to 180°C/350°F/Gas 4. Grease and line a deep round 20 cm/8 in cake tin. Sift the flour, baking powder and cinnamon into a mixing bowl, then mix in the dates and make a well in the centre.

2 Mix the sugar with the pear and apple spread in a small bowl. Gradually stir in the apple juice. Add to the dry ingredients with the eggs, oil and apples. Mix thoroughly.

COOK'S TIP

It is not necessary to peel the apples – the skin adds extra fibre and softens on cooking.

3 Spoon the mixture into the prepared cake tin, sprinkle with the walnuts and bake for 60–65 minutes or until a skewer inserted into the centre of the cake comes out clean. Transfer to a wire rack, remove the lining paper and leave to cool.

NUTRITIONAL NOTES

PER PORTION:

ENERGY 331 Kcals/1389 KJ
FAT 11.41 g **SATURATED FAT** 1.68 g
CHOLESTEROL 48.13 mg **FIBRE** 2.50 g

Wholemeal Herb Triangles

Stuffed with cooked chicken and salad these make a good lunchtime snack and are also an ideal accompaniment to a bowl of steaming soup.

Makes 8

INGREDIENTS
225 g/8 oz/2 cups wholemeal flour
115 g/4 oz/1 cup strong plain flour
5 ml/1 tsp salt
2.5 ml/½ tsp bicarbonate of soda
5 ml/1 tsp cream of tartar
2.5 ml/½ tsp chilli powder
50 g/2 oz/¼ cup soft margarine
60 ml/4 tbsp chopped mixed
    fresh herbs
250 ml/8 fl oz/1 cup skimmed milk
15 ml/1 tbsp sesame seeds

mixed fresh herbs

sesame seeds *wholemeal flour* *chilli powder* *bicarbonate of soda* *cream of tartar* *soft margarine* *skimmed milk* *salt* *strong plain flour*

1 Preheat the oven to 220°C/425°F/Gas 7. Lightly flour a baking sheet. Put the wholemeal flour in a mixing bowl. Sift in the remaining dry ingredients, including the chilli powder, then rub in the soft margarine.

2 Add the herbs and milk and mix quickly to a soft dough. Turn on to a lightly floured surface. Knead only very briefly or the dough will become tough. Roll out to a 23 cm/9 in round and place on the prepared baking sheet. Brush lightly with water and sprinkle evenly with the sesame seeds.

3 Carefully cut the dough round into 8 wedges, separate them slightly and bake for 15–20 minutes. Transfer to a wire rack to cool. Serve warm or cold.

NUTRITIONAL NOTES
PER PORTION:
ENERGY 222 Kcals/932 KJ
FAT 7.22 g **SATURATED FAT** 1.25 g
CHOLESTEROL 1.06 mg **FIBRE** 3.54 g

VARIATION
To make Sun-dried Tomato Triangles, replace the fresh mixed herbs with 30 ml/2 tbsp drained chopped sun-dried tomatoes in oil, and add 15 ml/1 tbsp each mild paprika, chopped fresh parsley and chopped fresh marjoram.

Caraway Bread Sticks

Ideal to nibble with drinks, these can be made
with all sorts of other seeds – try cumin seeds,
poppy seeds or celery seeds.

Makes about 20

INGREDIENTS
150 ml/¼ pint/⅔ cup warm water
2.5 ml/½ tsp dried yeast
pinch of sugar
225 g/8 oz/2 cups plain flour
2.5 ml/½ tsp salt
10 ml/2 tsp caraway seeds

*dried
yeast*

*caraway
seeds*

*plain
flour*

water

salt

NUTRITIONAL NOTES
PER PORTION:

ENERGY 45 Kcals/189 KJ
FAT 0.24 g SATURATED FAT 0.02 g
CHOLESTEROL 0 FIBRE 0.39 g

VARIATION

To make Coriander and Sesame
Sticks, replace the caraway seeds
with 15 ml/1 tbsp crushed coriander
seeds. Dampen the bread sticks
lightly and sprinkle them with
sesame seeds before baking.

1 Grease two baking sheets. Put the
warm water in a jug. Sprinkle the yeast
on top. Add the sugar, mix well and
leave for 10 minutes.

2 Sift the flour and salt into a mixing
bowl, stir in the caraway seeds and make
a well in the centre. Add the yeast
mixture and gradually incorporate the
flour to make a soft dough, adding a little
extra water if necessary.

3 Turn on to a lightly floured surface
and knead for 5 minutes until smooth.
Divide the mixture into 20 pieces and
roll each one into a 30 cm/12 in stick.
Arrange on the baking sheets, leaving
room to allow for rising, then leave for
30 minutes until well risen. Meanwhile,
preheat the oven to 220°C/425°F/Gas 7.

4 Bake the bread sticks for about
10–12 minutes until golden brown. Cool
on the baking sheets.

Poppy Seed Rolls

Pile these soft rolls in a basket and serve them for breakfast or with dinner.

NUTRITIONAL NOTES

PER PORTION:

ENERGY 160 Kcals/674 KJ
FAT 2.42 g **SATURATED FAT** 0.46 g
CHOLESTEROL 32.58 mg **FIBRE** 1.16 g

Makes 12

INGREDIENTS
300 ml/½ pint/1¼ cups warm
   skimmed milk
5 ml/1 tsp dried yeast
pinch of sugar
450 g/1 lb/4 cups strong white flour
5 ml/1 tsp salt
1 egg, beaten

FOR THE TOPPING
1 egg, beaten
poppy seeds

strong white flour

skimmed milk

poppy seeds   *egg*

salt   *dried yeast*

1 Put half the warm milk in a small bowl. Sprinkle the yeast on top. Add the sugar, mix well and leave for 30 minutes.

2 Sift the flour and salt into a mixing bowl. Make a well in the centre and pour in the yeast mixture and the egg. Gradually incorporate the flour, adding enough of the remaining milk to mix to a soft dough.

3 Turn the dough on to a floured surface and knead for 5 minutes until smooth and elastic. Return to the clean bowl, cover with a damp dish towel and leave in a warm place to rise for about 1 hour until doubled in bulk.

4 Lightly grease two baking sheets. Turn the dough on to a floured surface. Knead for 2 minutes, then cut into 12 pieces and shape into rolls.

5 Place the rolls on the prepared baking sheets, cover loosely with a large plastic bag (ballooning it to trap the air inside) and leave in a warm place until the rolls have risen well. Preheat the oven to 220°C/425°F/Gas 7.

6 Glaze the rolls with beaten egg, sprinkle with poppy seeds and bake for 12–15 minutes until golden brown. Transfer to a wire rack to cool.

COOK'S TIP
Use easy-blend dried yeast if you prefer. Add it directly to the dry ingredients and mix with hand-hot milk. The rolls will only require one rising (see package instructions). Vary the toppings. Linseed, sesame seeds and caraway seeds are all good; try adding caraway seeds to the dough, too, for extra flavour.

Chive and Potato Scones

These little scones should be fairly thin, soft and crisp on the outside. Serve them for breakfast.

Makes 20

INGREDIENTS
450 g/1 lb potatoes
115 g/4 oz/1 cup plain flour, sifted
30 ml/2 tbsp olive oil
30 ml/2 tbsp snipped chives
salt and freshly ground black pepper
low fat spread, for topping
   (optional)

potatoes

black pepper

olive oil

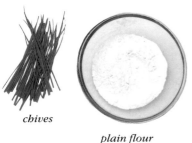

chives

plain flour

salt

1 Cook the potatoes in a saucepan of boiling salted water for 20 minutes or until tender, then drain thoroughly. Return the potatoes to the clean pan and mash them. Preheat a griddle or

2 Add the flour, olive oil and snipped chives with a little salt and pepper to the hot mashed potato in the pan. Mix to a soft dough.

COOK'S TIP

Cook the scones over a low heat so that the outsides do not burn before the insides are cooked through.

3 Roll out the dough on a well-floured surface to a thickness of 5 mm/¼ in and stamp out rounds with a 5 cm/2 in plain pastry cutter. Lightly grease the griddle or frying pan.

4 Cook the scones, in batches, on the hot griddle or frying pan for about 10 minutes, turning once, until they are golden brown on both sides. Keep the heat low. Top with a little low fat spread, if you like, and serve immediately.

Ham and Tomato Scones

These make an ideal accompaniment for soup. Choose a strongly flavoured ham and chop it fairly finely, so that a little goes a long way.

Makes 12

INGREDIENTS
225 g/8 oz/2 cups self-raising flour
5 ml/1 tsp dry mustard
5 ml/1 tsp paprika, plus extra for
   sprinkling
2.5 ml/¹/₂ tsp salt
25 g/1 oz/2 tbsp soft margarine
15 ml/1 tbsp snipped fresh basil
50 g/2 oz/¹/₃ cup drained sun-dried
   tomatoes in oil, chopped
50 g/2 oz Black Forest ham,
   chopped
90–120 ml/3–4 fl oz/¹/₂–²/₃ cup
   skimmed milk, plus extra
   for brushing

soft margarine

paprika

salt

skimmed milk

self-raising flour

fresh basil

dry mustard

sun-dried tomatoes

Black Forest ham

1 Preheat the oven to 200°C/400°F/ Gas 6. Flour a large baking sheet. Sift the flour, mustard, paprika and salt into a bowl. Rub in the margarine until the mixture resembles breadcrumbs.

2 Stir in the basil, sun-dried tomatoes and ham, and mix lightly. Pour in enough milk to mix to a soft dough.

3 Turn the dough out on to a lightly floured surface, knead lightly and roll out to a 20 × 15 cm/8 × 6 in rectangle. Cut into 5 cm/2 in squares and arrange on the baking sheet.

4 Brush lightly with milk, sprinkle with paprika and bake for 12–15 minutes. Transfer to a wire rack to cool.

NUTRITIONAL NOTES
PER PORTION:

ENERGY 113 Kcals/474 KJ
FAT 4.23 g **SATURATED FAT** 0.65 g
CHOLESTEROL 2.98 mg **FIBRE** 0.65 g

Granary Baps

These make excellent picnic fare, filled with cottage cheese, tuna, salad and low fat mayonnaise. They are also good served warm with soup.

NUTRITIONAL NOTES
PER PORTION:

ENERGY 223 Kcals/939 KJ
FAT 1.14 g **SATURATED FAT** 0.16 g
CHOLESTEROL 0 **FIBRE** 3.10 g

Makes 8

INGREDIENTS
300 ml/¹/₂ pint/1¹/₄ cups warm water
5 ml/1 tsp dried yeast
pinch of sugar
450 g/1 lb/4 cups malted
    brown flour
5 ml/1 tsp salt
15 ml/1 tbsp malt extract
15 ml/1 tbsp rolled oats

rolled oats

brown flour

water

malt extract

salt

dried yeast

VARIATION

To make a large loaf, shape the dough into a round, flatten it slightly and bake for 30–40 minutes. Test by tapping the base of the loaf – if it sounds hollow, it is cooked.

1 Put half the warm water in a jug. Sprinkle in the yeast. Add the sugar, mix well and leave for 10 minutes.

2 Put the malted brown flour and salt in a mixing bowl and make a well in the centre. Add the yeast mixture with the malt extract and the remaining water. Gradually incorporate the flour and mix to a soft dough.

3 Turn the dough on to a floured surface and knead for 5 minutes until smooth and elastic. Return to the clean bowl, cover with a damp dish towel and leave in a warm place to rise for about 2 hours until doubled in bulk.

4 Lightly grease a large baking sheet. Turn the dough on to a floured surface, knead for 2 minutes, then divide into eight pieces. Shape into balls and flatten with the palm of your hand to make neat 10 cm/4 in rounds.

5 Place the rounds on the prepared baking sheet, cover loosely with a large plastic bag (ballooning it to trap the air inside), and leave in a warm place until the baps are well risen. Preheat the oven to 220°C/425°F/Gas 7.

6 Brush the baps with water, sprinkle with the oats and bake for about 20–25 minutes or until they sound hollow when tapped underneath. Cool on a wire rack, then serve with the low fat filling of your choice.

Curry Crackers

These spicy, crisp little biscuits are very low fat and are ideal for serving with drinks.

Makes 12

INGREDIENTS
50 g/2 oz/¹/₂ cup plain flour
1.5 ml/¹/₄ tsp salt
5 ml/1 tsp curry powder
1.5 ml/¹/₄ tsp chilli powder
15 ml/1 tbsp chopped fresh
  coriander
30 ml/2 tbsp water

fresh coriander

chilli powder

salt

plain flour

water

curry powder

NUTRITIONAL NOTES
PER PORTION:

ENERGY 15 Kcals/65 KJ
FAT 0.11 g **SATURATED FAT** 0.01 g
CHOLESTEROL 0 **FIBRE** 0.21 g

1 Preheat the oven to 180°C/350°F/ Gas 4. Sift the flour and salt into a mixing bowl, then add the curry powder and chilli powder. Make a well in the centre and add the chopped fresh coriander and water. Gradually incorporate the flour and mix to a firm dough.

2 Turn on to a lightly floured surface, knead until smooth, then leave to rest for 5 minutes.

VARIATIONS
Omit the curry and chilli powders and add 15 ml/1 tbsp caraway, fennel or mustard seeds.

3 Cut the dough into 12 pieces and knead into small balls. Roll each ball out very thinly to a 10 cm/4 in round.

4 Arrange the rounds on two ungreased baking sheets, then bake for 15 minutes, turning over once during cooking. Cool on a wire rack.

Oatcakes

Try serving these oatcakes with reduced-fat hard cheeses. They are also delicious topped with thick honey for breakfast.

Makes 8

INGREDIENTS
175 g/6 oz/1 cup medium oatmeal,
   plus extra for sprinkling
2.5 ml/¹/₂ tsp salt
pinch of bicarbonate of soda
15 g/¹/₂ oz/1 tbsp butter
75 ml/5 tbsp water

medium oatmeal

bicarbonate of soda

salt

water

butter

NUTRITIONAL NOTES
PER PORTION:

ENERGY 102 Kcals/427 KJ
FAT 3.43 g **SATURATED FAT** 0.66 g
CHOLESTEROL 0.13 mg **FIBRE** 1.49 g

COOK'S TIP
To achieve a neat round, place a 25 cm/10 in cake board or plate on top of the oatcake. Cut away any excess dough with a palette knife, then remove the board or plate.

1 Preheat the oven to 150°C/300°F/ Gas 2. Mix the oatmeal with the salt and bicarbonate of soda in a mixing bowl.

2 Melt the butter with the water in a small saucepan. Bring to the boil, then add to the oatmeal mixture and mix to a moist dough.

3 Turn the dough on to a surface sprinkled with oatmeal and knead to a smooth ball. Turn a large baking sheet upside-down, grease it, sprinkle it lightly with oatmeal and place the ball of dough on top. Sprinkle the dough with oatmeal, then roll out to a 25 cm/10 in round.

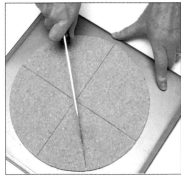

4 Cut the round into 8 sections, ease them apart slightly and bake for about 50–60 minutes until crisp. Leave to cool on the baking sheet, then remove the oatcakes with a palette knife.

Drop Scones

These little scones are delicious spread with jam.

Makes 18

INGREDIENTS
225 g/8 oz/2 cups self-raising flour
2.5 ml/¹/₂ tsp salt
15 ml/1 tbsp caster sugar
1 egg, beaten
300 ml/¹/₂ pint/1¹/₄ cups skimmed
 milk

egg

*self-raising
flour*

salt

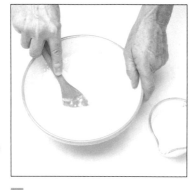

*skimmed
milk*

caster sugar

VARIATION

For savoury scones, omit the sugar and add 2 chopped spring onions and 15 ml/1 tbsp freshly grated Parmesan cheese to the batter. Serve with cottage cheese.

1 Preheat a griddle, heavy-based frying pan or an electric frying pan. Sift the flour and salt into a mixing bowl. Stir in the sugar and make a well in the centre.

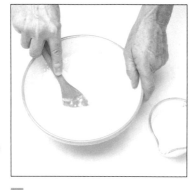

2 Add the egg and half the milk, then gradually incorporate the surrounding flour to make a smooth batter. Beat in the remaining milk.

NUTRITIONAL NOTES

PER PORTION:

ENERGY 64 Kcals/270 KJ
FAT 1.09 g **SATURATED FAT** 0.20 g
CHOLESTEROL 11.03 mg **FIBRE** 0.43 g

3 Lightly grease the griddle or pan. Drop tablespoons of the batter on to the surface, leaving them until they bubble and the bubbles begin to burst.

4 Turn the drop scones over with a palette knife and cook until the underside is golden brown. Keep the cooked drop scones warm and moist by wrapping them in a clean napkin while cooking successive batches.

Pineapple and Cinnamon Drop Scones

Making the batter with pineapple juice instead of milk cuts down on fat and adds to the taste.

Makes 24

INGREDIENTS

115 g/4 oz/1 cup self-raising wholemeal flour
115 g/4 oz/1 cup self-raising white flour
5 ml/1 tsp ground cinnamon
15 ml/1 tbsp caster sugar
1 egg
300 ml/½ pint/1¼ cups pineapple juice
75 g/3 oz/½ cup semi-dried pineapple, chopped

semi-dried pineapple

pineapple juice

egg

caster sugar

self-raising wholemeal flour

ground cinnamon

self-raising white flour

NUTRITIONAL NOTES

PER PORTION:

ENERGY 51 Kcals/215 KJ
FAT 0.81 g SATURATED FAT 0.14 g
CHOLESTEROL 8.02 mg FIBRE 0.76 g

1 Preheat a griddle, heavy-based frying pan or an electric frying pan. Put the wholemeal flour in a mixing bowl. Sift in the white flour, add the cinnamon and sugar and make a well in the centre.

2 Add the egg with half the pineapple juice and gradually incorporate the surrounding flour to make a smooth batter. Beat in the remaining juice with the chopped pineapple.

COOK'S TIP

Drop scones do not keep well and are best eaten freshly cooked.

3 Lightly grease the griddle or pan. Drop tablespoons of the batter on to the surface, leaving them until they bubble and the bubbles begin to burst.

4 Turn the drop scones with a palette knife and cook until the underside is golden brown. Keep the cooked scones warm and moist by wrapping them in a clean napkin while continuing to cook successive batches.

Soda Bread

Finding the bread bin empty need never be a problem when your repertoire includes a recipe for soda bread. It takes only a few minutes to make and needs no rising or proving. If possible eat soda bread while still warm from the oven as it does not keep well.

Serves 8

INGREDIENTS
450 g/1 lb/4 cups plain flour
5 ml/1 tsp salt
5 ml/1 tsp bicarbonate of soda
5 ml/1 tsp cream of tartar
350 ml/12 fl oz/1½ cups buttermilk

salt

buttermilk

bicarbonate of soda

plain flour

cream of tartar

1 Preheat the oven to 220°C/425°F/Gas 7. Flour a baking sheet. Sift all the dry ingredients into a mixing bowl and make a well in the centre.

2 Add the buttermilk and mix quickly to a soft dough. Turn on to a floured surface and knead lightly. Shape into a round about 18 cm/7 in in diameter and place on the baking sheet.

3 Cut a deep cross on top of the loaf and sprinkle with a little flour. Bake for 25–30 minutes, then transfer the soda bread to a wire rack to cool.

NUTRITIONAL NOTES
PER PORTION:

ENERGY 230 Kcals/967 KJ
FAT 1.03 g **SATURATED FAT** 0.24 g
CHOLESTEROL 0.88 mg **FIBRE** 1.94 g

COOK'S TIP
Soda bread needs a light hand. The ingredients should be bound together quickly in the bowl and kneaded very briefly. The aim is just to get rid of the largest cracks, as the dough will become tough if it is handled for too long.

Parma Ham and Parmesan Bread

This nourishing bread is almost a meal in itself.

Serves 8

INGREDIENTS
225 g/8 oz/2 cups self-raising
wholemeal flour
225 g/8 oz/2 cups self-raising
white flour
5 ml/1 tsp baking powder
5 ml/1 tsp salt
5 ml/1 tsp freshly ground
black pepper
75 g/3 oz Parma ham, chopped
25 g/1 oz/2 tbsp freshly grated
Parmesan cheese
30 ml/2 tbsp chopped fresh parsley
45 ml/3 tbsp Meaux mustard
350 ml/12 fl oz/1½ cups buttermilk
skimmed milk, to glaze

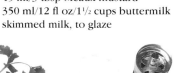
*self-raising
wholemeal flour*

parsley
salt
*Parmesan
cheese*

*black
pepper*

*self-raising
white flour*

*Meaux
mustard*

buttermilk
Parma ham

*baking
powder*

1 Preheat the oven to 200°C/400°F/
Gas 6. Flour a baking sheet. Place the
wholemeal flour in a bowl and sift in the
white flour, baking powder and salt. Add
the pepper and the ham. Set aside about
15 ml/1 tbsp of the grated Parmesan and
stir the rest into the flour mixture. Stir in
the parsley. Make a well in the centre.

2 Mix the mustard and buttermilk in a
jug, pour into the flour mixture and
quickly mix to a soft dough.

3 Turn the dough on to a floured
surface and knead briefly. Shape into an
oval loaf, brush with milk and sprinkle
with the remaining cheese. Place the loaf
on the prepared baking sheet.

4 Bake the loaf for 25–30 minutes, or
until golden brown. Transfer to a wire
rack to cool.

NUTRITIONAL NOTES
PER PORTION:

ENERGY 250 Kcals/1053 KJ
FAT 3.65 g **SATURATED FAT** 1.30 g
CHOLESTEROL 7.09 mg **FIBRE** 3.81 g

Austrian Three-Grain Bread

A mixture of grains gives this close-textured bread a delightful nutty flavour. Make two smaller twists if preferred.

Serves 8–10

INGREDIENTS
475 ml/16 fl oz/2 cups warm water
10 ml/2 tsp dried yeast
pinch of sugar
225 g/8 oz/2 cups strong white flour
7.5 ml/1½ tsp salt
225 g/8 oz/2 cups malted
  brown flour
225 g/8 oz/2 cups rye flour
30 ml/2 tbsp linseed
75 g/3 oz/½ cup medium oatmeal
45 ml/3 tbsp sunflower seeds
30 ml/2 tbsp malt extract

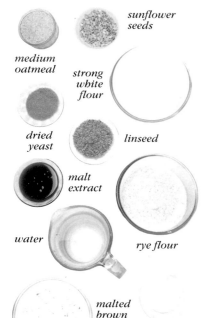

sunflower seeds

medium oatmeal

strong white flour

dried yeast

linseed

malt extract

water

rye flour

malted brown flour

salt

1 Put half the water in a jug. Sprinkle the yeast on top. Add the sugar, mix well and leave for 10 minutes.

2 Sift the white flour and salt into a mixing bowl and add the other flours. Set aside 5 ml/1 tsp of the linseed and add the rest to the flour mixture with the oatmeal and sunflower seeds. Make a well in the centre.

3 Add the yeast mixture to the bowl with the malt extract and the remaining water. Gradually incorporate the flour.

4 Mix to a soft dough, adding extra water if necessary. Turn out on to a floured surface and knead for about 5 minutes until smooth and elastic. Return to the clean bowl, cover with a damp dish towel and leave to rise for about 2 hours until doubled in bulk.

5 Flour a baking sheet. Turn the dough on to a floured surface, knead for 2 minutes then divide in half. Roll each half into a 30 cm/12 in long sausage.

6 Twist the two sausages together, dampen the ends and press to seal. Lift the twist on to the prepared baking sheet. Brush it with water, sprinkle with the remaining linseed and cover loosely with a large plastic bag (ballooning it to trap the air inside). Leave in a warm place until well risen. Preheat the oven to 220°C/425°F/Gas 7.

7 Bake the loaf for 10 minutes, then lower the oven temperature to 200°C/400°F/Gas 6 and cook for 20 minutes more, or until the loaf sounds hollow when it is tapped underneath. Transfer to a wire rack to cool.

NUTRITIONAL NOTES
PER PORTION:

ENERGY 367 Kcals/1540 KJ
FAT 5.36 g **SATURATED FAT** 0.60 g
CHOLESTEROL 0 **FIBRE** 6.76 g

Banana and Cardamom Bread

The combination of banana and cardamom is delicious in this soft-textured moist loaf. It is perfect for tea time, served with low fat spread and jam.

Serves 6

INGREDIENTS
150 ml/¼ pint/⅔ cup warm water
5 ml/1 tsp dried yeast
pinch of sugar
10 cardamom pods
400 g/14 oz/3½ cups strong
   white flour
5 ml/1 tsp salt
30 ml/2 tbsp malt extract
2 ripe bananas, mashed
5 ml/1 tsp sesame seeds

malt extract

dried yeast   *sesame seeds*

cardamom pods

bananas   *salt*

water

strong white flour

NUTRITIONAL NOTES
PER PORTION:

ENERGY 299 Kcals/1254 KJ
FAT 1.55 g **SATURATED FAT** 0.23 g
CHOLESTEROL 0 **FIBRE** 2.65 g

COOK'S TIP
Make sure the bananas are really ripe, so that they impart maximum flavour to the bread.

If you prefer, place the dough in one piece in a 450 g/1 lb loaf tin and bake for an extra 5 minutes.

1 Put the water in a small bowl. Sprinkle the yeast on top, add the sugar and mix well. Leave for 10 minutes.

2 Split the cardamom pods. Remove the seeds and chop them finely.

3 Sift the flour and salt into a mixing bowl and make a well in the centre. Add the yeast mixture with the malt extract, chopped cardamom seeds and bananas.

4 Gradually incorporate the flour and mix to a soft dough, adding a little extra water if necessary. Turn the dough on to a floured surface and knead for about 5 minutes until smooth and elastic. Return to the clean bowl, cover with a damp dish towel and leave to rise for about 2 hours until doubled in bulk.

5 Grease a baking sheet. Turn the dough on to a floured surface, knead briefly, then shape into a plait. Place the plait on the baking sheet and cover loosely with a plastic bag (ballooning it to trap the air). Leave until well risen. Preheat the oven to 220°C/425°F/Gas 7.

6 Brush the plait lightly with water and sprinkle with the sesame seeds. Bake for 10 minutes, then lower the oven temperature to 200°C/400°F/Gas 6. Cook for 15 minutes more, or until the loaf sounds hollow when it is tapped underneath. Cool on a wire rack.

Swedish Sultana Bread

A lightly sweetened bread that is delicious served warm. It is also excellent toasted and topped with low fat spread.

NUTRITIONAL NOTES
PER PORTION:

ENERGY 273 Kcals/1145 KJ
FAT 4.86 g SATURATED FAT 0.57 g
CHOLESTEROL 0.39 mg FIBRE 3.83 g

Serves 8–10

INGREDIENTS
150 ml/¼ pint/⅔ cup warm water
5 ml/1 tsp dried yeast
15 ml/1 tbsp clear honey
225 g/8 oz/2 cups wholemeal flour
225 g/8 oz/2 cups strong white flour
5 ml/1 tsp salt
115 g/4 oz/⅔ cup sultanas
50 g/2 oz/½ cup walnuts, chopped
175 ml/6 fl oz/¾ cup warm skimmed milk, plus extra for glazing

salt

strong white flour

walnuts

clear honey

water

skimmed milk

sultanas

dried yeast

wholemeal flour

VARIATION

To make Apple and Hazelnut Bread, replace the sultanas with 2 chopped eating apples and use chopped toasted hazelnuts instead of the walnuts. Add 5 ml/1 tsp ground cinnamon with the flour.

1 Put the water in a small bowl. Sprinkle the yeast on top. Add a few drops of the honey to help activate the yeast, mix well and leave for 10 minutes.

2 Put the flours in a bowl with the salt and sultanas. Set aside 15 ml/1 tbsp of the walnuts and add the rest to the bowl. Mix together lightly and make a well in the centre.

3 Add the yeast mixture to the flour mixture with the milk and remaining honey. Gradually incorporate the flour, mixing to a soft dough; add a little extra water if you need to.

4 Turn the dough on to a floured surface and knead for 5 minutes until smooth and elastic. Return to the clean bowl, cover with a damp dish towel and leave in a warm place to rise for about 2 hours until doubled in bulk. Grease a baking sheet.

5 Turn the dough on to a floured surface and knead for 2 minutes, then shape into a 28 cm/11 in long sausage shape. Place the loaf on the prepared baking sheet. Make some diagonal cuts down the whole length of the loaf.

6 Brush the loaf with milk, sprinkle with the reserved walnuts and leave to rise for about 40 minutes. Preheat the oven to 220°C/425°F/Gas 7. Bake the loaf for 10 minutes. Lower the oven temperature to 200°C/400°F/Gas 6 and bake for about 20 minutes more, or until the loaf sounds hollow when it is tapped underneath.

Rye Bread

Rye bread is popular in Northern Europe and makes an excellent base for open sandwiches – add a low fat topping of your choice.

Makes 2 loaves, each serving 6

INGREDIENTS
475 ml/16 fl oz/2 cups warm water
10 ml/2 tsp dried yeast
pinch of sugar
350 g/12 oz/3 cups wholemeal flour
225 g/8 oz/2 cups rye flour
115 g/4 oz/1 cup strong white flour
7.5 ml/1½ tsp salt
30 ml/2 tbsp caraway seeds
30 ml/2 tbsp molasses
30 ml/2 tbsp sunflower oil

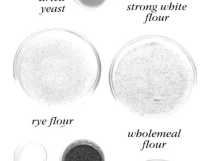

molasses
dried yeast
strong white flour

rye flour
wholemeal flour

salt
caraway seeds

sunflower oil
water

1 Put half the water in a jug. Sprinkle the yeast on top. Add the sugar, mix well and leave for 10 minutes.

2 Put the flours and salt in a bowl. Set aside 5 ml/1 tsp of the caraway seeds and add the rest to the bowl.

3 Make a well in the flour mixture, then add the yeast mixture with the molasses, oil and the remaining water. Gradually incorporate the flour and mix to a soft dough, adding a little extra water if necessary.

4 Turn the dough on to a floured surface and knead for 5 minutes until smooth and elastic. Return to the clean bowl, cover with a damp dish towel and leave in a warm place to rise for about 2 hours until doubled in bulk. Grease a baking sheet.

5 Turn the dough on to a floured surface and knead for 2 minutes, then divide the dough in half, shape into two 23 cm/9 in long oval loaves. Flatten the loaves slightly and place them on the baking sheet.

 Brush the loaves with water and sprinkle with the remaining caraway seeds. Cover and leave in a warm place for about 40 minutes until well risen. Preheat the oven to 200°C/400°F/Gas 6. Bake the loaves for 30 minutes, or until they sound hollow when they are tapped underneath. Cool on a wire rack. Serve the bread plain, or slice and add a low fat topping.

NUTRITIONAL NOTES
PER PORTION:

ENERGY 224 Kcals/941 KJ
FAT 3.43 g **SATURATED FAT** 0.33 g
CHOLESTEROL 0 **FIBRE** 6.04 g

VARIATION
Shape the dough into two loaves and bake in two greased 450 g/1 lb loaf tins, if you prefer.

Olive and Oregano Bread

This is an excellent accompaniment to all salads and is particularly good served warm.

NUTRITIONAL NOTES

Per portion:

ENERGY 202 Kcals/847 KJ
FAT 3.28 g **SATURATED FAT** 0.46 g
CHOLESTEROL 0 **FIBRE** 22.13 g

Serves 8–10

INGREDIENTS

300 ml/10 fl oz/1¼ cups warm water
5 ml/1 tsp dried yeast
pinch of sugar
15 ml/1 tbsp olive oil
1 onion, chopped
450 g/1 lb/4 cups strong white flour
5 ml/1 tsp salt
1.5 ml/¼ tsp freshly ground
  black pepper
50 g/2 oz/⅓ cup stoned black olives,
  roughly chopped
15 ml/1 tbsp black olive paste
15 ml/1 tbsp chopped fresh oregano
15 ml/1 tbsp chopped fresh parsley

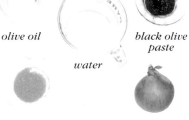

fresh oregano *fresh parsley* *black olives*

black pepper *strong white flour*

olive oil *black olive paste*

water

dried yeast *salt* *onion*

1 Put half the warm water in a jug. Sprinkle the yeast on top. Add the sugar, mix well and leave for 10 minutes.

2 Heat the olive oil in a frying pan and fry the onion until golden brown.

3 Sift the flour into a mixing bowl with the salt and pepper. Make a well in the centre. Add the yeast mixture, the fried onion (with the oil), the olives, olive paste, herbs and remaining water. Gradually incorporate the flour and mix to a soft dough, adding a little extra water if necessary.

4 Turn the dough on to a floured surface and knead for 5 minutes until smooth and elastic. Place in a mixing bowl, cover with a damp dish towel and leave in a warm place to rise for about 2 hours until doubled in bulk. Lightly grease a baking sheet.

5 Turn the dough on to a floured surface and knead again for a few minutes. Shape into a 20 cm/8 in round and place on the prepared baking sheet. Using a sharp knife, make criss-cross cuts over the top, cover and leave in a warm place for 30 minutes until well risen. Preheat the oven to 220°C/425°F/Gas 7.

6 Dust the loaf with a little flour. Bake for 10 minutes then lower the oven temperature to 200°C/400°F/Gas 6. Bake for 20 minutes more, or until the loaf sounds hollow when it is tapped underneath. Transfer to a wire rack to cool slightly before serving.

Cheese and Onion Herb Sticks

An extremely tasty bread which is very good with soup or salads. Use an extra-strong cheese to give plenty of flavour without piling on the fat.

Makes 2 sticks, each serving 4–6

INGREDIENTS
300 ml/½ pint/1¼ cups warm water
5 ml/1 tsp dried yeast
pinch of sugar
15 ml/1 tbsp sunflower oil
1 red onion, chopped
450 g/1 lb/4 cups strong white flour
5 ml/1 tsp salt
5 ml/1 tsp dry mustard powder
45 ml/3 tbsp chopped fresh herbs,
    such as thyme, parsley, marjoram
    or sage
75 g/3 oz/¾ cup grated reduced-fat
    Cheddar cheese

fresh herbs

sunflower oil

reduced-fat Cheddar cheese

salt

mustard powder

strong white flour

red onion

water

dried yeast

1 Put the water in a jug. Sprinkle the yeast on top. Add the sugar, mix well and leave for 10 minutes.

2 Heat the oil in a frying pan and fry the onion until well coloured.

3 Sift the flour, salt and mustard into a mixing bowl. Add the herbs. Set aside 30 ml/2 tbsp of the cheese. Stir the rest into the flour mixture and make a well in the centre. Add the yeast mixture with the fried onions and oil, then gradually incorporate the flour and mix to a soft dough, adding extra water if necessary.

4 Turn the dough on to a floured surface and knead for 5 minutes until smooth and elastic. Return to the clean bowl, cover with a damp dish towel and leave in a warm place to rise for about 2 hours until doubled in bulk. Lightly grease two baking sheets.

5 Turn the dough on to a floured surface, knead briefly, then divide the mixture in half and roll each piece into a 30 cm/12 in long stick. Place each stick on a baking sheet and make diagonal cuts along the top.

NUTRITIONAL NOTES

Per portion:

ENERGY 210 Kcals/882 KJ
FAT 3.16 g **SATURATED FAT** 0.25 g
CHOLESTEROL 3.22 mg **FIBRE** 1.79 g

6 Sprinkle the sticks with the reserved cheese. Cover and leave for 30 minutes until well risen. Preheat the oven to 220°C/425°F/Gas 7. Bake the sticks for 25 minutes or until they sound hollow when they are tapped underneath. Cool on a wire rack.

VARIATION
To make Onion and Coriander Sticks, omit the cheese, herbs and mustard. Add 15 ml/1 tbsp ground coriander and 45 ml/3 tbsp chopped fresh coriander instead.

Sun-dried Tomato Plait

This is a marvellous Mediterranean-flavoured bread to serve at a summer buffet or barbecue.

Serves 8–10

NUTRITIONAL NOTES
PER PORTION:

ENERGY 294 Kcals/1233 KJ
FAT 12.12 g SATURATED FAT 2.13 g
CHOLESTEROL 3.40 mg FIBRE 3.39 g

COOK'S TIP

If you are unable to locate red pesto, use 30 ml/2 tbsp chopped fresh basil mixed with 15 ml/1 tbsp sun-dried tomato paste.

INGREDIENTS

300 ml/½ pint/1¼ cups warm water
5 ml/1 tsp dried yeast
pinch of sugar
225 g/8 oz/2 cups wholemeal flour
225 g/8 oz/2 cups strong white flour
5 ml/1 tsp salt
1.5 ml/¼ tsp freshly ground
  black pepper
115 g/4 oz/⅔ cup drained sun-dried
  tomatoes in oil, chopped, plus
  15 ml/1 tbsp oil from the jar
25 g/1 oz/¼ cup freshly grated
  Parmesan cheese
30 ml/2 tbsp red pesto
5 ml/1 tsp coarse sea salt

Parmesan cheese *red pesto* *black pepper*
wholemeal flour *salt*
dried yeast *sun-dried tomatoes*

water
strong white flour
coarse sea salt *tomato oil*

 Put half the warm water in a jug. Sprinkle the yeast on top. Add the sugar, mix well and leave for 10 minutes.

2 Put the wholemeal flour in a mixing bowl. Sift in the white flour, salt and pepper. Make a well in the centre and add the yeast mixture, oil, sun-dried tomatoes, Parmesan, pesto and the remaining water. Gradually incorporate the flour and mix to a soft dough, adding a little extra water if necessary.

3 Turn the dough on to a floured surface and knead for 5 minutes until smooth and elastic. Return to the clean bowl, cover with a damp dish towel and leave in a warm place to rise for about 2 hours until doubled in bulk. Lightly grease a baking sheet.

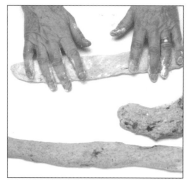

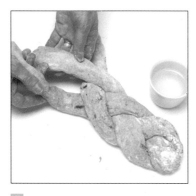

4 Turn the dough on to a lightly floured surface and knead for a few minutes. Divide the dough into three equal pieces and shape each into a 33 cm/13 in long sausage.

5 Dampen the ends of the three "sausages". Press them together at one end, plait them loosely, then press them together at the other end. Place on the baking sheet, cover and leave in a warm place for 30 minutes until well risen. Preheat the oven to 220°C/425°F/Gas 7.

 Sprinkle the plait with the coarse sea salt. Bake for 10 minutes, then lower the temperature to 200°C/400°F/Gas 6 and bake for a further 15–20 minutes, or until the loaf sounds hollow when tapped underneath. Cool on a wire rack.

Focaccia

This flat Italian bread is best served warm. It makes a delicious snack with low fat cheese and chunks of fresh tomato.

Serves 8

INGREDIENTS

300 ml/½ pint/1¼ cups warm water
5 ml/1 tsp dried yeast
pinch of sugar
450 g/1 lb/4 cups strong white flour
5 ml/1 tsp salt
1.5 ml/¼ tsp freshly ground
   black pepper
15 ml/1 tbsp pesto
115 g/4 oz/⅔ cup stoned black
   olives, chopped
25 g/1 oz/3 tbsp drained sun-dried
   tomatoes in oil, chopped, plus
   15 ml/1 tbsp oil from the jar
5 ml/1 tsp coarse sea salt
5 ml/1 tsp roughly chopped
   fresh rosemary

black pepper

sun-dried tomatoes

pesto

strong white flour

black olives

coarse sea salt

salt

water

dried yeast

fresh rosemary

tomato oil

1 Put the water in a bowl. Sprinkle the yeast on top. Add the sugar, mix well and leave for 10 minutes. Lightly grease a 33 x 23 cm/13 x 9 in Swiss roll tin.

2 Sift the flour, salt and pepper into a bowl and make a well in the centre.

3 Add the yeast mixture with the pesto, olives and sun-dried tomatoes (reserve the oil). Mix to a soft dough, adding a little extra water if necessary.

5 Turn the dough on to a floured surface, knead briefly, then roll out to a 33 x 23 cm/13 x 9 in rectangle. Lift the dough over the rolling pin and place in the prepared tin. Preheat the oven to 220°C/425°F/Gas 7.

4 Turn the dough on to a floured surface and knead for 5 minutes until smooth and elastic. Return to the clean bowl, cover with a damp dish towel and leave in a warm place to rise for about 2 hours until doubled in bulk.

NUTRITIONAL NOTES
PER PORTION:

ENERGY 247 Kcals/1038 KJ
FAT 6.42 g **SATURATED FAT** 0.93 g
CHOLESTEROL 0.35 mg **FIBRE** 2.18 g

 Using your fingertips, make small indentations all over the dough. Brush with the reserved oil from the sun-dried tomatoes, then sprinkle with the salt and rosemary. Leave to rise for 20 minutes, then bake for 20–25 minutes, or until golden. Transfer to a wire rack, but serve while still warm.

VARIATION
To make Oregano and Onion Focaccia, omit the pesto, olives and sun-dried tomatoes. Add 15 ml/ 1 tbsp chopped fresh oregano or 5 ml/1 tsp dried oregano to the flour. Slice 1 onion very thinly into rounds and scatter over the rolled out dough. Drizzle with olive oil and sprinkle with sea salt before baking.

Spinach and Bacon Bread

This bread is so tasty that it is a good idea to make double the quantity and freeze one of the loaves. Use smoked lean back bacon for the best possible flavour with the minimum of fat.

NUTRITIONAL NOTES
PER PORTION:
ENERGY 172 Kcals/723 KJ
FAT 2.17 g **SATURATED FAT** 0.36 g
CHOLESTEROL 1.97 mg **FIBRE** 1.68 g

Makes 2 loaves, each serving 8

INGREDIENTS
450 ml/³/₄ pint/2 cups warm water
10 ml/2 tsp dried yeast
pinch of sugar
15 ml/1 tbsp olive oil
1 onion, chopped
115 g/4 oz rindless smoked bacon
   rashers, chopped
225 g/8 oz chopped spinach, thawed
   if frozen
675 g/1¹/₂ lb/6 cups strong
   plain flour
7.5 ml/1¹/₂ tsp salt
2.5 ml/¹/₂ tsp grated nutmeg
25 g/1 oz/¹/₄ cup grated reduced-fat
   Cheddar cheese

dried yeast

bacon rashers

grated nutmeg

olive oil

salt

onion

reduced-fat Cheddar cheese

strong plain flour

spinach

water

COOK'S TIP
If using frozen spinach, be sure to squeeze out any excess liquid or the resulting dough will be too sticky.

1 Put the water in a small bowl. Sprinkle the yeast on top and add the sugar. Mix well and leave for 10 minutes. Lightly grease two 23 cm/9 in cake tins.

2 Heat the oil in a frying pan and fry the onion and bacon for 10 minutes until golden brown. Meanwhile, if using frozen spinach, drain it thoroughly.

3 Sift the flour, salt and nutmeg into a mixing bowl and make a well in the centre. Add the yeast mixture. Tip in the fried bacon and onion (with the oil), then add the spinach. Gradually incorporate the flour mixture and mix to a soft dough.

4 Turn the dough on to a floured surface and knead for 5 minutes until smooth and elastic. Return to the clean bowl, cover with a damp dish towel and leave in a warm place to rise for about 2 hours until doubled in bulk.

5 Turn the dough on to a floured surface, knead briefly then divide it in half. Shape each half into a ball, flatten slightly and place in a tin, pressing the dough so that it extends to the edges. Mark each loaf into eight wedges and sprinkle with the cheese. Cover loosely with a plastic bag and leave in a warm place until well risen. Preheat the oven to 200°C/400°F/Gas 6.

6 Bake the loaves for 25–30 minutes, or until they sound hollow when they are tapped underneath. Transfer to a wire rack to cool.

Malt Loaf

This is a rich and sticky loaf. If it lasts long enough to go stale, try toasting it for a delicious tea-time treat.

NUTRITIONAL NOTES

Per portion:

ENERGY 279 Kcals/1171 KJ
FAT 2.06 g **SATURATED FAT** 0.33 g
CHOLESTEROL 0.38 mg **FIBRE** 1.79 g

Serves 8

INGREDIENTS
150 ml/¼ pint/⅔ cup warm
    skimmed milk
5 ml/1 tsp dried yeast
pinch of caster sugar
350 g/12 oz/3 cups plain flour
1.5 ml/¼ tsp salt
30 ml/2 tbsp light muscovado sugar
175 g/6 oz/generous 1 cup sultanas
15 ml/1 tbsp sunflower oil
45 ml/3 tbsp malt extract

FOR THE GLAZE
30 ml/2 tbsp caster sugar
30 ml/2 tbsp water

malt extract

sultanas

salt

plain flour

skimmed milk

light muscovado sugar

dried yeast

sunflower oil

VARIATION

To make buns, divide the dough into 10 pieces, shape into rounds, leave to rise, then bake for about 15–20 minutes. Brush with the glaze while still hot.

1 Place the warm milk in a bowl. Sprinkle the yeast on top and add the sugar. Leave for 30 minutes until frothy. Sift the flour and salt into a mixing bowl, stir in the muscovado sugar and sultanas, and make a well in the centre.

2 Add the yeast mixture with the oil and malt extract. Gradually incorporate the flour and mix to a soft dough, adding a little extra milk if necessary.

3 Turn on to a floured surface and knead for about 5 minutes until smooth and elastic. Grease a 450 g/1 lb loaf tin.

4 Shape the dough and place it in the prepared tin. Cover with a damp dish towel and leave in a warm place for 1–2 hours until well risen. Preheat the oven to 190°C/375°F/Gas 5.

5 Bake the loaf for 30–35 minutes, or until it sounds hollow when it is tapped underneath.

6 Meanwhile, prepare the glaze by dissolving the sugar in the water in a small pan. Bring to the boil, stirring, then lower the heat and simmer for 1 minute. Place the loaf on a wire rack and brush with the glaze while still hot. Leave the loaf to cool before serving.

Cinnamon Apple Gâteau

Make this lovely cake for an autumn celebration.

Serves 8

NUTRITIONAL NOTES

PER PORTION:

ENERGY 244 Kcals/1023 KJ
FAT 4.05 g **SATURATED FAT** 1.71 g
CHOLESTEROL 77.95 mg **FIBRE** 1.50 g

INGREDIENTS
3 eggs
115 g/4 oz/¹/₂ cup caster sugar
75 g/3 oz/³/₄ cup plain flour
5 ml/1 tsp ground cinnamon

FOR THE FILLING AND TOPPING
4 large eating apples
60 ml/4 tbsp clear honey
15 ml/1 tbsp water
75 g/3 oz/¹/₂ cup sultanas
2.5 ml/¹/₂ tsp ground cinnamon
350 g/12 oz/1¹/₂ cups low fat
  soft cheese
60 ml/4 tbsp reduced-fat
  fromage frais
10 ml/2 tsp lemon juice
45 ml/3 tbsp Apricot Glaze
mint sprigs, to decorate

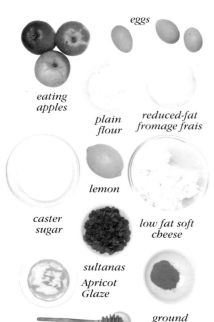

eggs

eating apples

plain flour

reduced-fat fromage frais

lemon

caster sugar

low fat soft cheese

sultanas

Apricot Glaze

ground cinnamon

clear honey

1 Preheat the oven to 190°C/375°F/Gas 5. Grease and line a 23 cm/9 in sandwich cake tin. Place the eggs and caster sugar in a bowl and beat with a hand-held electric whisk until thick and mousse-like (when the whisk is lifted, a trail should remain on the surface of the mixture for at least 15 seconds).

2 Sift the flour and cinnamon over the egg mixture and carefully fold in with a large spoon. Pour into the prepared tin and bake for 25–30 minutes or until the cake springs back when lightly pressed. Slide a palette knife between the cake and the tin to loosen the edge, then turn the cake on to a wire rack to cool.

To make the filling, peel, core and slice three of the apples and put them in a saucepan. Add 30 ml/2 tbsp of the honey and the water. Cover and cook over a gentle heat for about 10 minutes until the apples have softened. Add the sultanas and cinnamon, stir well, replace the lid and leave to cool.

3

4 Put the soft cheese in a bowl with the remaining honey, the fromage frais and half the lemon juice. Beat until the mixture is smooth.

5 Halve the cake horizontally, place the bottom half on a board and drizzle over any liquid from the apples. Spread with two-thirds of the cheese mixture, then top with the apple filling. Fit the top of the cake in place.

6 Swirl the remaining cheese mixture over the top of the sponge. Core and slice the remaining apple, sprinkle with lemon juice and use to decorate the edge of the cake. Brush the apple with Apricot Glaze and place mint sprigs on top, to decorate.

Chestnut and Orange Roulade

This moist cake is ideal to serve as a dessert.

NUTRITIONAL NOTES

PER PORTION:

ENERGY 185 Kcals/775 KJ
FAT 4.01 g **SATURATED FAT** 1.47 g
CHOLESTEROL 76.25 mg **FIBRE** 1.40 g

Serves 8

INGREDIENTS
3 eggs, separated
115 g/4 oz/½ cup caster sugar
½ x 439 g/15½ oz can unsweetened chestnut purée
grated rind and juice of 1 orange
icing sugar, for dusting

FOR THE FILLING
225 g/8 oz/1 cup low fat soft cheese
15 ml/1 tbsp clear honey
1 orange

eggs

unsweetened chestnut purée

clear honey

caster sugar

oranges

low fat soft cheese

COOK'S TIP

Do not whisk the egg whites too stiffly, or it will be difficult to fold them into the mixture and they will form lumps in the roulade.

1 Preheat the oven to 180°C/350°F/Gas 4. Grease a 30 x 20 cm/12 x 8 in Swiss roll tin and line with non-stick baking paper. Whisk the egg yolks and sugar in a bowl until thick and creamy.

2 Put the chestnut purée in a separate bowl. Whisk in the orange rind and juice, then whisk the flavoured chestnut purée into the egg mixture.

3 Whisk the egg whites in a grease-free bowl until fairly stiff. Using a metal spoon, stir a generous spoonful of the whites into the chestnut mixture to lighten it, then fold in the rest.

4 Spoon the roulade mixture into the prepared tin and bake for 30 minutes until firm. Cool for 5 minutes, then cover with a clean damp dish towel and leave until completely cold.

5 Meanwhile, make the filling. Put the soft cheese in a bowl with the honey. Finely grate the orange rind and add to the bowl. Peel away all the pith from the orange, cut the fruit into segments, chop roughly and set aside. Add any juice to the cheese mixture, then beat until it is smooth. Mix in the chopped orange.

6 Sprinkle a sheet of greaseproof paper thickly with icing sugar. Carefully turn the roulade out on to the paper, then peel off the lining paper. Spread the filling over the roulade and roll up like a Swiss roll. Transfer to a plate and dust with some more icing sugar.

Nectarine Amaretto Cake

Try this delicious cake with low fat fromage frais for dessert, or serve it solo for afternoon tea. The syrup makes it moist but not soggy.

NUTRITIONAL NOTES

PER PORTION:

ENERGY 264 Kcals/1108 KJ
FAT 5.70 g **SATURATED FAT** 0.85 g
CHOLESTEROL 72.19 mg **FIBRE** 1.08 g

Serves 8

INGREDIENTS
3 eggs, separated
175 g/6 oz/³/₄ cup caster sugar
grated rind and juice of 1 lemon
50 g/2 oz/¹/₃ cup semolina
40 g/1¹/₂ oz/¹/₃ cup ground almonds
25 g/1 oz/¹/₄ cup plain flour
2 nectarines or peaches, halved
  and stoned
60 ml/4 tbsp Apricot Glaze

FOR THE SYRUP
75 g/3 oz/6 tbsp caster sugar
90 ml/6 tbsp water
30 ml/2 tbsp Amaretto liqueur

Amaretto liqueur

water

Apricot Glaze

ground almonds

nectarines

eggs

semolina

caster sugar

plain flour

lemon

1 Preheat the oven to 180°C/350°F/ Gas 4. Grease a 20 cm/8 in round loose-bottomed cake tin. Whisk the egg yolks, caster sugar, lemon rind and juice in a bowl until thick, pale and creamy.

2 Fold in the semolina, almonds and flour until smooth.

3 Whisk the egg whites in a grease-free bowl until fairly stiff. Using a metal spoon, stir a generous spoonful of the whites into the semolina mixture to lighten it, then fold in the remaining egg whites. Spoon the mixture into the prepared cake tin.

4 Bake for 30–35 minutes until the centre of the cake springs back when lightly pressed. Remove the cake from the oven and carefully loosen around the edge with a palette knife. Prick the top of the cake with a skewer and leave to cool slightly in the tin.

VARIATION
Use drained canned mandarin orange segments for the topping, if preferred, and use an orange-flavoured liqueur instead of the Amaretto.

5 Meanwhile, make the syrup. Heat the sugar and water in a small pan, stirring until dissolved, then boil without stirring for 2 minutes. Add the Amaretto liqueur and drizzle slowly over the cake.

6 Remove the cake from the tin and transfer it to a serving plate. Slice the nectarines or peaches, arrange them over the top and brush with the warm Apricot Glaze.

Strawberry Gâteau

It is hard to believe that this delicious gâteau is
low in fat, but it is true, so enjoy!

Serves 6

INGREDIENTS
2 eggs
75 g/3 oz/6 tbsp caster sugar
grated rind of ½ orange
50 g/2 oz/½ cup plain flour
strawberry leaves, to decorate
icing sugar, for dusting

FOR THE FILLING
275 g/10 oz/1¼ cups low fat
    soft cheese
grated rind of ½ orange
30 ml/2 tbsp caster sugar
60 ml/4 tbsp low fat
    fromage frais
225 g/8 oz strawberries, halved
25 g/1 oz/¼ cup chopped
    almonds, toasted

low fat
fromage frais

eggs

strawberries

low fat soft
cheese

caster
sugar

almonds

orange

plain flour

NUTRITIONAL NOTES

PER PORTION:

ENERGY 213 Kcals/893 KJ
FAT 6.08 g **SATURATED FAT** 1.84 g
CHOLESTEROL 70.22 mg **FIBRE** 1.02 g

VARIATION

Use other soft fruits in season, such
as currants, raspberries, blackberries
or blueberries, or try a mixture of
different berries.

1 Preheat the oven to 190°C/375°F/
Gas 5. Grease a 30 x 20 cm/12 x 8 in
Swiss roll tin and line with non-stick
baking paper.

2 In a bowl, whisk the eggs, sugar and
orange rind together with a hand-held
electric whisk until thick and mousse-like
(when the whisk is lifted, a trail should
remain on the surface of the mixture for
at least 15 seconds).

3 Fold in the flour with a metal spoon,
being careful not to knock out any air.
Turn into the prepared tin. Bake for
15–20 minutes, or until the cake springs
back when lightly pressed. Turn the cake
on to a wire rack, remove the lining
paper and leave to cool.

4 Meanwhile make the filling. In a
bowl, mix the soft cheese with the
orange rind, sugar and fromage frais until
smooth. Divide between two bowls.
Chop half the strawberry halves and add
to one bowl of filling.

5 Cut the sponge widthways into
three equal pieces and sandwich them
together with the strawberry filling.
Spread two-thirds of the plain filling over
the sides of the cake and press on the
toasted almonds.

6 Spread the rest of the filling over the
top of the cake and decorate with the
strawberry halves, and strawberry leaves
if liked. Dust with icing sugar and transfer
to a serving plate.

Tia Maria Gâteau

A feather-light coffee sponge with a creamy liqueur-flavoured filling.

NUTRITIONAL NOTES
PER PORTION:

ENERGY 226 Kcals/951 KJ
FAT 3.14 g **SATURATED FAT** 1.17 g
CHOLESTEROL 75.03 mg **FIBRE** 0.64 g

Serves 8

INGREDIENTS
75 g/3 oz/³/₄ cup plain flour
30 ml/2 tbsp instant coffee powder
3 eggs
115 g/4 oz/¹/₂ cup caster sugar
coffee beans, to decorate (optional)

FOR THE FILLING
175 g/6 oz/³/₄ cup low fat soft cheese
15 ml/1 tbsp clear honey
15 ml/1 tbsp Tia Maria
50 g/2 oz/¹/₄ cup stem ginger,
   roughly chopped

FOR THE ICING
225 g/8 oz/1³/₄ cups icing
   sugar, sifted
10 ml/2 tsp coffee essence
15 ml/1 tbsp water
5 ml/1 tsp fat-reduced cocoa powder

clear honey
eggs
coffee beans
coffee essence
low fat soft cheese
coffee powder
stem ginger
plain flour
icing sugar
caster sugar
fat-reduced cocoa powder
Tia Maria

1 Preheat the oven to 190°C/375°F/ Gas 5. Grease and line a 20 cm/8 in deep round cake tin. Sift the flour and coffee powder together on to a sheet of greaseproof paper.

2 Whisk the eggs and sugar in a bowl with a hand-held electric whisk until thick and mousse-like (when the whisk is lifted, a trail should remain on the surface of the mixture for at least 15 seconds).

3 Gently fold in the flour mixture with a metal spoon, being careful not to knock out any air. Turn the mixture into the prepared tin. Bake the sponge for 30–35 minutes or until it springs back when lightly pressed. Turn on to a wire rack and leave to cool completely.

4 Make the filling. Mix the soft cheese with the honey in a bowl. Beat until smooth, then stir in the Tia Maria and chopped stem ginger.

5 Split the cake in half horizontally and sandwich the two halves together with the Tia Maria filling.

6 Make the icing. In a bowl, mix the icing sugar and coffee essence with enough of the water to make an icing which will coat the back of a wooden spoon. Pour three-quarters of the icing over the cake, spreading it evenly to the edges. Stir the cocoa into the remaining icing until smooth. Spoon into a piping bag fitted with a writing nozzle and pipe the mocha icing over the coffee icing. Decorate with coffee beans, if liked.

VARIATION

To make a Mocha Gâteau, replace the coffee powder with 30 ml/2 tbsp fat-reduced cocoa powder, sifting it with the flour. Omit the chopped ginger in the filling.

Raspberry Vacherin

Meringue rounds filled with orange-flavoured fromage frais and fresh raspberries make a perfect dinner party dessert.

NUTRITIONAL NOTES
PER PORTION:

ENERGY 248 Kcals/1041 KJ
FAT 2.22 g SATURATED FAT 0.82 g
CHOLESTEROL 4.00 mg FIBRE 1.06 g

Serves 6

INGREDIENTS
3 egg whites
175 g/6 oz/³/₄ cup caster sugar
5 ml/1 tsp chopped almonds
icing sugar, for dusting
raspberry leaves, to decorate

FOR THE FILLING
175 g/6 oz/³/₄ cup low fat soft cheese
15–30 ml/1–2 tbsp clear honey
15 ml/1 tbsp Cointreau
120 ml/4 fl oz/¹/₂ cup low fat
    fromage frais
225 g/8 oz raspberries

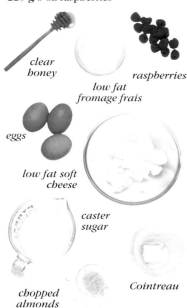

clear
honey

low fat
fromage frais

raspberries

eggs

low fat soft
cheese

caster
sugar

chopped
almonds

Cointreau

COOK'S TIP

When making the meringue, whisk the egg whites until they are so stiff that you can turn the bowl upside-down without them falling out.

1 Preheat the oven to 140°C/275°F/ Gas 1. Draw a 20 cm/8 in circle on two pieces of non-stick baking paper. Turn the paper over so the marking is on the underside and use it to line two heavy baking sheets.

2 Whisk the egg whites in a grease-free bowl until very stiff, then gradually whisk in the caster sugar to make a stiff meringue mixture.

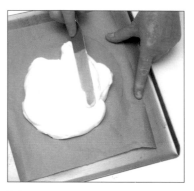

3 Spoon the mixture on to the circles on the prepared baking sheets, spreading the meringue evenly to the edges. Sprinkle one meringue round with the chopped almonds.

4 Bake for 1¹/₂–2 hours, then carefully lift the meringue rounds off the baking sheets, peel away the paper and cool on a wire rack.

5 To make the filling, cream the soft cheese with the honey and liqueur in a bowl. Fold in the fromage frais and raspberries, reserving three of the best for decoration.

6 Place the plain meringue round on a board, spread with the filling and top with the nut-covered round. Dust with icing sugar, transfer to a serving plate and decorate with the reserved raspberries, and a sprig of raspberry leaves, if liked.

Lemon Chiffon Cake

Lemon mousse provides a tangy filling for this light lemon sponge.

Serves 8

INGREDIENTS
2 eggs
75 g/3 oz/6 tbsp caster sugar
grated rind of 1 lemon
50 g/2 oz/½ cup sifted plain flour
Lemon Shreds, to decorate

FOR THE FILLING
2 eggs, separated
75 g/3 oz/6 tbsp caster sugar
grated rind and juice of 1 lemon
30 ml/2 tbsp water
15 ml/1 tbsp gelatine
125 ml/4 fl oz/½ cup low fat
   fromage frais

FOR THE ICING
115 g/4 oz/scant 1 cup icing
   sugar, sifted
15 ml/1 tbsp lemon juice

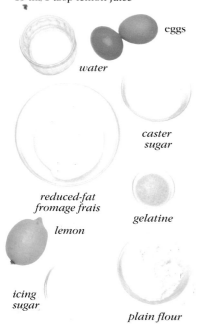

eggs

water

caster
sugar

reduced-fat
fromage frais

gelatine

lemon

icing
sugar

plain flour

1 Preheat the oven to 180°C/350°F/ Gas 4. Grease and line a 20 cm/8 in loose-bottomed cake tin. Whisk the eggs, sugar and lemon rind together with a hand-held electric whisk until thick and mousse-like. Gently fold in the flour, then turn the mixture into the prepared tin.

2 Bake for 20–25 minutes until the cake springs back when lightly pressed in the centre. Turn on to a wire rack to cool. Once cold, split the cake in half horizontally and return the lower half to the clean cake tin. Set aside.

3 Make the filling. Place the egg yolks, sugar, lemon rind and juice in a bowl. Beat with a hand-held electric whisk until thick, pale and creamy.

4 Pour the water into a small heat-proof bowl and sprinkle the gelatine on top. Leave until spongy, then place over simmering water and stir until dissolved. Cool slightly, then whisk into the yolk mixture. Fold in the fromage frais. When the mixture begins to set, quickly whisk the egg whites to soft peaks. Fold a spoonful into the mousse mixture to lighten it, then fold in the rest.

5 Pour the lemon mousse over the sponge in the cake tin, spreading it to the edges. Set the second layer of sponge on top and chill until set.

6 Slide a palette knife dipped in hot water between the tin and the cake to loosen it, then carefully transfer the cake to a serving plate. Make the icing by adding enough lemon juice to the icing sugar to make a mixture thick enough to coat the back of a wooden spoon. Pour over the cake and spread evenly to the edges. Decorate with the Lemon Shreds.

NUTRITIONAL NOTES
PER PORTION:

ENERGY 202 Kcals/849 KJ
FAT 2.81 g **SATURATED FAT** 0.79 g
CHOLESTEROL 96.41 mg **FIBRE** 0.20 g

COOK'S TIP
The mousse mixture should be just on the point of setting when the egg whites are added. This setting process can be speeded up by placing the bowl of mousse in a bowl of iced water.

INDEX

January

Spring passes and one remembers one's innocence.
Summer passes and one remembers one's exuberance.
Autumn passes and one remembers one's reverence.
Winter passes and one remembers one's perseverance.
Yoko Ono

31 Monday   New Year's Eve

1 Tuesday   New Year's Day

2 Wednesday

3 Thursday

4 Friday

5 Saturday

6 Sunday   Epiphany

If you do one thing

Go easy on the New Year resolutions. You're much more likely to succeed if you choose to tackle one thing at a time. So instead of resolving to lose weight, get fit and give up smoking all at once, pick the one that matters to you the most. Once you've reached that goal move onto the next.

School days

Here is my school photo taken in 1958. I am seated forth from the left. It was the local Village Church School at Bodenham, Herefordshire. Sadly, I did not enjoy my time there, as we had a very strict headmaster who ran the school with a rod of iron. One of the best things, though, was the lovely roast dinners we had at lunchtime, followed by pudding, which nearly always had custard with it.

Jennifer Phillipson, Hereford, Herefordshire

Mini Puzzle

Can you unscramble this conundrum to form a nine-letter word?

U	L	T	R	A	C	O	N	N

(answer Nocturnal)

Recipe of the week

Cranberry, Ginger and Mascarpone Filo Stacks

Serves: 6
Preparation time: 20 minutes
Cooking time: 10 minutes

4 sheets filo pastry
50g (2oz) butter, melted
65g (2^1/$_2$oz) caster sugar
50g (2oz) pistachio nuts, finely chopped
3 oranges
4 balls stem ginger, finely chopped
500g (1lb 2oz) tub mascarpone cheese
4 tbsp brandy or orange liqueur
4 tbsp cranberry sauce
Icing sugar, for dusting

1 Preheat the oven to 180°C/350°F/Gas Mark 4. Layer the four sheets of filo pastry with melted butter, one on top of each other. Scatter with 15g (^{1}/$_2$ oz) caster sugar and the pistachio nuts, then cut into 18 equal–sized squares.
2 Lay the squares on two foiled baking sheets and bake for eight minutes, or until golden brown.
3 Segment the oranges over a bowl to catch any juices, then add the ginger to it. Beat in the mascarpone, half the liqueur and remaining sugar, until smooth. In a separate bowl, whisk the cranberry sauce with the remaining liqueur.
4 Arrange six squares of filo pastry onto individual serving plates. Top each with a spoonful of the mascarpone mixture, a couple of pieces of orange and drizzle with a spoonful of cranberry sauce. Repeat, before finally topping with another layer of filo pastry. Dust with icing sugar and serve immediately. Decorate with holly and berries if desired.
© Ocean Spray Cranberries, www.oceanspray.co.uk

January 2013

7 Monday

8 Tuesday

9 Wednesday

10 Thursday

11 Friday

12 Saturday

13 Sunday

If you do one thing

Treat yourself to a bit of bronzer. Giving your skin a bit of a glow at this time of year could really lift your spirits. Use a large brush to sweep a light dusting of bronzing powder over your cheeks, nose and forehead – anywhere the sun would usually hit.

School days

Here is a photo of my Nan, Emily Minnie, and her class at Totteridge Road School, High Wycombe, in 1898. She is in the centre of the photograph with a necklace on, looking a little grumpy! Funnily enough, I remember my Nan as a very jolly person, who loved to sing and do little jigs to the Billy Cotton Band Show on the radio. I can still hear her voice saying 'Wakey, Wakey!'
Maureen Oaten, Christchurch, Dorset

Mini Puzzle

Can you unscramble this conundrum to form a nine-letter word?

L	O	A	D	S	T	O	T	O

(answer Toadstool)

Recipe of the week

Almond Granola Bars

Makes: 12
Preparation time: 10 minutes
Cooking time: 40 minutes

110g (4oz) butter, plus extra for greasing
150g (5oz) rolled porridge oats
75g (2^1/$_2$oz) sunflower seeds
125g (4^1/$_2$oz) blanched almonds, roughly chopped
50g (2oz) sesame seeds
110g (4oz) light muscavado sugar
50g (2oz) honey

1 Preheat the oven to 180°C/350°F/Gas Mark 4. Grease and line a 15 x 20cm (6 x 8inch) baking tin. Roast the nuts and seeds for ten minutes, or until golden brown. Watch these to make sure they don't burn.
2 In a saucepan, heat the butter, honey and sugar, until melted. Mix in the oats and the toasted nuts, then press into the greased and lined baking tin.
3 Bake for 30 minutes, or until golden brown. Remove from the heat and score into 12 pieces – leave to cool completely before cutting apart. These will keep for up to a week in an airtight container. They're perfect for a nutritious, on-the-go breakfast; or make a great dessert when served with a scoop of good quality ice-cream.
© Californian Almonds, www.almondboard.com

14 Monday

15 Tuesday

16 Wednesday

17 Thursday

18 Friday

19 Saturday

20 Sunday

If you do one thing

Have soup for lunch. It's a great way to warm up on a cold winter's day and it will fill you up without too many calories. Look for one that's made with beans or lentils – both good sources of protein and fibre to help you feel fuller for longer.

School days

I was seven years old in this class photo taken in 1958 at Glenfields Infants, Southampton. I am fifth from the left in the bottom row. Note the bootees I was wearing, which were popular at the time. The school was surrounded by woods and I remember my class being taken on some beautiful nature rambles to study the plants and insects. School was fun at that age.

Mrs C Barrow, Plymouth, Devon

Mini Puzzle

Can you unscramble this conundrum to form a nine-letter word?

D	U	D	E	G	I	S	I	S

(answer: Disguised)

Recipe of the week

Thai Beef Noodle Salad

Serves: 2
Preparation time: 30 minutes + 20 minutes marinating time
Cooking time: On each side: Rare 2¹/₂ minutes; medium 4 minutes; well done 6 minutes.

2 x 2cm (³/₄inch) thick lean rump or fillet steaks
3 tbsp ready-made Teriyaki sauce
1 tsp sesame oil
For the dressing:
2 tbsp fresh lime juice
1 tbsp Thai fish sauce
Handful of fresh mint, chopped
For the salad:
100g (3¹/₂oz) rice noodles, cooked and cooled
8 radishes, finely sliced
¹/₂ cucumber, thinly peeled to form ribbons
1 red chilli, de-seeded and finely chopped

1 Place the steaks in a shallow dish and coat with the Teriyaki sauce, oil and black pepper. Mix well, cover and chill for 20 minutes. Meanwhile, make the dressing by mixing all the ingredients together and set aside.
2 Heat a non-stick griddle pan and cook the steaks according to your preference. Alternatively, cook under a preheated moderate grill. Transfer to a warm plate and leave to rest for 1-2 minutes.
3 Meanwhile, mix the salad ingredients in a large bowl and transfer to a serving plate. Thinly slice the steaks and arrange over the salad. Stir the dressing before drizzling over the salad. Serve immediately.
© Simply Beef and Lamb, www.simplybeefandlamb.co.uk

January 2013

21 Monday

22 Tuesday

23 Wednesday

24 Thursday

25 Friday

Burns' Night

26 Saturday

27 Sunday

Holocaust Memorial Day

Recipe of the week

If you do one thing

Take a Vitamin D supplement. This wonder vitamin has been found to boost immunity, bolster your bone strength and even help you live longer. Your body makes Vitamin D from sunshine – but in the winter months most people in the UK don't get enough. Take 10 micrograms a day.

School days

This school photo was taken about sixty years ago. We had to dress as people from other countries. I am the girl in a Scottish costume on the right side of the photograph. I am still in touch with some of the pupils as, 20 years ago, we had our first school reunion. We have met every year since then and have rekindled friendships after all this time.

Monica Norris, Blackpool, Lancashire

Extra-Light Fruity Scones

Makes: 8
Preparation time: 20 minutes
Cooking time: 15 minutes

50g (2oz) margarine, plus extra for greasing
250g (9oz) self-raising flour, plus extra for kneading
1 tsp baking powder
1 medium cooking apple, peeled, cored and grated
25g (1oz) caster sugar
50g (2oz) low-fat cream cheese
5 tbsp skimmed milk
100g (3½ oz) light cream cheese, to serve
1 tbsp no-added-sugar fruit jam per scone

1 Preheat the oven to 200°C/400°F/Gas Mark 6. Lightly grease a baking tray. In a large mixing bowl, rub the fat into the flour until it resembles breadcrumbs. Add the remaining dry ingredients and mix well. Separately, mix a tablespoon of the milk with the cream cheese, to form a runny paste. Stir into the dry ingredients. Then add enough milk to form a stiff dough (saving some to brush the top of the scones).
2 Roll out the dough on a lightly floured surface 2cm (²/₃ inch) thick. Using a scone cutter, make eight scones and place on the baking tray. Brush the tops with milk and bake for 10-15 minutes, or until golden brown.
3 Cool on a wire rack and eat warm or cold, filled with the cream cheese and jam.

Top Tip: Try adding a sprinkle of ground cinnamon when mixing the dry ingredients.
© Philadelphia, www.philadelphia.co.uk

Mini Puzzle

Can you unscramble this conundrum to form a nine-letter word?

C	A	R	E	R	F	A	N	G

(answer Fragrance)

January 2013

28 Monday

29 Tuesday

30 Wednesday

31 Thursday

1 Friday

2 Saturday

3 Sunday

If you do one thing

Write a note. Whether it's a thank you card or a letter to a friend you haven't seen in a while, putting pen to paper could improve your wellbeing. Scientists have found that people who write letters expressing their gratitude are happier and more satisfied with their lives, while other studies have shown that expressing yourself on paper could boost immunity and lower your blood pressure.

School days

This photo is of class 4A at Fareham Modern Secondary School, which I attended from 1945-49. Our teacher was Miss Nuttall, who eventually married one of the boys' teachers and became Mrs Barker. We did wonder how she managed to meet the boys' teachers, as we were not allowed to cross the invisible line between us and the boys!

Mooneen Truckle, Salisbury, Wiltshire

Mini Puzzle

Can you unscramble this conundrum to form a nine-letter word?

| F | I | N | E | H | A | R | M | S |

(answer Fisherman)

Recipe of the week

Saintly Roasted Rhubarb and Vanilla Dessert

Serves: 4
Preparation time: 15 minutes
Cooking time: 10 minutes

400g (14oz) rhubarb, roughly chopped
50g (2oz) golden caster sugar
Juice of ½ lemon
500g (1lb 2oz) good-quality custard
Ground cinnamon, to decorate

1 Preheat the oven to 200°C/400°F/Gas Mark 6. Line a baking sheet with baking parchment, or grease well and spread the rhubarb out over this.
2 Sprinkle on the golden caster sugar and pour over the lemon juice. Mix well and roast for ten minutes, or until the rhubarb is just tender. Remove from the heat and leave to cool for five minutes.
3 Divide the custard between four glass serving dishes, spooning over the rhubarb. Sprinkle a pinch of cinnamon over each one and serve immediately. This can be eaten cold too.
© Alpro Soya, www.alprosoya.co.uk

A grand day out

Celebrate a classic — literally — at Chatsworth, one of England's best-loved stately homes in the Peak District

It was 200 years ago this month that Jane Austen's classic, Pride and Prejudice, was first published in the UK. Today, you can experience a taste of the novel at Chatsworth House in the Peak District. While staying in nearby Bakewell, the grandeur of the place was thought to have inspired Jane to create Pemberley House – and one of the most romantic love stories of all time. For the 2005 film adaption, the Pemberley scenes were actually filmed there, and Chatsworth really did become Mr Darcy's residence for a short while.

Parts of The Duchess (2008) were also filmed at Chatsworth; Georgiana, Duchess of Devonshire had indeed lived there, with her Duke and Lady Elizabeth Foster.

Many of the house's historic rooms are open to the public. It is home to one of Europe's most significant art collections, as well as a beautiful, 105-acre garden. There's plenty to keep the grandchildren entertained, including a woodland adventure playground, a farmyard with animal handling, and a choice of eateries. Visit www.chatsworth.org for further information.

While in the area, make time to visit Bakewell itself, which is the charming capital of the Peaks. Walk along the River Wye, and admire the 14th Century gothic bridge with its five arches, or wander through the town's pretty streets. And be sure to sample the famous Bakewell Pudding, quite unlike Bakewell Tart, but still delicious!

Also, nearby are the popular towns of Matlock and Buxton, and, of course, the Peak District has wonderful countryside to explore. One of the best views is from the Heights of Abraham at Matlock Bath – you can reach the top via cable car. As well as looking out over Derwent Valley, take a look inside the caverns; and youngsters will enjoy the fabulous adventure playground.

For more details visit www.heightsofabraham.com.

Fact: The highest point in the Peak District is moorland plateau Kinder Scout, at 636 metres.

With thanks to VisitEngland, the national tourist board for England, visit www.visitengland.com.

Quiz of the month

Many great novels have been adapted for TV – how many of these literary series have you seen? If you get stuck the answers are below.

1 Which actor played Mister Tom in the ITV adaptation of Goodnight Mister Tom by by Michelle Magorian?

2 Which Dickens novel featuring the orphan Pip was adapted for the BBC?

3 Who was the author of Birdsong – recently adapted by the BBC?

4 Who played the older Logan Mountstuart in the Channel 4 adaptation of Any Human Heart by William Boyd?

5 Colin Firth played Mr Darcy – but who was his Elizabeth Bennett in the BBC series of Jane Austen's Pride and Prejudice?

6 Which BBC series starring James Nesbit was said to be a sequel to the Strange Case of Dr Jekyll and Mr Hyde by Robert Louis Stephenson rather than an adaptation of it?

7 Which BBC detective series left viewers in suspense in January 2012 with the apparent death of its super sleuth star?

8 Which ITV adaptation of a novel by Evelyn Waugh starring Jeremy Irons won seven BAFTAs in 1982

9 Recently a Hollywood hit, which John le Carré novel was also a BBC series in 1979 starring Alec Guiness?

10 Which wordless Raymond Briggs book became a Channel 4 cartoon that is shown almost every Christmas?

11 Which actress played Roberta in both the 1968 BBC version and the 1970 film version of The Railway Children by Edith Nesbit?

PIC. REX FEATURES

12 Miranda Hart stars as Chummy in which BBC adaptation of a book by Jennifer Worth?

13 The BBC produced a highly popular 26 episode series of which Nobel Prize-winning novel by John Galsworthy

14 Who played Pa in the television version of Laura Ingalls Wilder's Little House on the Prairie?

15 Which novel by Canadian author Lucy Maud Montgomery was turned into a series of television movies starring Megan Follows and Jonathan Crombie?

16 Which Emmy Award winning television series set in Australia and starring Christopher Plummer was based on a novel by Colleen McCullough

17 Anna Maxwell Martin plays a spirited Yorkshire headmistress in a BBC adaptation of which book by Winifred Holtby?

18 David Powlett-Jones has just returned to England from the trenches of First World War to become a school teacher in the TV adaptation of which novel by R. F. Delderfield?

Answers: 1 John Thaw, 2 Great Expectations, 3 Sebastian Faulks, 4 Jim Broadbent, 5 Jennifer Ehle, 6 Jekyll, 7 Sherlock, 8 Brideshead Revisited, 9 Tinker Tailor Soldier Spy, 10 The Snowman, 11 Jenny Agutter, 12 Call the Midwife, 13 The Forsyte Saga, 14 Michael Landon, 15 Anne of Green Gables, 16 The Thornbirds, 17 South Riding, 18 To Serve Them All My Days

A winter miracle

BY: DOROTHY BENNETT

With no experience of dogs or children, can Imogen really help Ellie–Mae?

Drawing back the curtains in her sitting room, Imogen gazed with delight at the sight that met her eyes. It had snowed during the night and the frozen earth was covered with a crisp meringue of snow. Children were busily scooping up handfuls to build a snowman. Dogs skittered crazily in the unfamiliar white stuff. The sky was a cloudless blue and a solitary plane left a trail of silver vapour in its wake.

Imogen's eye was caught by the figure of little Ellie-Mae Parsons who lived in one of the old council houses on the other side of the village green. She was treading a solitary path accompanied only by a puppy, a long-legged creature of dubious parentage.

Ellie-Mae was a girl of whom Imogen was very fond. She was just such a child she would have liked as her own but, to her regret, marriage and babies had not come her way. Ellie was a plain little girl with dark eyes too large for her face and a shock of unruly hair, but with a sweet, loving nature that Imogen suspected was not appreciated at home.

As she watched, the child fell suddenly to her knees. She threw her arms around the dog and appeared to be crying. Opening the window and letting in a rush of icy air, Imogen called out: "Ellie – Ellie-Mae, come over here, dear."

Getting to her feet, the child made her way slowly, head hung down, towards the cottage. At the front door, she lifted a tear-stained face. "I can't come in, Miss Gray. I've got Buster and he's all wet. He'll make a mess in your house."

On cue, the puppy shook himself, sending particles of snow and ice in all directions. Ellie started to apologise but Imogen interrupted her with a laugh. "Don't worry, he's just making himself comfy. Come along in, the pair of you."

She took Ellie's coat and put it to dry, then sat in a big armchair facing her. "Now, my dear, what are all these tears about?"

"It's Buster. Mum says I can't keep him now we've got a new baby. He's got to go and I shall never see him again." Her eyes filled with tears again as she spoke.

Imogen thought rapidly. She had as little experience of looking after dogs as children but she made a decision and asked impulsively: "Would you like me to look after him?"

Ellie's tear-filled eyes opened wide. "Oh, Miss Gray, would you? Would you really? He's ever so good – well, most of the time. I know he'd be good if he lived with you. Would you really have him?"

"Yes, I'd love to. As you know, I don't go out much these days but he can run round the garden and you could take him for walks so you'd see him every day. I'm sure that between us we could look after Buster and give him a happy life."

Ellie looked thoughtful for a moment, then said: "But he wouldn't really be my dog any more, would he? He'd be yours."

Imogen took Ellie's hand in hers. "Of course he'd still be your dog. I'd just be a sort of guardian."

The little girl still looked unsure, then said: "Perhaps he could be our dog, belonging to both of us?"

Imogen smiled: "That's a lovely idea. Would you like that, Buster?"

Buster thumped the floor enthusiastically with his stump of a tail. He behaved so nicely in her neat little cottage that Imogen forgot any qualms she might have had about taking on a lively puppy.

After a mug of hot chocolate, Ellie went home with a happier heart. The next morning, she staggered over the green, loaded down with Buster's basket, toys and a large tin of dog food. Once again, her face wore a worried frown.

'Don't worry, he's just making himself comfy'

PIC: KATE DAVIES

'I wish I was old enough to do a paper round'

"What are we going to do about buying his food, Miss Gray? You can have all my pocket money, but I don't think it would be enough. Buster does seem to eat a lot – Mum complained he sent her supermarket bills sky-high," she sighed. "I wish I was old enough to do a paper round or something."

"Now don't you worry yourself. You can be in charge of making sure he gets enough exercise and I'll be in charge of his food. After all, he is going to be our dog so I must do my part in his care."

Ellie's face lit up with a gap-toothed smile and, looking down at her, Imogen hoped that one day

some discerning male would see the beauty of her character behind that rather plain little face and give her all the happiness she deserved.

Reaching up, Ellie put her arms round Imogen's neck and whispered: "Thank you, dear Miss Gray. I'm so glad Buster is coming to live with you and I can come here every day."

With the child's thin frame pressed lovingly to her, Imogen felt enveloped by a great glow of happiness. Soon, she was to have the company of a loveable puppy and daily visits from this equally loveable little girl.

Speaking softly, she asked: "Do you believe in miracles, Ellie?"

Ellie gave a deep sigh. "I do now, Miss."

"So do I, Ellie. So do I."

Sister act

Kath (left) with her sister Josie

Josie and I never got on as children; she once threw a dart at my leg and said she hated me. I sobbed my heart out and told her, 'You have to love your sister!'. She was always a tomboy and mucked in with our four brothers whereas I liked playing with dolls, especially the bride doll that I kept hidden under my bed. One day, Josie found it and pulled its arms and legs off. Things got a little better when we were teenagers and when I got married I asked Josie to be my bridesmaid. She only agreed as Millwall were not playing at home that day. She was okay with wearing a dress for once but drew the line at having her hair put in rollers. We argued and she flounced out of the house, but when she came back she was perfectly coiffed, having been to the hairdresser for a shampoo and set. I was proud of her – at last she looked ladylike. Until after the reception when she hitched up her skirt and went out on the green for a kick-about with the boys.

We are both happily married now with grown-up children (of course, Josie had boys and I had girls) and, as you can see from the photo, we are always laughing when we are together.

Kath Tuck, Isle of Sheppey

What's in a word

Brobdingnagian
(adjective) gigantic, huge, immense. From the novel Gulliver's Travels, where Brobdingnag is a land occupied by giants

Pet of the month

NAME: Bryan

AGE: 4 years

BREED: Daschund

OWNER: Debi Clarke, Torquay, Devon

PET LIKES: Pushing his ball under the sofa

PET HATES: His human mummy's vacuum cleaner – he barks and runs away whenever it is being used

HUMAN TRAIT: Enjoys going out to the local pub quiz, and occasionally sharing a small shandy!

February

Winter is the time for comfort, for good food and warmth,
for the touch of a friendly hand
and for a talk beside the fire – it is the time for home.
Poet, Edith Sitwell

February 2013

4 Monday

5 Tuesday

6 Wednesday

7 Thursday

8 Friday

9 Saturday

Chinese New Year (Year of the Snake)

10 Sunday

If you do one thing

Treat chapped lips by gently buffing them with a soft toothbrush to remove dry skin. Then apply a nourishing lip balm or gloss. Well moisturised lips look fuller and plumper which, in turn, could help you to look younger.

School days

Here is a photo of me on the day I started school in September 1949. Despite the strictness, I loved school, perhaps, because I was an only child and it was lovely being with other girls my age. I loved the teachers too, even the headmistress. I was sad when the school closed down when I was 13, but I went on to commercial college and became a secretary.

C Neville, Axminster, Devon

Mini Puzzle

Can you unscramble this conundrum to form a nine-letter word?

| C | L | E | A | N | P | A | D | S |

(answer Landscape)

Recipe of the week

Savoury Cheese Canapé Balls
Makes: 30
Preparation time: 30 minutes

200g (7oz) tub low-fat soft cheese
200g (7oz) mature cheddar cheese, finely grated
1 spring onion, very finely chopped
3 tbsp paprika
5 tbsp fresh chives, finely chopped
3 tbsp sesame seeds, lightly toasted

1 Put the soft cheese into a large mixing bowl and mash with a fork, or wooden spoon, to soften. Add the grated cheddar and spring onion, working it through until well combined. Season with ground pepper.
2 Roll the cheese mixture into 30 small balls. Roll one third into the paprika, one third into the chopped chives and the final third into the sesame seeds. Chill for 30 minutes, or until ready to serve.

Top tip: The cheese balls can also be rolled in finely chopped pistachio nuts, cashews or almonds; or finely chopped parsley or coriander. The mixture could then be used to top tiny crackers or mini bruschetta, topped with fresh herb sprigs.
© Pilgrims Choice Cheese, www.pilgrimschoice.com

February 2013

11 Monday

Shrove Tuesday (Pancake Day)

12 Tuesday

Ash Wednesday

13 Wednesday

St Valentine's Day

14 Thursday

15 Friday

16 Saturday

17 Sunday

If you do one thing

Have a hug or squeeze your partner's hand – it could lower your stress levels and your blood pressure. It's especially helpful to hold a loved one's hand in a stressful situation or if you're feel anxious. A hug could be just the tonic you need.

School days

This school photo of me was taken in 1945. Although I am now 71, I remember my early days at school clearly. No computers in those days – I learned my letters in a sand tray. Knitting was one of my favourite lessons, and we were also taught to darn. There was an air-raid shelter in the school playground and playtime was spent with lots of us skipping in one long rope and bouncing balls.

Mrs A Lee, Witham, Essex

Mini Puzzle

Can you unscramble this conundrum to form a nine-letter word?

D	R	A	T	L	E	A	C	H

(answer Cathedral)

Recipe of the week

Chocolate Berry Pancakes with Minted Creamy Custard

Serves: 4
Preparation time: 10 minutes, plus 15 minutes chilling time
Cooking time: 20 minutes

For the pancakes:
100g (3½oz) plain flour
15g (½oz) cocoa powder
1 egg
1 egg yolk
1 tsp vegetable oil, plus extra for frying
250ml (9fl.oz) semi-skimmed milk
For the filling:
170g (6oz) fat-free Greek yoghurt
150g (5oz) ready-made custard
4 tsp fresh mint, chopped
175g (6oz) raspberries
225g (8oz) strawberries, sliced
50g (2oz) dark chocolate, melted at end (optional)

1 Make the pancakes by mixing the flour and cocoa into a bowl. Add the egg, egg yolk and oil. Then gradually whisk in the milk until smooth. Leave to chill for 15 minutes.
2 For the filling, mix the yoghurt, custard and mint together – and in a separate bowl, mix the berries. Chill while you cook the pancakes.
3 Heat a little oil in an 18cm (7in) pan, then add 2-3 tablespoons of pancake batter. Cover the base in a thin layer and cook until browned on the underside. Flip and cook the other side until browned. Keep hot while you cook the remaining pancakes.
4 Fold the pancakes into quarters and arrange two on each serving plate. Spoon on the yoghurt mix and sprinkle berries. Drizzle with melted chocolate, if using. Serve immediately.
(C) Seasonal Berries, www.seasonalberries.co.uk

18 Monday

19 Tuesday

20 Wednesday

21 Thursday

22 Friday

23 Saturday

24 Sunday

If you do one thing

Have a cuppa – if you need an excuse to have another cup of tea just consider the fact that tea drinkers are thought to have a lower risk of stroke than non-tea drinkers. The benefits are thought to be due to the antioxidants and amino acids in both black and green teas. Go easy on the milk and sugar though.

School days

This photo is of the 1953 pageant at Kings Cliffe School, with me as Maid Marion, aged 13. I was at the school from 1951 to 1955, and cycled there every day with a girl called Jean Morris. On one occasion, I had made lemon meringue pie in cooking class and wedged it in my bike basket to go home, but a draught from a passing lorry completely took the top off it!

Margaret Black, Peterborough, Cambridgeshire

Mini Puzzle

Can you unscramble this conundrum to form a nine-letter word?

C	I	T	E	D	D	E	A	D

(answer Dedicated)

Recipe of the week

Lamb with Harissa Yoghurt

Serves: 4
Preparation time: 10 minutes, plus 2 hours marinating time
Cooking time: 6 minutes

4 lamb steaks

For the marinade:
1 clove garlic
4 tbsp harissa paste
250g (9oz) plain set yoghurt
Squeeze of lemon

For the couscous:
200g (9oz) couscous
_ pomegranate, de-seeded
150g (5oz) tinned chickpeas
10 large green olives, stoned and sliced
Handful of chopped fresh mint and flat-leaf parsley
4 tbsp extra virgin olive oil
2 tbsp white wine vinegar
2 tbsp lemon juice

For the sauce:
2 tbsp harissa paste
100g (3^1/$_2$ oz) plain set yoghurt
1 tbsp honey

1 Add the lamb steaks to the marinade ingredients and mix until well coated. Marinate in the fridge for about two hours. Towards the end, cook the couscous in a heat-proof bowl with 250ml (9 fl oz) boiling water. Cover with cling film and leave for 5–10 minutes.
2 Now prepare the lamb by cooking in a frying pan, for two to three minutes on each side. Remove and allow to rest for a few minutes.
3 Continue preparing the couscous by separating the grains with a fork. Add the herbs, pomegranate seeds, olives and chickpeas and stir to combine. Then whisk the rest of the ingredients together and stir through.
4 In a small saucepan, gently heat the sauce ingredients until warm. Divide the couscous between four serving plates, top with the lamb steaks and drizzle over the sauce.

© Alpro Soya, www.alprosoya.co.uk

February 2013

25 Monday

26 Tuesday

27 Wednesday

28 Thursday

1 Friday
St David's Day

2 Saturday

3 Sunday

If you do one thing

Put down the remote. If you can't quite drag yourself away from your favourite TV programmes you can still increase your activity levels by getting up to change the channel manually. An Australian study found that people who do even a small amount of light activity while doing something sedentary had smaller waists than those who just sat there. You could use the advert break to march on the spot or climb the stairs too.

School days

I love this photo of my granddaughters, Jade and Lauren, with their cheeky little faces. They are now aged 19 and 20, but would have been about 5 or 6 at this time. Jade is studying beauty therapy at college and Lauren is working as a PA. I have this picture in the hallway, and I just can't part with it as it cheers me up whenever I feel down.

Lilian Smith, Preston, Lancashire

Mini Puzzle

Can you unscramble this conundrum to form a nine-letter word?

| H | O | T | A | L | I | E | N | S |

(answer Hailstone)

Recipe of the week

Low-fat Banana Chip Tea bread

Makes: 1 loaf/10-12 slices
Preparation time: 10 minutes, plus 30 minutes soaking time
Cooking time: 1–1$^1/_4$ hours

1 Earl Grey tea bag
150g (5oz) dried banana slices
100g (3$^1/_2$ oz) sultanas
100ml (3$^1/_2$ fl oz) rapeseed oil
175g (6oz) soft brown sugar
2 eggs
225g (8oz) self-raising wholemeal flour

1 Preheat the oven to 180°C/350°F/Gas Mark 4 and base line a 1kg (2lb 1oz) loaf tin.
2 Soak the tea bag in 300ml (11 fl oz) of boiling water for around five minutes, then discard the bag and pour the tea over the fruit. Leave to soak for 30 minutes.
3 Whisk the oil, sugar and eggs in a large bowl, until the mixture is pale and creamy. Then add the soaked fruit, including any leftover juices. Fold in the flour, and pour into the prepared tin. Bake for 1–1$^1/_4$ hours, or until your loaf cake is golden brown on top and a skewer comes out clean from the middle. Leave to cool slightly before removing from the tin. Serve alongside a cup of tea, or with a warm fruit compote for dessert.

© Wholegrain goodness, www.wholegraingoodness.com

Wander in Winchester

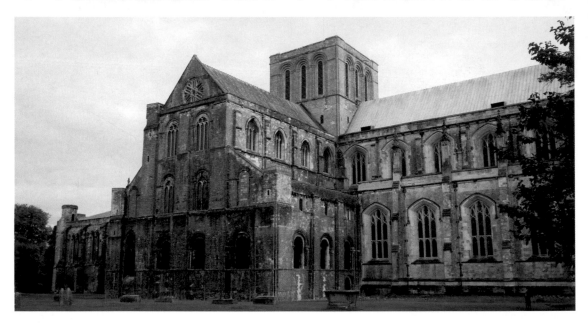

Head to this medieval city for a spot of culture

Perhaps, most famous for King Arthur's legendary Round Table, Winchester's 13th Century architecture is steeped in history. The Great Hall was the heart of Winchester Castle, where Henry III – and later, Edward I – would have dined. It is open to the public all year round, and entry is free (however all donations go towards the hall's upkeep).

A visit wouldn't be complete without a look around the city's stunning cathedral. Europe's longest medieval cathedral, it houses beautiful carvings, a 12th Century bible, and wall paintings; as well as more contemporary artwork. Tours around the main building and crypt run regularly during the day, and there is also a children's trail. Events are held throughout the year, and there's a lovely refectory, where you can enjoy afternoon tea overlooking the site.
Visit www.winchester-cathedral.org.uk.

The popular farmers' market takes place in the cathedral's shadow on the third Saturday of each month, and there's a great selection of independent shops, award-winning pubs, and restaurants. History buffs will also enjoy having a nose around the city's museums and the debtors' prison.
Visit www.visitwinchester.co.uk.

If keeping the grandchildren entertained is your priority, then a visit to the INTECH Science Centre and Planetarium should do the trick. It features hands-on exhibits and the UK's largest planetarium – perfect for rainy day fun.
For opening times call 0196 286 3791, or visit www.intech-uk.com.

Fact: Jane Austen spent her last days living at nearby Chawton House, which is now a dedicated museum.
For visitor information call 0142 083 262 or visit www.jane-austens-house-museum.org.uk.

Quiz of the month

Love is all around — test your knowledge of storybook sweethearts. If you get stuck, the answers are below

PIC. REX FEATURES

1 Which Victorian heroine wrote, 'Reader, I married him'?

2 In which book do Dexter and Emma meet every year on St Swithin's Day?

3 Who wrote The Pursuit of Love?

4 Which young diarist has a crush on Pandora Braithwaite?

5 Name the gentleman detective who married Harriet Vane.

6 In Pride and Prejudice who admired 'a pair of fine eyes in the face of a pretty woman'?

7 Who wrote The End of the Affair?

8 In A Woman of Substance who is the father of Emma Harte's first child?

9 On which Greek island does Antonio Corelli fall in love with Dr Iannis' daughter, Pelagia?

10 Name the prolific romantic novelist who was famous for wearing pink.

11 In The Young Visiters, who wrote, 'My life will be sour grapes and ashes without you'?

12 Who teases Anne of Green Gables about her red hair but eventually falls in love with her?

13 In The Thorn Birds, why can Meggie never marry her true love, Ralph de Bricassart?

14 Founded in 1908 by two men, which publishing company is most famous for its romantic fiction?

15 In which epic novel, set in India, does the hero Ash fall in love with the princess Anjuli?

16 'Love means never having to say you're sorry' is a quote from which book by Erich Segal?

17 Whose first novel, published in 2004, is called P.S. I Love You?

18 Connie and Mellors were lovers — in which novel that was banned in this country until 1960?

19 Beatrice flirts wittily with Benedick in which Shakespearean comedy?

20 Which poet compared his love to a red, red rose?

Answers: 1. Jane Eyre 2. One Day 3. Nancy Mitford 4. Adrian Mole 5. Lord Peter Wimsey 6. Mr Darcy 7. Graham Greene 8. Edwin Fairley 9. Cephallonia 10. Barbara Cartland 11. Daisy Ashford 12. Gilbert Blythe 13. He is a Catholic priest 14. Mills & Boon 15. The Far Pavilions 16. Love Story 17. Cecelia Ahern 18. Lady Chatterley's Lover 19. Much Ado About Nothing 20. Robert Burns

Storm in a teacup

BY: CHRIS RODGERS

Flo's old-fashioned ways irritate her bossy sister

It started the day Flo slipped and fell in her kitchen. Since Alf died she'd managed very well but just one stray drip of paraffin on the floor when she was filling the heater had done for her.

The hospital said her arm was broken and now she was in plaster up to her elbow and in a bit of a fix. They had arranged for carers to come in the mornings to help her wash and dress, they would even cook a meal if she wanted. But that was the trouble – she didn't want them to. The carers were very nice but she could manage like she'd always done and that was a fact. When they came in and found yet again that she had already washed and dressed and done all her chores, they stopped coming.

But Gladys still came! Oh, what a nag her sister was. She lived nearby in a house very like Flo's but her home was bright and contemporary and equipped with every modern convenience.

"You should get a proper electric kettle," Gladys said sharply as she bustled about with teacups and saucers. "If you stopped fiddling about with this battered old thing you put on the gas stove, you wouldn't need matches – so dangerous at your age!"

'Your age indeed!' thought Flo. 'What a cheek'. Gladys was six years younger and considered herself superior in every way.

"You know very well that I haven't got anywhere to plug one in," Flo said defensively.

"And a microwave would be much easier and quicker than your gas oven," Gladys continued as though Flo hadn't spoken.

"Now look here, Glad, don't you keep coming round here, telling me how to live my life. I'm fine the way I am," said Flo, made tetchier than usual by the pain in her arm and the frustration of not being able to carry out her familiar household routine.

"Of course you're not!" Gladys snapped in exasperation. "Messing about with a paraffin heater when you could just turn on a switch. You're still living like we did in the war, for goodness' sake, and there's no need. You and your funny old ways."

"Well, I'm not going to change now, so there," Flo shouted, marching to the front door. "You'd better go – and don't bother coming back if you think it's so awful here."

Puffing with indignation, Gladys left. Flo slammed the door behind her. She had heard it all before and was thoroughly fed up with the way Gladys bullied her. So what if she didn't have central heating or a washing machine or any of the other things that Gladys felt she needed to make life bearable?

Deep down, Flo knew that her life would be more comfortable if she made some changes and moved into the twenty-first century, but she wasn't going to admit that. The thought of the upheaval frightened her. The house would have to be rewired and she didn't have that sort of money. A microwave would scare her to death – all those dials, never mind the harmful rays going into her food.

After their row, Gladys didn't come round, even to enquire after Flo's broken arm. 'Sulky so-and-so', thought Flo. 'See if I care!'

But, oddly enough, she did care. She even missed her sister's nagging about improvements. Despite Gladys' bossy ways, they hadn't seriously fallen out before and Gladys never missed her weekly visits. But Flo began to fear that she'd never come back. Surely Gladys knew that she hadn't really meant those words spoken in temper, and now rather regretted.

Eventually, the hospital removed her plaster and gave her some exercises to do. Once again, Flo could do all her housework and pop across the road to the launderette where the girl kindly loaded the machine and helped her put her money

She even missed her sister's nagging

PIC: KATE DAVIES

'What's wrong with writing a letter?'

in. From time to time, she wistfully wondered what Gladys was up to these days.

Then one day there was a knock on the door, and there she was. Secretly pleased and relieved, Flo nevertheless braced herself for the usual onslaught from her sister.

"Hello, dear, how's your arm?" Gladys asked as she breezed in without waiting for an answer. "Sorry I haven't been round lately but I've had the flu and as you don't have anything as modern as a telephone, I couldn't let you know."

Flo bridled, ready for another argument. 'What's wrong with writing a letter? We do still have a postal service,' she wondered to herself. Aloud, she asked: "Would you like a cup of tea, Gladys?"

"Brought you this, dear. Thought you could do with it. Got it in the camping shop in town."

From her shopping trolley, Gladys produced a kettle which she proceeded to fill with water and placed it on the much-maligned gas stove. The old battered one was thrown merrily into the recycling bin by the back door.

To her surprise, Flo found that for once she wasn't riled by her sister's bossy ways. She beamed fondly at Gladys as the gleaming new kettle came to the boil. Her heavy heart lifted with a surge of happiness. Gladys was back in her life. Was it possible that she had come to accept Flo's 'funny old ways' after all this time?

"Come on then, dear," said Gladys briskly, getting out the cups and saucers. "Let's have a good old-fashioned cuppa."

Very Woolly Finger Puppets

These are a great project if you're just starting out in the world of knitting

You will need:

Wool (scraps will do) or a couple of balls of 8-ply (DK)
wool in your favourite colours
Felt (again scraps are good) or several 10x10cm
(4x4in) squares of coloured felt for the details (trunks,
ears, spikes etc)
Crafting googly eyes!
Scissors
4-mm (Size 6) knitting needles
Wool needle
Regular sewing needle and thread
to match your felt scraps
Crafting glue (or a good all-purpose glue will do)

1 Knit the basic finger puppet shape by casting on 15
   stitches; knitting 20 rows; then cast off, leaving a
   long tail of wool (about 30cm/12in).

2 Plan the shapes for the puppet's face, e.g. ears,
   crown, antennae etc. Simply hand draw onto felt
   and cut out carefully.

3 Sew up your puppet. With the short end at the top,
   fold your knitted rectangle in half. Thread your
   needle with the wool tail and sew up the side and
   across the top. Turn your puppet the right way out.

4 Now it's time to embellish your puppet. Stick on the
   felt pieces and googly eyes using glue. Small items
   such as ears and antennae can be sewn on with
   matching thread.

Fold in half

Safety notes

Please don't give these puppets to very small children, who might pull the glued-on bits off and swallow them.

Other ideas and variations

◆ These make great presents for grandchildren or party favours.
◆ Once you've learned the basics get inventive and add stripes, scarves and horns.
◆ Theme your puppets to be farmyard animals or storybook characters.
◆ Use thinner yarn and finer needles to make tiny puppets for smaller fingers.

© Make Hey While the Sun Shines by Pip Lincolne is published by Hardie Grant, £17.99 (Hardback).

Sister act

A family bond from childhood has seen the sisters through heartache and happiness

I have three amazing sisters, Sarah, Liz and Dorothy, who are among my greatest blessings. There are only seven years between the oldest and the youngest and we were brought up in comfortable middle-class suburbia in the Sixties and Seventies.

During childhood, we were always around for each other although we all had our own friends. As we grew into teenagers, we inevitably had different interests and priorities.

Although we might have had disagreements, nothing pulled us apart. As adults, we always shared in each other's family celebrations as well as dealing with life's crises, ranging from losing our parents to coping with miscarriages, divorce, health scares and bankruptcy. Throughout all of these, we've always been able to build each other up, give practical support, offer sensible advice and, above all, to laugh and cry together. We have precious memories that we share; catchphrases that mean nothing to anyone else, guiding songs that we sing with gusto, and a verbal shorthand that goes beyond words.

Friends who don't have siblings, or who don't have much of a relationship with their sisters, envy our special bond. We bring out the best in each other, recognising one another's faults as well as their strengths and talents.

Sue Richards, Newport Pagnell, Bucks

What's in a word

Prestidigitator

(noun) conjuror, someone who can perform tricks. From the French preste (nimble) and Latin digitus (finger)

Pet of the month

NAME: Louis

AGE: 18 months

BREED: Yorkshire terrier, Bichon and Papillon cross

OWNER: Ann Atterbury Thomas, Lewes, East Sussex

PET LIKES: Cuddles, treats and chasing squirrels in the garden

PET HATES: Walking in his cold weather jacket

HUMAN TRAIT: Curling up in front of the log fire and watching TV, especially in winter

March

The spring came suddenly,
bursting upon the world as a child bursts into a room,
with a laugh and a shout and hands full of flowers.
Henry Wadsworth Longfellow, poet

4   Monday

5   Tuesday

6   Wednesday

7   Thursday

8   Friday

9   Saturday

Mothering Sunday

10   Sunday

If you do one thing

Floss between your teeth. Regardless of how well you brush your teeth, if you don't floss they won't be completely clean – and that puts you at an increased risk of gum disease and heart disease. Plaque bacteria could affect your heart by causing inflammation in your blood vessels, which, in turn, could affect your cholesterol and blood pressure.

School days

Here are my daughters at school in Australia in 1971. Julie was 10, Susan 8. When we emigrated on the Assisted Passage scheme, it was the summer holidays in England, so having to go to school after just two weeks in Sydney didn't go down too well with the girls! Julie was thrilled with the attaché case after using a satchel in England, and said it was like taking her own desk to school each day!

Barbara Bignell, Kettering, Northamptonshire

Mini Puzzle

Can you unscramble this conundrum to form a nine-letter word?

| E | O | H | U | S | R | K | O | W |

(answer Housework)

Recipe of the week

Crumbed Lamb Chops with Crushed Vegetables

Serves: 4
Preparation time: 30 minutes
Cooking time: 30 minutes

4 lean chump chops or boneless leg steaks
2 tbsp olive oil
50g (2oz) fresh white breadcrumbs
Grated zest and juice of 1 lemon
1 tbsp fresh chives, chopped
For the dressing:
2 tbsp good balsamic vinegar
3 tbsp clear honey
3 tbsp Dijon or wholegrain mustard
2 tbsp rapeseed or olive oil
For the vegetables:
450g (1lb) waxy potatoes, cubed
100g (3½ oz) broccoli, in small florets
100g (3½ oz) cauliflower, in small florets
2 tbsp garlic and herb cream cheese

1 Heat the oil in a non-stick pan and fry the breadcrumbs with the lemon zest and juice: do this for two to three minutes, tossing frequently, until golden brown. Remove from the heat and add the chives.
2 For the dressing, mix all the ingredients together before transferring to two separate bowls. Season the steaks and brush each side with the dressing, from one of these bowls.
3 Boil the potatoes for 15-20 minutes, adding the broccoli and cauliflower ten minutes before the end. Drain, roughly mash, season, and stir through the cream cheese.
4 Meanwhile, heat a non-stick pan and cook for six to eight minutes on each side. During the last few minutes, sprinkle the breadcrumbs over the lamb and warm the remaining dressing.
5 Serve the vegetables with a piece of lamb on top, and drizzled with warm dressing. Serve immediately.
Top tip: This also works well with lamb cutlets or loin chops.
© Simply Beef and Lamb, www.simplybeefandlamb.co.uk

March 2013

11 Monday

12 Tuesday

13 Wednesday

14 Thursday

15 Friday

16 Saturday

St Patrick's Day

17 Sunday

If you do one thing

See your pharmacist for a drug check-up. If you take a cocktail of prescription pills, over-the-counter medicines and supplements, ask your pharmacist for a medicine review. They can look at what you're taking and make sure none of the drugs interact in a harmful way or cancel each other out.

School days

This is our Girl Guide Troop, of the Rye Collegiate School, taken in about 1942. I am sitting front left with the bushy hair. My memories are wartime ones, once crouching beneath our tables when a plane dropped a bomb so close we could see the debris of what was left of our cinema shooting into the air. But we managed to keep cheerful in spite of air-raids, rationing and shortages.

Joy King, Burgess Hill, West Sussex

Mini Puzzle

Can you unscramble this conundrum to form a nine-letter word?

| G | I | A | N | T | S | P | I | N |

(answer Paintings)

Recipe of the week

Blueberry Frangipane Tarts

Makes: 6
Preparation time: 20 minutes, plus 20 minutes cooling
Cooking time: 40 minutes

400g (14oz) sweet shortcrust pastry
Plain flour for dusting
100g (3½ oz) butter, at room temperature
100g (3½ oz) caster sugar
2 eggs, lightly beaten
100g (3½ oz) ground almonds
Few drops almond essence
125g (4½ oz) blueberries
2 tbsp flaked almonds
Icing sugar to decorate (optional)

1 Grease six 10cm (4in) loose-bottomed and fluted tart tins. Roll out the pastry, thinly, on a lightly dusted surface. Then arrange five tart tins on top, cutting out the pastry a little larger than the tins. Press into the tins, and trim just above the top. Then use the trimmings to line the sixth tart tin. Prick the base and chill for 15 minutes.
2 Meanwhile, preheat the oven to 190°C/375°F/Gas Mark 5. Line the tart cases with greaseproof or non-stick baking paper and fill with baking beans (or use dried macaroni/ other small pasta shapes). Blind-bake for ten minutes, before baking normally for five to six minutes, until beginning to brown.
3 Meanwhile, make the filling by beating the butter and sugar together, until light and fluffy. Gradually beat in the eggs, then stir in the ground almonds and almond essence. Divide between the tart cases, then sprinkle with blueberries and flaked almonds.
4 Bake at 180°C/350°F/Gas Mark 4 for 20-25 minutes, or until golden. Leave to cool for 20 minutes, or until ready to serve. Remove from the tart tins and dust with icing sugar. Serve with spoonfuls of crème fraiche.
© Seasonal Berries, www.seasonalberries.co.uk

March 2013

18 Monday

19 Tuesday

20 Wednesday

21 Thursday

22 Friday

23 Saturday

Palm Sunday

24 Sunday

If you do one thing

Don't forget to use up your ISA allowance. Individual Savings Accounts are tax-free savings accounts where you can save up to £5,640 in a cash ISA. It means you don't pay any tax on the interest accrued, so, if you have spare cash in your current account, put it into your ISA.

School days

This is the Infants' class 1928/29 from Queens Road School, Dalston. Most of us are happily smiling for the camera. I am in the front row, fifth from the left with long black stockings. I was then Joan Osborne. I'd love to get in touch with any of the other pupils from those years – hopefully some are reading Yours!

J Gingell, Tunbridge Wells, Kent

Mini Puzzle

Can you unscramble this conundrum to form a nine-letter word?

| I | F | A | V | I | D | F | A | T |

(answer Affidavit)

Recipe of the week

Hot Cross Bun Pudding

Serves: 4
Preparation time: 10 minutes
Cooking time: 5–10 minutes

4 hot cross buns
100ml (3½ fl.oz) milk
2 eggs, beaten
1 tsp oil
170g (6oz) Greek yoghurt
4 tbsp sugar-free blueberry jam
1 tbsp honey
50g (2oz) flaked almonds, toasted
250g (9oz) fresh blueberries

1 Slice the hot cross buns in half. Mix together the milk and eggs and soak the sliced buns in the mixture for a couple of minutes.
2 Using a large, non–stick frying pan, heat the oil and gently fry the buns on each side until golden brown.
3 To serve, put the buns onto serving plates. Divide the yoghurt and jam on top, then drizzle with honey and sprinkle on the almonds. Garnish with fresh blueberries and serve immediately.

Top tip: This is a good way to use up slightly stale hot cross buns. The recipe can be easily halved and would make a fun breakfast choice to enjoy with your grandchildren.

© Total Greek Yoghurt, www.totalgreekyoghurt.com

March 2013

25 Monday

26 Tuesday

27 Wednesday

28 Thursday
Maundy Thursday

29 Friday
Good Friday

30 Saturday

31 Sunday
Easter Sunday / British Summer Time begins (clocks go forward)

If you do one thing

Get a professional eyebrow shape – it could really help to lift your face and give a bit of a visual face lift. Once you've got a good shape you can just tweeze away any new hairs as they come through. If your brows have faded over time consider a brow tint too – in a slightly darker shade than your hair colour.

School days

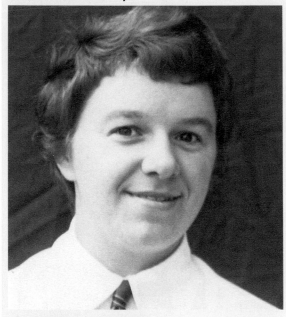

This is a photograph of me, taken in 1957 when I was a prefect at Ilkley Grammar School. I spent seven very happy years at IGS, which was situated on the edge of Ilkley Moor, so we were able to go for cross-country runs on the moor and, in winter, we went sledging. The only part of school I didn't like was receiving our reports on the last morning of each term.

Barbara Cox, Hexham, Northumberland

Mini Puzzle

Can you unscramble this conundrum to form a nine-letter word?

| R | O | U | T | S | A | T | A | N |

(answer Astronaut)

Recipe of the week

St Clement's Roast Lamb

Serves: 8-10
Preparation time: 10 minutes
Cooking time:
Medium: 25 minutes per 450g (1lb) +25 minutes;
Well done: 30 minutes per 450g (1lb) + 30 minutes

1.3kg (3lb) lean, half leg joint of lamb
4 tbsp fresh thyme leaves, chopped
Grated zest of 2 oranges (reserve oranges)
2 lemons, sliced
3 tbsp dry white wine or white grape juice

1 Preheat the oven to 180°C/350°F/Gas Mark 4. Place the joint on a large chopping board. Make several incisions over the joint and season well on both sides. Press the thyme and orange zest over the surface of the lamb and into the slits.
2 Slice the reserved oranges and place in a large, non-stick roasting tin with the lemon slices. Place the joint on top and open roast for the preferred cooking time, basting occasionally with any meat juices. Cover with foil if it is browning too quickly.
3 Then, 30 minutes before the cooking time ends, pour the wine or grape juice over the lamb and return to the oven uncovered.

Top tip: This tastes great served with baked vegetables (try fennel) and roasted white or sweet potatoes.
© Simply Beef and Lamb, www.simplybeefandlamb.co.uk

Ticket to ride

Explore Liverpool, the birthplace of Britain's best-loved band

The story began with four teenagers from Liverpool, hungry for fame, who went on to form The Beatles. Fans will love a tour of Mendips and 20 Forthlin Road (the childhood homes of John Lennon and Paul McCartney) where some of their most popular songs were penned. The experience provides real insight into the beginning of what was Britain's best-loved band. It includes a look at original family photographs, a peak into John's bedroom, and a chance to encounter two very different homes. Tours are operated by the National Trust; **for details call 0844 800 4791 or visit www.nationaltrust.org.uk.**

Don't miss out on the Cavern Club, which was a regular haunt for the boys in their early days. They first played the club in 1961,

going on to perform at the venue nearly 300 times in just a few years. And if music really is your thing, take a trip to the famous Liverpool Philharmonic Hall (visit www.liverpoolphil.com).

Yet Liverpool isn't only known as the birthplace of British pop. It's also a mecca for shoppers and has a great restaurant scene. Head to the popular Albert Dock (www.albertdock.com), where you'll find restaurants, museums, and water tours, set in the largest group of Grade I listed buildings in the UK. Here you'll find the Merseyside Maritime Museum, where you can discover the story of the Titanic and learn about Liverpool's nautical past. It's also home to Tate Liverpool – the most visited gallery of contemporary art in the North.

PIC: REX FEATURES

Fact: During her teens, Liverpool lass Cilla Black worked at the Cavern Club as a cloakroom girl... and went on to have the same manager as The Beatles.

Quiz of the month

Which of these furry friends can you recall? If you get stuck the answers are below

1 Whose bacon does Charlotte save in E B White's Charlotte's Web?

2 Name the fifth member of the Famous Five by Enid Blyton?

3 Tintin was always ably assisted by a white Fox Terrier called...?

4 What's the name of Hermione Granger's cat in the Harry Potter books?

5 Name the much-loved horse created by Anna Sewell in 1877?

6 Which character in George Orwell's Animal Farm was thought to be based on Joseph Stalin?

7 A dedicated washer woman, name Peter Rabbit's prickly friend?

8 Who leads a band of rabbits from Sandleford Warren to Watership Down?

9 Which of Kenneth Grahame's characters is obsessed with cars?

10 The Hundred Acre Wood is home to which honey-loving bear?

11 In The Jungle Book Mowgli and Baloo the bear have to fight against a tiger called...?

12 Who looks after the Darling children in J M Barrie's Peter Pan?

13 Which Collie dog created by Eric Knight has been read about by millions and even starred in a film with Elizabeth Taylor?

PIC: REX FEATURES

14 Which stuffed toy hopes that the love of his owner will make him real?

15 What's the name of the Lion in C S Lewis' Chronicles of Narnia?

16 In My Family and Other Animals what was the name of Gerald Durrell's dog?

17 Dick King-Smith's novel The Sheep Pig is about a gallant pig called?

18 Alice is often baffled by this disappearing creature during her adventures in Wonderland?

19 In The Wonderful Wizard of Oz by L. Frank Baum Dorothy gets transported to Oz with her faithful four legged friend called...?

20 The Incredible Journey by Sheila Burnford charts the adventures of three very loyal pets in their quest to find their owners – what where their names?

1 Wilbur the Pig, 2 Timmy the dog, 3 Snowy, 4 Crookshanks, 5 Black Beauty, 6 Napoleon, 7 Mrs Tiggywinkle, 8 Hazel, 9 Toad of Toad Hall, 10 Winnie the Pooh, 11 Shere Khan, 12 Nana the Newfoundland Dog, 13 Lassie, 14 The Velveteen Rabbit, 15 Aslan, 16 Roger, 17 Babe, 18 The Cheshire Cat, 19 Toto, 20 Luath (the Labrador), Bodger (the old English Bull Terrier) and Tao (the Siamese Cat)

No more new

BY: EVE CHAPMAN

Giving up his allotment is a grim rite of passage for Frank

Frank swept the last of the dust out of the shed door. It was truly empty now. He gazed at his weed-covered allotment: undug, unattended. He should be planting his potatoes today. The March sun had some warmth in it at last and he could see the other allotment holders bent over the soil.

He sighed as he limped towards his car, leaning on his stick. He would have been planting his potatoes now if it weren't for his hip. He'd had one replaced but now the other one needed doing and he knew it was time to give up. Thirty years he'd been coming here, ever since the boys were small and he and Wilma had decided an allotment would be good for all the family.

And it had been, but the one who had gained most pleasure from it was Frank. Wilma had soon found other interests but for him the joy of driving to the outskirts of town, opening up his shed and getting out his garden tools had never waned. He wondered how many pounds of vegetables he'd grown over the years, how many baskets of fruit and crisp salad leaves.

He'd said goodbye to the few allotment holders he was on friendly terms with and he'd seen the look of sympathy in their eyes. Slowly, without looking back, he drove home.

In the bungalow's small kitchen, Wilma kept glancing at the clock. He should be home soon and she'd made sardine sandwiches with cucumber for their lunch – Frank's favourite. She knew it would be small consolation. This was a sad day for Frank.

She would miss the vegetables, of course she would – especially the early potatoes, small waxy ovals that were the first taste of summer. She had been glad the allotment was such an absorbing hobby for her husband while she was taken up with choir singing and her craft work. But maybe it had absorbed him too much and sometimes it seemed

Wilma wanted him to be at home more

that time on the allotment was preferable to time spent with her. Wilma wanted him to be at home more so that they could enjoy their retirement together. And if the truth were told, she no longer wanted the bother of fresh produce.

When their boys were home, it was fine. Growing boys could devour quantities of vegetables as well as the pies and crumbles she made with the fruit. Now it had become a burden. All the washing, slicing, storing and freezing, giving surplus produce away – Wilma thought it simply wasn't worth the effort.

And she'd had to give up things, as well. Their house, for a start. She missed her spacious kitchen and missed having an upstairs to retreat to. Sometimes the bungalow felt claustrophobic but they'd had to move when it became painful for Frank to climb the stairs. Neither of them was getting any younger.

Wilma heard Frank's key in the lock and went into the hall to greet him. "Well?" she said. "All done?"

He nodded. "Yes, I left the shed keys under a stone. I think the new fellow is taking over this weekend. Young man with a family – just like I was when I started. There are as many women as men now, though. When I first went there, it was all old blokes in flat caps…"

Frank stopped and smiled wryly. "Well, just like I am now, I suppose!"

Wilma put her arms round him. "It will be okay," she said. "You'll feel better about everything when the other hip is done. And when you're mobile again there's your new greenhouse in the garden here – you can still grow us tomatoes and salad stuff."

He smiled at her. He knew she was doing her best to comfort him, so why did he feel this bleakness, this sense of everything ending?

Wilma brought the tray of sandwiches into the sitting room and they sat down to eat. She said: "We'll be able to go out more, now. Coach trips

potatoes

PIC: KATE DAVIES

'We're both getting old and we have to face it'

and things. Pub lunches." Facing him squarely, she went on: "Look, Frank, it can't be helped. You are seventy-five. We're both getting old and we just have to face it."

"I know," he said, "but there was never anything like it, you know. Bringing home those first potatoes – never anything like it. We'll never replace that."

Wilma chewed her sardine sandwich and thought about it. In her mind's eye she pictured rows of neat, clean bags of potatoes in the supermarket. All washed and ready to use. She saw packages of ready-trimmed beans, sprouts in green nets, soft fruit in punnets – all picked, all ready to eat with minimum preparation.

She felt a little surge of pleasure which grew and grew until she was smiling broadly – almost laughing out loud. She wanted to sing and dance and rush out and buy ready-meals and put them straight in the microwave. The thought of never having to peel a vegetable again filled her with joy, but she restrained herself. She knew how sad Frank was.

In time he would see, as she did, that although parts of their lives were coming to an end, other things were just beginning. Patting his hand, she said: "It will be fine, love. Just fine."

Sister act

Friends envy the closeness of sisters Marie and Betty

Pet of the month

NAME: Radcliffe (Raddy for short)

AGE: 13 weeks

OWNER: Sue Farrow, Ely, Cambridgeshire

PET LIKES: Apples, carrots and climbing in her cage

PET HATES: Sleeping in her bed

ENDEARING TRAIT: Chasing Sue around the house in her ball!

INTERESTING FACT: Sue is a competitive runner, and named her pet after Paula Radcliffe because she darts around so quickly

I am the older of two sisters by nearly four years so mother always told me to look after Betty. She was a thin child and I had to make sure she always drank her milk at school and was not bullied. When I was seven our father died and mother had a hard time bringing us up on her own. Betty had to go to school at an early age so our mother could go out to work. When war broke out, all three of us were evacuated first to Northampton and later to Bedford. Betty and I had to share a bed with the daughter of the lady with whom we were billeted. One night, I woke and realised my sister was not next to me. I panicked until I found she had fallen out of bed on to the floor where she was still sleeping. We look back and laugh at this. Now that we are both widowed, we each have our own flat in the same apartment block. We do have our own lives but are always there to help each other. No one could wish for a more caring and loving sister and friends envy our togetherness.

Marie Hearley, Plymouth, Devon

April

Aprils have never meant much to me,
autumns seem that season of beginning, spring.
Truman Capote (Breakfast at Tiffany's)

April 2013

1 Monday Easter Monday / All Fools' Day

2 Tuesday

3 Wednesday

4 Thursday

5 Friday

6 Saturday

7 Sunday

If you do one thing

There's nothing like a bit of spring cleaning to blow away the cobwebs – literally and metaphorically. Some experts believe that a good clear out could help you to reduce your stress levels. If you need to declutter and find the idea overwhelming – start small – perhaps with a draw or cupboard – you'll soon get the bug.

School days

Here is my school photograph from around 1940. I remember coming home from school one day to find I had a new baby sister. I already had two younger siblings so didn't really want another baby in the house. At school, I enjoyed reading, and was sometimes asked to read to the younger children to keep them quiet while the teacher had a break.

Mrs M Mansfield, Worthing, Sussex

Mini Puzzle

Can you unscramble this conundrum to form a nine-letter word?

O	K	A	S	G	R	O	A	N

(answer Kangaroos)

Recipe of the week

Chocolate and Mini Egg Masterpiece

Serves: 4
Preparation time: 5 minutes,
plus 2 hours/overnight chilling
Cooking time: 25 minutes

600ml (1pt) whole milk
6 egg yolks
50g (2oz) sugar
100g (3$\frac{1}{2}$ oz) plain chocolate, grated
100g (3$\frac{1}{2}$ oz) mini chocolate-filled eggs, plus extra to decorate

1 In a saucepan, bring the milk almost to the boil and remove from the heat.
2 Whisk the egg yolks and sugar together until thick and fluffy. Then gradually pour in the milk, whisking continuously.
3 Return the saucepan and stir the mixture over a very gentle heat, until it coats the back of a spoon. Remove from the heat and add the chocolate. Stir until dissolved then chill for around two hours, or until cold. Place dampened greaseproof paper directly on to the surface to stop a 'skin' from forming.
4 Lightly crush a handful of mini chocolate eggs and place in the bottom of four glass dishes. Spoon the chocolate custard over and sprinkle a few more crushed or whole mini eggs, then serve.

Top Tip: If time is tight, make the custard beforehand and chill overnight.
© Alpro Soya, www.alprosoya.co.uk

April 2013

8   Monday

9   Tuesday

10   Wednesday

11   Thursday

12   Friday

13   Saturday

14   Sunday

If you do one thing

Start slapping on sun cream. The sun is strong enough at this time of year to cause sunburn on warm days so get into the habit of applying a minimum of SPF 15 everyday if you're going to be outside for longer than 10 minutes. It will help you to reduce your risk of skin cancer and it could help to prevent age spots and wrinkles.

School days

I was 13 years old when this photo was taken in 1944. We had to make this school uniform dress from rose-pink cotton and trim it with white braid. I remember I was so quick I had finished tacking my dress long before the others, and the teacher made me unpick it all and start again so we would all finish together! I went on to do dressmaking all my working life.

Mrs E Newman, Bolsover, Derbyshire

Mini Puzzle

Can you unscramble this conundrum to form a nine-letter word?

A	M	E	H	P	O	S	E	R

(answer Semaphore)

Recipe of the week

Speedy Mackerel in Black Bean Sauce

Serves: 4
Preparation time: 10 minutes
Cooking time: 15 minutes

2 x 110g (4oz) cans of cooked mackerel fillets in spring water, drained
225g (8oz) pak choi, chopped
125g (4$^1/_2$oz) black bean sauce
1 onion, peeled and diced
1 red chilli, finely diced
1 tbsp olive oil

1. Heat the oil in a medium saucepan over a medium heat. Add the onion and chilli. Cook for two minutes before adding the pak choi. Cook for a further five minutes, or until it starts to wilt. Stir in half the black bean sauce and cook for three minutes. Then remove from the heat and set aside.
2. Return the pan to a medium heat; add the mackerel and remaining bean sauce. Bring to the boil and gently simmer for two minutes. Remove from the heat.
3. Divide the pak choi between four serving plates and arrange the mackerel fillets on top. Drizzle with any pan juices and serve with egg or rice noodles.

© James Martin for John West, www.domorewithfish.co.uk

15 Monday

16 Tuesday

17 Wednesday

18 Thursday

19 Friday

20 Saturday

21 Sunday

If you do one thing

If you've not yet got to grips with the internet, twitter or skype head to your local library for advice. Not only will it connect you to a whole new world it could help to enhance your memory too. Learning a new skill is a great way to keep your mind active. Make sure the first website you visit is **www.yours.co.uk** of course.

School days

This is my school photo from Walton Church of England Infants' School, when I was about six years old. I'm on the back row with long, curled pigtails. I only remember a few of the other pupils, particularly one boy who used to chase me home from school! The school had a lovely playground which backed on to the church, but horrible outside toilets!
Mrs A Bloor, Market Harborough, Leicestershire

Mini Puzzle

Can you unscramble this conundrum to form a nine-letter word?

S	A	N	E	S	T	I	L	E

(answer Essential)

Recipe of the week

Green Tea Ice Cream

Serves: 12
Preparation time: 5 minutes
Cooking time: 20 minutes (plus 4^1/$_2$ hours cooling and freezing time)

500ml (1pint) semi-skimmed milk
100ml (3^1/$_2$ fl oz) low-fat double cream
3 egg yolks
15g (^{1}/$_2$ oz) granulated sweetener
1 tsp green tea powder, or the contents of 1 green tea bag
Sliced mango and papaya or almond biscotti, to serve (optional)

1 Pour the milk and cream into a medium saucepan and bring to almost boiling point over a medium heat, then remove.
2 In a large mixing bowl, whisk together the egg yolks, sweetener and green tea, until it starts to thicken. Then slowly add the hot milk mixture in batches, stirring as you go.
3 Pour this mixture back into the saucepan and heat on a medium-low heat, stirring continuously for 10-12 minutes, or until it begins to thicken slightly. Do not overheat it as it may curdle. Sieve into a clean bowl and cool to room temperature.
4 Pour into a freezer-proof container and freeze for two hours. Then take it out and blend in a food processor until smooth. Repeat this stage before leaving to freeze until serving. Take out five minutes beforehand, to serve with fruit and biscotti, if desired.

Top tip: Replace the sweetener with caster sugar if preferred. Once frozen, cover the ice cream with a double layer of cling film or ice crystals will form. This can be frozen for up to a month.
© Canderel, www.canderel.co.uk

22 Monday

23 Tuesday   St George's Day

24 Wednesday

25 Thursday

26 Friday

27 Saturday

28 Sunday

If you do one thing

Look back through old photographs and choose some of the ones that make you feel happiest to frame and display. UK researchers found that looking at pictures of happy times made most people feel more cheerful than eating a bar of chocolate.

School days

Here are myself and classmates at Westcote Girls' School, Leicester, in our final year in 1961, aged 15. A lot of the girls had moved from Junior School with me, and I am still in contact with some of them now. One particular memory I have of school is breaking my arm during relay running in the playground and being unable to write for a while.

Mary Waren, Melton Mowbray, Leicestershire

Mini Puzzle

Can you unscramble this conundrum to form a nine-letter word?

V	E	I	N	E	N	T	E	R

(answer *Intervene*)

Recipe of the week

Speedy Garlic and Rosemary Focaccia-Style Bread

Makes: 1 loaf/12 slices
Preparation time: 40 minutes
Cooking time: 15–20 minutes

500g (1lb 1oz) ciabatta or white bread mix
3 cloves garlic, chopped
3 tsp chopped rosemary
4 tbsp cold-pressed rapeseed oil
$\frac{1}{4}$ tsp coarse sea salt

1 Preheat the oven to 230°C/450°F/Gas Mark 8.
2 Take a large mixing bowl and blend the bread mix with a pinch of salt, the garlic, and two-thirds of the rosemary. Mix in three-quarters of the oil and 320ml (12 fl.oz) lukewarm water to form a rough dough.
3 Knead on a floured surface for five minutes, or until you have a smooth dough. Shape into a rough 23cm (9in) round, and place on a large greased baking tray. Brush the dough with the remaining oil and sprinkle on the reserved rosemary and sea salt.
4 Cover with cling film and leave to prove in a warm place for 30 minutes, or until it has doubled in size. Then press shallow dimples into the top of the bread with a wooden spoon handle and bake for 15–20 minutes, or until the bread is golden-brown and sounds hollow when tapped. Allow to cool slightly before serving – with a dip of olive oil and balsamic vinegar as a starter, or with soup.
© Wholegrain goodness, www.wholegraingoodness.com

April 2013

29 Monday

30 Tuesday

1 Wednesday

2 Thursday

3 Friday

4 Saturday

5 Sunday

If you do one thing

Start thinking about your feet. If you want to wear sandals this summer now is the time to turn your attention to your toes. Use a pumice or foot file to slough off dry skin after giving your feet a soothing soak once a week. Massage in a rich moisturiser every day and cut your toenails straight across. See a chiropodist to tackle more serious foot problems.

School days

This is from the May Day celebrations at my school in 1953, when I was aged seven. My sister, Patricia, was the retiring May Queen, and I was one of the attendants, third from the right at the back. The garlands we are holding were made from hula-hoops! I remember all the nominees for Queen being marched around the classes and standing there while we voted for who we wanted.

Sylvia Worsdall, via email

Mini Puzzle

Can you unscramble this conundrum to form a nine-letter word?

| S | C | A | R | E | H | E | R | O |

(answer Racehorse)

Recipe of the week

Showstopping Mocha Choca Pavlova

Serves: 6-8
Preparation time: 30 minutes
Cooking time: 2¹/₂ hours

For the meringue:
6 egg whites
300g (11oz) caster sugar
25g (1oz) cocoa powder
1 tbsp instant coffee
25g (1oz) hazelnuts, chopped and roasted
For the filling:
500g (1lb 2oz) Greek yoghurt
400g (14oz) hazelnut chocolate spread
For the topping:
200g (7oz) seasonal fresh fruit of your choice
75g (3oz) chocolate, grated
(a mix of milk, dark and white works well)

1 Preheat oven to 120°C/250°F/Gas Mark¹/₂. On baking parchment, draw four 23cm (9in) diameter circles and place on to baking trays.
2 Take a large bowl and whisk the egg whites with one third of the sugar until thick and fluffy. Then gradually whisk in the remaining sugar until you have a thick and silky texture. Now gently fold in the cocoa and coffee.
3 Divide the mixture into four and gently spread in the pre-drawn circles to form four perfect circles. Then sprinkle the hazelnuts on and bake for 2¹/₂ hours, or until completely dry and hard. Leave to cool to room temperature.
4 Meanwhile, make the filling by mixing the hazelnut chocolate spread and yoghurt (chill until required). To serve, layer the meringue circles with the chocolate hazelnut mixture and garnish with fresh fruit and chocolate shavings.

Top tip: Make this even more indulgent by adding a splash of cherry brandy to the yoghurt mixture.
© Total Greek Yoghurt, www.totalgreekyoghurt.com

Shakespeare's country

Stratford–upon–Avon: theatre fans will love this pretty town

As the birthplace of William Shakespeare, Stratford-upon-Avon is rich in cultural history, and there are lots of attractions that celebrate his life and works. Visit the five houses connected to Shakespeare – including his birthplace, and wife Anne Hathaway's Cottage. Anne lived in the cottage before marrying the playwright; it's picture-postcard pretty, and set in beautiful gardens. For more information, visit www.shakespeare.org.uk.

Of course, a visit to Stratford-upon-Avon wouldn't be complete without a trip to the Royal Shakespeare Theatre. Here you can enjoy classic works of Shakespeare, and contemporary works from the Royal Shakespeare Company. **To find out what's on, call 0844 800 1110 or visit www.rsc.org.uk.**

Grandchildren will love Stratford's Butterfly Farm.

As well as some of the most spectacular butterflies, they can get close to all kinds of creepy-crawlies. **For opening times, call 01789 299288 or visit www.butterflyfarm.co.uk.**

History buffs can encounter the past at Tudor World, with an educational and fun journey through Tudor England. It's set in one of the town's oldest buildings, which is also known as one of England's spookiest, and has featured on TV show Most Haunted. **To find out more, call 01789 298070, or visit www.falstaffexperience. co.uk.** Alternatively, make the most of the town's beautiful setting on the River Avon, with a short ride on the historic chain ferry or a sightseeing boat trip.

Fact: William Shakespeare's birthday is widely believed to be April 23rd, but there's little evidence to support this.

Quiz of the month

Maps out – test your knowledge of places real and imaginary. If you get stuck, the answers are below.

1 Which seaside town features in both The French Lieutenant's Woman and Persuasion?

2 The area around Thirsk in North Yorkshire is associated with whose veterinary practice?

3 Name the poet who invited friendly bombs to fall on Slough.

4 Tyneside features in many of the novels of which bestselling author born in South Shields in 1906?

5 Who wrote a collection of poems known as The Shropshire Lad?

6 In which county does Detective Superintendent Charles Wycliffe represent the long arm of the law?

7 Supply the missing word in the title, Lorna Doone: A Romance of − − − − − −

8 Wessex was an imaginary county created by which Dorset-born writer?

9 Which poet was inspired by the daffodils growing on the shores of Lake Ullswater?

10 New Quay in West Wales has claims to be the original Llareggub in which radio drama by Dylan Thomas?

11 Bram Stoker's Count Dracula visited which town on the Yorkshire coast?

12 Born in Staffordshire in 1867, which author set his novels in the five towns of the Potteries?

13 The city of Edinburgh is said to be as much of a character as Inspector Rebus in whose crime novels?

PIC: REX FEATURES

14 A A Milne based the Hundred Acre Wood in his Winnie-the-Pooh stories on which forest in East Sussex?

15 In which Noel Coward play did Amanda say that Norfolk was very flat?

16 The Forest of Dean is the setting of Blue Remembered Hills by which TV dramatist who was born there in 1935?

17 Which Irish writer celebrates her birthplace in Dublin?

18 Virginia Woolf belonged to a group of writers named after which residential area in London?

19 Which poet who died in the First World War celebrated the village of Grantchester in verse?

20 Barsetshire is the invention of which Victorian novelist?

Answers: 1. Lyme Regis 2. James Herriot 3. John Betjeman 4. Catherine Cookson 5. A E Housman 6. Cornwall 7. Exmoor 8. Thomas Hardy 9. William Wordsworth 10. Under Milk Wood 11. Whitby 12. Arnold Bennett 13. Ian Rankin 14. Ashdown Forest 15. Private Lives 16. Dennis Potter 17. Maeve Binchy 18. Bloomsbury 19. Rupert Brooke 20. Anthony Trollope

Easter egg hunt

BY: RUTH SPENCER

Sandra is desperate to find the Easter egg she bought many years ago

The egg had always been important, even though as the years had gone by its appearance became less and less attractive. The paper lace joining its two halves had become frayed and tatty. The bright yellow of the chicks had faded. But the egg still held its charm for Sandra.

"I can't understand why you don't buy a new one," Emily said, swinging her legs backwards and forwards as she sat on the table.

"Because that's not the point!" Sandra replied impatiently. Her hair was a mess from rummaging frantically in the big cupboard that contained everything from the vacuum cleaner to an ancient rucksack. But no egg.

"Perhaps you threw it away," seven-year-old Rachel suggested helpfully, but her remark met with a look of disdain from her older sister and a frantic waving of her arms from their mother.

After the girls had been collected by the neighbour who was doing the school run, Sandra made a cup of coffee, sat down at the kitchen table, and cried. Her tears were a mixture of sadness and frustration. She quickly wiped them away and told herself she had to think this thing out logically.

The egg was somewhere in the house and it would be found. And when she had found it she would do what she had done in the week leading up to Easter Sunday ever since she was a teenager. She'd buy a small gift, place it in the egg, wrap it with care and post it to her friend Barbara.

The following year Barbara would return the egg to Sandra. It was a longstanding ritual of love and friendship. The two girls had been inseparable when they had attended the local High School together. Even the teaching staff had made good-natured comments about their closeness.

Then a terrible thing happened – Barbara's family had moved to Scotland when her father's job was relocated. The girls wept and vowed to keep in touch.

The girls wept and vowed to keep in touch

Despite the hundreds of miles between them, the friendship did survive. As well as keeping up through letters and phone calls, they spent holidays together. It was while they were on holiday in Devon one year that they saw the egg in a shop window and the idea of sending it to each other every Easter was born.

Sipping her coffee, Sandra reflected on the happy times they had enjoyed over the years – they had attended each other's weddings and been godmother to each other's children. Over the phone, they had shared life's ups and downs and felt each was the sister they'd never had.

Her daydreaming was interrupted when her neighbour, Jane, returned from the school run and put her head round the back door. Smiling, she said: "The girls were telling me about the egg…"

Sandra laughed. "I know it must sound silly to get worked up about it but it really does mean a lot to Barbara and me. It has been flying from north to south and back again through engagements, weddings, births, illness – nothing ever prevented us sending it. I've got to find it."

Jane was sympathetic. "My guess is that you've put it in a place you'd never dream of putting it if you hadn't been busy. Don't forget you were rushed off your feet with the Easter bazaar last year. I bet you put it somewhere you'd never think of looking."

Reassured by Jane's comments, Sandra resumed her search, looking in all the most unlikely places she could imagine. It was crazy to suppose the egg had found its way up into the attic, but it was just possible. She fetched the ladder from the garage and set it up on the landing. As she was about to climb it, the phone rang in the hall.

Picking up the receiver, she heard a familiar voice. "Barbara?"

"Hullo, Sandra. Bet you didn't expect it to be me!"

Blushing guiltily, Sandra was glad her friend couldn't see her. She replied: "Well, no I didn't. Actually, I was just… "

"Can't stop to natter, lovey. This has got to be a

PIC: KATE DAVIES

'You know what I won't be able to do?'

really quick call. I'm in a mad rush. Tony's mother has had an accident and I'm flying over to the island. It's nothing serious, thank goodness, but I said I'd go right away so you know what I won't be able to do?"

"Er, no – I don't."

"Of course you do! I won't be able to send you the egg in time for Easter."

Sandra couldn't believe her ears – or her luck!

"You still there?" Barbara asked.

"Yes, I'm still here."

"Well, as I said, I'm in a terrific rush. Tom's waiting for me at the airport. I'll be in touch when I get back. Have a lovely Easter. Bye!"

Sandra leaned weakly against the wall. Had it really been such a hectic year that she'd forgotten it wasn't even her turn to send the egg?

When the girls returned from school, they entered the house a little warily and were surprised to find their mother in an exceptionally good mood.

"Did you find the egg, then?" asked Rachel.

"Um, not exactly. I'll tell you about it later. Now, who's going to help me put the marzipan balls on the Simnel cake I made this afternoon?"

Sister act

A double wedding in 1951 for Sylvia and her older sister Joan

My sister, Joan, is four years older than me. When we were children we slept together and used to tell each other stories. When I was evacuated for a year during the war I missed Joan very much. Later, in 1951, we shared a double wedding. Dresses were hard to come by so we went with our mum to Selfridge's where we used our clothing coupons and money to buy identical dresses. Sadly, Joan was widowed after 13 years but she remarried and these days we keep in touch by phone. Recently, she sent me this poem.

'Treasured is the right word, when it comes to you.
There's not a sister in this world as wonderful as you.
If I need someone to lean on, I can always use your shoulder;
My whole life you have been there but I find that now I'm older
I appreciate you even more, and when I'm faced with strife,
It's then I thank my lucky stars I've got you in my life.'

Sylvia Luck, Ashford, Kent

Joan (left) and Sylvia still remain close friends

What's in a word

Floccinaucinihilipilification
(noun) the act of estimating something as worthless, of little or no value. Of Latin origin.

Pet of the month

NAME: Jaspa

AGE: 10 months

BREED: Lhasa Apso

OWNERS: Harvey and Glennys Wood, Alvaston, Derbyshire

PET LIKES: Playing with his ball and chasing gulls

PET HATES: The vacuum cleaner

HUMAN TRAIT: Using his paws like hands, even sitting next to people and putting his paws on their shoulders like an old friend.

May

Nothing is so beautiful as Spring
When weeds, in wheels, shoot long and lovely and lush;
Thrush's eggs look little low heavens, and thrush
Through the echoing timber does so rinse and wring
The ear, it strikes like lightning to hear him sing.
Poet, Gerard Manley Hopkins, extract from 'Spring'

May 2013

6 Monday

7 Tuesday

8 Wednesday

9 Thursday

10 Friday

11 Saturday

12 Sunday

If you do one thing

Take stock of your summer wardrobe. With the help of an honest friend try on every item in your cupboard and decide its fate. Send anything unflattering or badly fitting to the charity shop, repair any loose hems, seams or buttons, make a list of what you have and what you need to buy to look great all summer long.

School days

This is a photograph of myself and my school friend Vera, taken in 1961, aged 14. We were good friends through Burnhope Secondary School, but lost touch when I left Durham. After my husband died I moved back, and tried to find my old friend. It was by chance that a friend spoke of someone with the same surname, who turned out to be Vera's cousin. I am hoping to meet up with her soon.

Christine Chiesa, Stanley, County Durham

Mini Puzzle

Can you unscramble this conundrum to form a nine-letter word?

| A | C | E | D | U | N | G | I | T |

(answer Educating)

Recipe of the week

Salmon and Herb Croquettes

Serves: 4
Preparation time: 10 minutes, plus 2 hours cooling time
Cooking time: 25 minutes

1 x 180g (6oz) canned skinless and boneless salmon, drained
750g (1lb 11oz) Charlotte potatoes, peeled and roughly chopped
1 tbsp fresh dill, chopped
2 eggs, beaten
100g (3½ oz) fresh white breadcrumbs
100g (3½ oz) plain flour, for dusting
Oil, for deep frying
200ml (7 fl.oz) sweet Thai chili dipping sauce
80g (3 oz) watercress

1 Place the potatoes in salted water and bring to the boil. Simmer for 15 minutes, or until tender. Drain and season before mashing. Leave to cool for one hour.
2 Then add in the salmon and dill. Mix well and season to taste. Divide the mixture into 25g (1oz) pieces and roll into cylinder shapes on a lightly floured surface − you should end up with 20 in total.
3 In separate bowls, lay out the flour, eggs and breadcrumbs. Using that order, coat the cakes; then repeat to give them a double coating. Chill for an hour.
4 Preheat the oil to 180°C/350°F/Gas Mark 4 and deep fry the croquettes in batches, for one to two minutes, or until golden brown. Drain on kitchen paper and serve immediately with the chilli sauce and watercress.

Top Tip: This recipe works well with leftover mashed potato too.
© James Martin for John West, www.domorewithfish.co.uk

13 Monday

14 Tuesday

15 Wednesday

16 Thursday

17 Friday

18 Saturday

Pentecost (Whit Sunday)

19 Sunday

If you do one thing

Get a make-up overhaul. If you've been wearing the same make up for years the chances are it's making you look older than you actually are. An update could turn back the clock – and you can get expert advice for free. Just go to your local department store pick your favourite beauty brand and ask for advice, most counters now offer a mini makeover at no cost.

Recipe of the week

Easy–Peasy Lemon and Blueberry Tart
Serves: 8
Cooking time: 15 minutes
Chilling time: 3–4 hours

250g (9oz) digestive biscuits
100g (3½oz) butter
2 tbsp golden syrup
300ml (½ pint) double cream
400g (14oz) condensed milk
2 lemons, grated rind and juice
125g (4½oz) blueberries
For the sauce:
2 tsp cornflour
6 tbsp water
2 tbsp caster sugar
125g (4½oz) blueberries

1 Grease a 23cm (9in) spring-form tin. Crush the biscuits until they resemble fine crumbs. Heat the butter and golden syrup in a saucepan until the butter has just melted. Take off the heat and stir in the biscuits, until they are evenly coated. Then tip into the tin and press into an even layer over the base.
2 Whip the cream in a large mixing bowl until it forms soft swirls. Gradually whisk in the condensed milk, add the lemon rind, and then gradually whisk in the lemon juice until the mixture is smooth and thick. Fold in the blueberries. Pour into the tin, spread into an even layer and chill for three to four hours.
3 Meanwhile, make the sauce by mixing the cornflour and water together in the base of a small saucepan. Add the sugar and blueberries and cook for four to five minutes over a gentle heat; stirring until the juices run from the blueberries and the sauce thickens. Leave to cool to room temperature.
4 To serve, remove carefully from tin and transfer to a serving plate. Cut into wedges and serve with a drizzle of sauce.
© Seasonal Berries, www.seasonalberries.co.uk

School days

This is the last photo I had taken with my class at Albany Secondary Modern School in Enfield, Middlesex. I grew up there, but was one of the children evacuated to the countryside during the war. We went to Hitchin, then my two brothers and I were sent on to Great Wakering, Essex, to our grandparents and aunts.

Sylvia Langridge, Luton, Bedfordshire

Mini Puzzle

Can you unscramble this conundrum to form a nine-letter word?

D	U	M	P	Y	N	O	S	E

(answer Pseudonym)

20 Monday

21 Tuesday

22 Wednesday

23 Thursday

24 Friday

25 Saturday

26 Sunday

If you do one thing

Measure your waist. Grab a tape measure, find the point midway between the bottom of your ribs and the top of your hips, breathe out naturally and measure your waist size. If your waist is more than 80cm (31½ inches) if you're a woman, or 94cm (37 inches) if you're a man then you have an increased risk of serious health problems such as heart disease or diabetes. Visit your GP for advice on losing weight.

School days

This photo was taken at St Margaret's Church of England School, Bowers Gifford, in 1946. Our teacher, Miss Margaret Faulkes, was adored by all. She had the most wonderful voice when reading to us, and taught me the descants to hymns which we sang in assembly. She left in the year this photo was taken to get married, and I wrote to her until her death in 2011, 65 years later.

Valerie Holdsworth, Wickford, Essex

Mini Puzzle

Can you unscramble this conundrum to form a nine-letter word?

| T | O | A | N | I | R | I | S | H |

(answer Historian)

Recipe of the week

Baked Strawberry Tart

Serves: 8
Preparation time: 10 minutes
Cooking time: 45 minutes,
plus 10 minutes cooling time

1 x 20cm (8in) ready-made raw flan case (preferably sweet pastry but short crust will do)
300g (11oz) strawberries
2 eggs
50g (2oz) caster sugar
½ tsp vanilla extract
75ml (3fl.oz) double cream
75g low-fat Greek yoghurt
25g (1oz) icing sugar, to sprinkle

1 Preheat the oven to 180°C/350°F/Gas Mark 4 and blind-bake the flan case for ten minutes. Then remove the baking beans and bake for a further five minutes. This ensures the bottom of the tart doesn't go soggy. Remove from oven and reduce the heat to 160°C/325°F/Gas Mark 3.
2 Cut the strawberries in half and arrange them neatly in the baked flan case.
3 In a separate bowl, mix the eggs, sugar, vanilla extract, cream and yoghurt to form a custard. Pour this over the strawberries and bake the case for 25-30 minutes, or until the top is lightly brown and the custard has just set (you don't want this too set).
4 Leave the tart to cool for ten minutes, then sprinkle with icing sugar and serve immediately – with a scoop of ice cream if you want.

Top tip: You can use any fresh summer fruits in this tart; frozen fruit will make the tart base too soggy.
© Total Greek Yoghurt, www.totalgreekyoghurt.com

May 2013

27 Monday

28 Tuesday

29 Wednesday

30 Thursday

31 Friday

1 Saturday

2 Sunday

If you do one thing

Visit a local market and see if you can save money on your weekly shop. Fruit and veg is often much cheaper from a market stall because they have lower overheads. You might have to shop around a bit more but you could make a good saving.

School days

I came across this old photo of a school play, taken in around 1959. I am the one on the far left in the back row. I can remember having the dress made by a dressmaker, but can only remember the names of about four of my classmates. My school days were not the happiest, but I love to look back at the old black and white photos.

Mrs S Foster, Bridlington, East Yorkshire

Mini Puzzle

Can you unscramble this conundrum to form a nine-letter word?

| P | R | A | Y | E | R | S | B | R |

(answer Raspberry)

Recipe of the week

Baby Strawberry Mousses

Makes: 8
Preparation time: 15 minutes, plus 4 hours chilling time
Cooking time: 5 minutes

625g (1lb 6oz) strawberries
3 limes, grated rind only
3 tbsp runny honey
3 tsp powdered gelatine
250ml (9fl.oz) double cream
250g (9oz) low-fat natural yoghurt
100g (3½oz) extra-small strawberries to decorate (optional)

1 Purée 225g (8oz) of the strawberries, then press through a sieve. Reserve this for the top layer and chill. Then purée the remaining strawberries, sieve, and mix with the lime rind and honey.
2 Add four tablespoons of water to a small heatproof bowl and sprinkle the gelatine over it. Leave to stand for five minutes, or until the water absorbs all the powder. Then heat this in a small saucepan of simmering water, until it is a clear liquid.
3 Then, whip the cream until it forms soft swirls. Fold in the yoghurt, puréed strawberry and lime mix, then the gelatine in a thin trickle. Pour into eight 120ml (4fl oz) small liqueur glasses or coffee cups. Chill for three to four hours, or until the mousses have set.
4 To serve, stir the reserved strawberry purée and divide over each mousse. Decorate with the whole strawberries, if using, and serve immediately.

Top tip: These taste delicious served with shortbread wafers.
© Seasonal Berries, www.seasonalberries.co.uk

Book lovers' heaven

Enjoy a great day out in Hay-on-Wye

If you're a self-confessed bookworm, you'll love the charms of Welsh market town Hay-on-Wye, where the Hay Festival of Literature and the Arts is held every May. Lasting ten days, the festival attracts writers, film makers, comedians, musicians, and even politicians. Bill Clinton once described it as a 'Woodstock of the mind', and with plenty to see and do, you don't have to be a literary buff to enjoy a great day out. Plus there's something for the grandchildren – dedicated mini-festival 'Hay Fever' is especially for 'tots, teens and inbetweens'. Many events are free, but some require tickets and sell out quickly, so make sure you buy well in advance. For further information visit **www.hayfestival.com**.

Ensure you find time to nose around the town too. It is home to almost 40 bookshops, including the novelty of Hay Castle Bookshop where you pay into an honesty box! Then there's the traditional market every Thursday, where you can pick up delicious local produce; and craft and antique shops to explore.

Located just inside the Brecon Beacons National Park, Hay-on-Wye is surrounded by stunning countryside and offers some great walks. For a spectacular view, head to Hay Bluff, at the northern tip of the Black Mountains. **For more information about the area, visit www.hay-on-wye.co.uk.**

Fact: Hay-on-Wye sits on the Welsh and English border, and at one time was divided into English Hay and Welsh Hay. Most of the town lies in Wales, but England lays claim to some of its eastern parts.

Quiz of the month

The books we read as children hold a special place in our hearts – how many of these can you remember?

PIC REX FEATURES

1 Which book by Dodie Smith, who also wrote 101 Dalmations, tells the story of Cassandra, her beautiful older sister, Rose, her eccentric stepmother, Topaz and their life in a crumbling castle?

2 Judy Blume charts one girls struggle to find religion, and deal with growing up in which novel?

3 Evacuee Will finds a new and happy life with a grumpy old man in which story by Michelle Magorian?

4 Which super intelligent, but much maligned, Roald Dahl heroine escapes her rotten family and goes to live with her teacher Miss Honey?

5 Mary, Dickon and Colin become firm friends in which novel by Frances Hodgson Burnett?

6 Carrie and her brother Nick are billeted to Wales during the Second World War and their lives become entwined with those of the family who live at Druid's Bottom in which novel by Nina Bawden?

7 Who are the tiny people who live secretly in the houses of 'human beans' in Mary Norton's story of the same name?

8 Eight-year-old loner, Barney, befriends a stone-age caveman in which children's classic by Clive King?

9 Name the band of young, lemonade drinking, rock cake munching, super-sleuths led by Peter in the popular Enid Blyton series?

10 A lonely little boy discovers that his soul-less London home returns to its former Victorian glory at midnight in which Philippa Pearce story?

11 Accident prone trainee witch, Mildred Hubble, comes up against her irascible teacher, Miss Hardbroom in which story by Jill Murphy?

12 Dave loses his beloved stuffed toy in which tale by Shirley Hughes?

13 The eternally scruffy William Brown is the lead character of which series of stories by Richmal Crompton?

14 What is the title of Laura Ingalls Wilder's first book that begins the story of her pioneer family's journey across America?

15 Outspoken orphan Anne Shirley finds a home with Marilla and Matthew in which L M Montgomery classic?

16 When their father mysteriously disappears, Roberta, Peter and Phyllis move with their mother to a house called Three Chimney's in which Edith Nesbit novel?

17 Katy Carr is a tomboy who dreams of being beautiful and beloved in which book by Susan Coolidge?

18 Rebecca Rowena Randall goes to live with her two aunts to learn to be a 'proper young lady' in which set of stories by Kate Douglas Wiggin?

Answers: 1 I Capture the Castle, 2 Are You There, God, It's Me Margaret? 3 Goodnight Mr Tom, 4 Matilda, 5 The Secret Garden, 6 Carrie's War, 7 The Borrowers, 8 Stig of the Dump, 9 The Secret Seven, 10 Tom's Midnight Garden, 11 The Worst Witch, 12 Dogger, 13 Just William, 14 Little House in the Big Woods, 15 Anne of Green Gables, 16 The Railway Children, 17 What Katy Did, 18 Rebecca of Sunnybrook Farm

Rags to riches

BY: MARION FELLOWS

Cissie's little dog leads her a merry dance…

Cissie Markham glanced at the calendar. May 23, 1968. Her forty-fourth birthday. Where had the time gone?

She watched a group of teenage girls in mini skirts stroll past her window. Her teenage years had borne no comparison to theirs – the war had seen to that. She'd met and married Jim in 1943 when she was nineteen. Their happiness was brief as he was killed in action the following year.

Since then she'd dedicated her life to nursing, but she had her memories. She smiled as she saw a young couple walking hand in hand. The boy was serenading his girl with the Beatles' song, From Me to You. Not quite the same as We'll Meet Again, Cissie reflected wryly.

Giving herself a shake, she said briskly: "Come on, Rags, time for your walk. I think we'll go along by the canal." The mongrel wagged his tail and sat while she clipped on his lead.

There was only one boat moored on the canal, its red and green livery shining in the spring sunlight. Cissie recognised the name, The Lady Elizabeth. It had been moored in the same place last year.

At that moment, she stumbled on the uneven towpath and Rags seized the chance to slip his lead and dash towards the narrow boat. "Come back, you rascal!"

Too late. The dog had jumped aboard, wagging his tail furiously at the man who opened the door to see what was happening.

"I'm so sorry – he slipped his lead."

The man beamed. "That's all right. We don't mind, do we, boy?" He bent down and patted Rags on the head. "In fact, I believe I have something for you." Reaching inside, he produced a doggie chew and Rags became even more excited at this unexpected treat.

"That's very kind of you, Mr – "

"Oh, call me Bill, please," he smiled, stroking his bushy white beard. "And you are?"

"Cissie – Cissie Markham. And this little scoundrel is Rags."

Rags cocked his head to one side and Bill laughed: "Your mistress is right – you are a little scoundrel!"

Cissie felt surprisingly at ease with the stranger with the twinkling blue eyes. Sporting a Breton cap and striped jersey, he looked a typical sailor. She guessed him to be in his fifties; his weatherbeaten face testament to an outdoor life.

He said: "I remember you and Rags passing by my window the last time I was this way."

"I remember your boat, but not you," Cissie replied, then blushed. "I'm sorry, that sounds quite rude."

Bill laughed: "Not at all!" He raised his cap and ran his fingers through his shock of white hair. "Would you think it forward of me if I invited you in for a cup of tea?"

Before she could reply, Rags bounded through the open door. She smiled: "Seems like Rags has made the decision for me."

Cissie gasped in surprise at the boat's neat interior with its shiny black-leaded range and beautiful ribbon plates on the walls. "This is beautiful, Bill. I had no idea! Do you live on board?"

He nodded. "It's something I've always wanted to do, so when I took early retirement, I bought The Lady Elizabeth."

The kettle on the range began to whistle and soon they were drinking tea while Rags played with an old toy that Bill told her used to belong to his dog, Buster. "I lost him a few months back. A finer friend a man never had."

He sat quietly, deep in thought, before saying: "Life can be lonely, don't you find, Cissie? I lost my Elizabeth in the Blitz and there has never been

'Seems like Rags has made the decision'

PIC: KATE DAVIES

'As it happens, I also lost my Jim in the war'

anyone to take her place."

Cissie murmured sympathetically and Bill said: "I presume that you, too, are on your own?" Blushing, he immediately apologised: "Please forgive me – that was too outspoken by far. I'm sorry."

"There's no need to apologise. You are right, I am on my own. As it happens, I also lost my Jim in the war. His ship, The Serendipity, was torpedoed."

The colour drained from Bill's face. "You mean your husband served on The Serendipity?"

Cissie nodded.

Bill clasped her hands in his. "I was on that ship, Cissie!"

As if dazed, he got to his feet, went over to the sideboard and picked up a framed photograph. "I knew your husband. I knew Jim Markham." Looking at the picture, he went on: "In fact, we shared a cabin; we were buddies. He was a grand fellow."

He handed the photo to Cissie and her eyes met those of the smiling, handsome sailor standing at the back of the group. A single tear fell on the glass. She looked up: "Then you must be Bill Baxter."

"Well, I'll be blowed." He shook his head in disbelief. "Cissie Markham. Jim told me so much about you, I feel I know you already." Taking her hand, he said with a catch in his voice: "I think Jim would be pleased to know we'd found each other."

Cissie looked once more at the photo and then at Bill and responded to the affectionate squeeze of his hand. "So do I, Bill."

Then they laughed as Rags jumped up and excitedly tried to lick them both at once.

Dainty Bicycle Seat Cover

This will add a touch of style to any bicycle.

You will need:

1 piece of decorative cotton fabric large enough for the main bike seat piece

4 pieces of fabric 15x30cm (6x12in) for the sides/front/back of the seat

50cm (20in) of elastic 1½cm (¾in) wide

60cm (24in) of pretty ribbon around 4cm (1½in) wide

Large sheet of baking parchment.

Scissors

Pins

Sewing machine and thread to match fabric

Note:

The finished size depends on the size of bike seat. Before sewing, wash and iron your fabric to prevent shrinkage and dyes running.

1 Lie the baking paper on the bike seat and trace around the shape, with a seam allowance of 1½cm (¾in). Fold in half lengthways (to ensure it's symetrical) and carefully cut out.

2 Laying your bike seat template onto another sheet of parchment draw lines extending 10cm (4in) from each corner to create templates for the sides, front and back as per the diagram.

3 Pin the pattern templates on to your fabric, right-side-up and cut out. Now, with the right sides together, pin the front, sides and back pieces in place around the main seat piece and stitch together with a 5 mm (¼in) seam. Stitch again for extra strength.

4 Still with right sides facing sew up the vertical seams. Next, sew a hem 2 cm (¾in) all the way around the bottom edges of the seat cover – this will create a channel through which you can thread the elastic.

5 Snip a small hole on the inside of this channel at the back of the seat and thread the elastic through (temporarily holding one end in place with a pin). Pull the elastic tightly so the bottom of the seat cover is gathered – sew both ends securely in place.

6 Attach the ribbon to the front for decoration. Trim your loose threads and pop the cover over your bike seat. Tie up the ribbon and away you go!

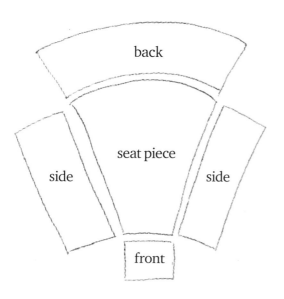

back

seat piece

side

side

front

Variation

To make your seat waterproof, use plastic fabric-backed tablecloth material – remember you can't iron and wash this.

© Make Hey While the Sun Shines by Pip Lincolne is published by Hardie Grant, £17.99 (Hardback).

Sister act

Above: A treasured picture of childhood and inset as the sisters are today. Shirley is on the left in both snapshots

There were six children in our family; four boys, my sister Shirley, and me. Shirley was 11 months older and I always wished I had her blonde, curly hair instead of my brown rats' tails. Everyone thought we were twins as Mam dressed us alike. I hated the way we were always compared at school because Shirley was the brighter one of the two of us. We shared a bedroom and one night we secretly took up a bag of sugar and a box of cocoa powder which we ate by sticking a wet finger first in one, then the other, but we fell asleep and woke up to sheets covered in chocolate. Mam went mad! We were also in big trouble when we tried walking down the stairs with both our legs in one pyjama leg and tore the pyjamas. When we were teenagers, we were allowed to go by bus to the next village for the Friday night bop. One week we'd wear our cardigans buttoned up the front and the following week buttoned up the back. Shirley started work at Woolworth's and bought some whalebone which we stitched into the hem of our skirts to make them stick out – but we couldn't sit down because the front of our skirts rose up over our heads!

Eileen Hawkes, Wigan, Lancs

What's in a word

Mumpsimus

(noun) a traditional view, custom or idea stubbornly held, even when shown to be unreasonable. From mid 16th century Latin.

Pet of the month

NAME: Jasmine (Jas for short)

AGE: 3 years

OWNER: Mrs C. Barrow, Plymouth, Devon

PET LIKES: Pouncing on our legs in bed, and being scratched under her chin

PET HATES: The doorbell

HUMAN TRAIT: Vocalising what she wants at an increasing volume until someone responds!

JASMINE'S STORY: Jasmine came from a local animal shelter after being handed in by the RSPCA

June

Long stormy spring-time, wet contentious April,
winter chilling the lap of very May;
but at length the season of summer does come.
Scottish writer and historian, Thomas Carlyle

June 2013

3   Monday

4   Tuesday

5   Wednesday

6   Thursday

7   Friday

8   Saturday

9   Sunday

If you do one thing

Give your hands a scrub. Mix together a tablespoon of caster sugar with two tablespoons of olive or almond oil and massage into your hands for a few minutes. This simple exfoliator will help to remove dry, dead skin cells and nourish your skin to leave it super smooth.

School days

Here is a school photo of my gorgeous daughter, Sophie. She is doing really well at school, excelling in literacy, numeracy and science. She loves school, has lots of lovely friends, adores her teacher and is always smiling and giggling. Like all girls of her age, she loves princesses and Hello Kitty! I am so proud of her.

David Knapp, Crowland, Lincolnshire

Mini Puzzle

Can you unscramble this conundrum to form a nine-letter word?

| G | R | R | S | A | T | I | R | E |

(answer Registrar)

Recipe of the week

Crispy Roast Beef with Cherry Tomato Pasta

Serves: 8-10
Preparation time: 15 minutes
Cooking times:
Rare: 20 minutes per 450g (1lb) + 20 minutes
Medium: 25 minutes per 450g (1lb) + 25 minutes
Well done: 30 minutes per 450g (1lb) + 30 minutes

1.3kg (3lb) lean beef topside joint
2 tbsp dried mixed herbs
2 tsp fennel seeds, crushed
2 tsp olive oil
For the pasta:
375g (13oz) cooked pasta shapes
350g (12oz) whole asparagus, halved, lightly cooked and cooled
100g (3^1/$_2$oz) cherry tomatoes, thinly sliced
For the dressing:
2 tbsp freshly chopped chives
2 tbsp white wine or cider vinegar
2 tsp caster sugar
1 tbsp olive oil

1 Preheat the oven to 180°C/350°F/Gas Mark 4. In a small bowl, mix together the dried herbs, fennel seeds and olive oil, then season. Place the joint on a chopping board, score the skin and rub the herb mixture all over.
2 Place the joint on a rack in a non-stick roasting tin, and open roast for your preferred cooking time; basting occasionally with any meat juices. Cover the joint with foil if it browns too quickly.
3 Remove the joint from the roasting tin, transfer to a warm plate and cover. Leave to rest for 15 minutes before carving.
4 Meanwhile, mix the pasta, asparagus and cherry tomatoes into a large bowl. Put the dressing ingredients into a screw-topped jar, season and shake well until combined. Pour over the salad and serve with the beef, immediately.
© Simply Beef and Lamb, www.simplybeefandlamb.co.uk

10 Monday

11 Tuesday

12 Wednesday

13 Thursday

14 Friday

15 Saturday

Fathers' Day

16 Sunday

If you do one thing

Scrunch up your face as if someone is going to drop something on your toe. Hold it for 15 seconds, then release. Repeat it several times. It's a great way to release the tension in your head and face and could help to soothe a headache.

School days

This is a photo of class 2B at Adeyfield School, Hemel Hempstead, in July 1955, when I was 13 years old. My best friends at school were Daphne and Jennifer. I remember we hated school dinners, so we used to take our lunch money to the local shop and buy a bag of chips, a cream doughnut and a fizzy drink! I was not happy at school, and still dread going past the building.
Christine Terry, Hemel Hempstead, Hertfordshire

Mini Puzzle

Can you unscramble this conundrum to form a nine-letter word?

H	O	T	S	C	A	R	E	R

(answer Orchestra)

Recipe of the week

Deeply Dippy and Decadent Strawberries

Makes: 30
Preparation time: 30 minutes
Chilling time: 2-3 hours

30 medium strawberries, tops left on
300g (11oz) of good quality dark chocolate
(or milk or white)
Options for decorating the strawberries:
100g ($3^1/_2$ oz) shelled pistachio,
chopped and toasted.
100g ($3^1/_2$ oz) hazelnuts, chopped and toasted
100g ($3^1/_2$ oz) desiccated coconut, toasted

1 Melt the chocolate (if you're using a mix of all three keep them in separate smaller bowls). Lay out your decorating options in separate bowls.
2 Then dip each strawberry in the chocolate to cover half the berry, then dip in one of the decorating options. Lay them on a baking sheet lined with non-stick baking paper. Chill, or leave in a cool place, until the chocolate has set. Serve alongside strong coffee or a choice of liqueurs after dinner, or at a picnic for a fun dessert.
© Seasonal Berries, www.seasonalberries.co.uk

17 Monday

18 Tuesday

19 Wednesday

20 Thursday

21 Friday   Longest Day (Summer Solstice)

22 Saturday

23 Sunday

If you do one thing

Pick up a pen after every meal. Writing down what you've eaten as soon as you've eaten it is a great way to keep track of your diet. It could help you see where you're comfort eating or giving into bad habits and could help you to lose weight. If you write down the time you ate too you'll be able to see if you really need to eat again.

School days

Here I am in the school netball team, which I belonged to in 1951-52. I dearly loved netball, and most dinnertimes you would find the team practising in the school yard, especially if there was a match on the Saturday, which there was most weeks. I played in the position of Goal Attack as I was quite small, able to run around a lot and scored lots of goals.

Joyce Clifford, Ledbury, Herefordshire

Mini Puzzle

Can you unscramble this conundrum to form a nine-letter word?

M	E	R	I	T	N	E	A	T

(answer Terminate)

Recipe of the week

Pork, Nectarine and Pistachio Terrine

Serves: 10
Preparation time: 30 minutes
(plus overnight marinating time)
Cooking time: 1 hour

300g (11oz) pork fillet, trimmed and diced
2 garlic cloves, crushed
2 sprigs thyme, leaves only, plus 3 sprigs with leaves on
2 tbsp brandy
250g (9oz) dry-cured streaky bacon
750g (1lb 11oz) good-quality sausage meat or skinned sausages
50g (2oz) parsley, chopped
50g (2oz) chives, chopped
100g (3½oz) shelled, unsalted pistachios
2 nectarines, stoned and sliced

1 Mix the pork fillet, garlic, thyme leaves and brandy in a bowl. Cover and leave overnight to marinate.
2 Heat the oven to 180°C/350°F/Gas Mark 4. Line a 1kg (2¼lb) terrine mould or loaf tin with foil, and lay the thyme sprigs on the bottom. Then line with overlapping strips of bacon, leaving any extra hanging over the edge. Loosen the sausage meat with a fork, add it to the marinated pork, and mix well. Stir through the herbs and pistachio; season well.
3 Pack the mould with half the pork. Lay the nectarine slices in a row down the centre, then add the remaining pork and flatten. Stretch the bacon over the top and cover with buttered foil. Then wrap the whole mould in a double layer of clingfilm.
4 Place in a roasting tin, half-filled with boiling water and bake for one hour. Cool and chill overnight. For a firmer texture, place a board and a couple of tins on top. To serve, remove the top foil and flip on to a serving platter. Remove the rest of the foil and serve immediately, with good bread.
© South African Fruit, www.beautifulcountrybeautifulfruit.com

June 2013

Wimbledon tennis tournament begins

24 Monday

25 Tuesday

26 Wednesday

27 Thursday

28 Friday

29 Saturday

30 Sunday

If you do one thing

Count your blessings – being grateful for what you have won't just make you happier it could boost your immunity too, according to researchers. Try writing down five things every day that you're thankful for.

Recipe of the week

Red Berry Meringue Roulade

Serves: 8
Preparation time: 20 minutes, plus 2 hours cooling
Cooking time: 15 minutes

For the roulade:
4 large egg whites
250g (9oz) caster sugar, plus extra for sprinkling
1 tsp cornflour
1 tsp white wine vinegar
For the filling:
300ml (1/2pint) double cream
4 tsp lemon curd
150g (5oz) raspberries
225g (8oz) strawberries, sliced

1 Preheat the oven to 190°C/375°F/Gas Mark 5. Line a 33x23cm (13x9in) swiss roll tin. Whisk the egg whites into stiff peaks. Gradually whisk in the sugar until thick. Mix the cornflour and vinegar, then fold into the meringue.
2 Spoon the meringue into the tin and shape gently into a thin layer. Bake for ten minutes, or until well risen and just colouring; then reduce heat to 160°C/325°F/Gas Mark 3 and cook for five minutes, or until just firm to the touch and beginning to crack.
3 Put a tea cloth on to the work surface, cover with a sheet of baking paper, and sprinkle with the extra sugar. Invert the hot meringue on to the paper; remove the tin and leave to cool for one to two hours.
4 Peel off the baking paper. Whip the cream until it forms soft swirls, then spoon over the meringue. Spread the lemon curd on top and sprinkle with berries. Roll up the meringue, starting at one short edge, using the paper and teacloth to help. Carefully transfer to a serving plate and remove rolling aids. Serve immediately with extra berries.
© Seasonal Berries, www.seasonalberries.co.uk

School days

Here I am in my school uniform, aged about six. My schooldays in Devon were mostly happy ones. I had my best friend, John, to walk to school with. We did not have the luxury of the 'school run' in those days! One of my favourite memories is of being taken into the assembly hall to watch the first film I ever saw on a big screen, 'The Wizard of Oz'.
Adrian Williams, Broadstairs, Kent

Mini Puzzle

Can you unscramble this conundrum to form a nine-letter word?

| M | R | D | U | M | M | I | E | S |

(answer Midsummer)

Beside the sea

The grandchildren will love marvellous Margate

For a traditional trip to the seaside you can't beat timeless Margate, with its nostalgic charm. This year should hopefully see the re-opening of a newly revamped Dreamland after years of campaigning to restore the historic site.

The original attraction and the popular Scenic Railway rollercoaster were opened in the 1920s, and the ride carried nearly half a million riders in its first year. Since then, Dreamland underwent many changes before its eventual closure in 2005, when all rides but the Grade II listed Scenic Railway ride were removed. Now, work is underway to reinstate it as one of the UK's best-loved amusement parks, based around the railway and the famous Dreamland Cinema, which dates back to the 1930s. The Dreamland Heritage Park will be the world's first authentic recreation of a good, old-fashioned seaside amusement park, and will include rides rescued from other British amusement parks that also faced closure. For more information, and to share your memories of the original Dreamland, **visit www. dreamlandmargate.com.**

While in Margate, be sure to visit Shell Grotto, a collection of underground passages that lead to a chamber where the walls are covered with a mosaic of millions of shells. The mystery surrounding the place makes for a truly intriguing visit. **Call 0184 322 0008, or visit www.shellgrotto.co.uk.**

For art enthusiasts, there's the Turner Contemporary, which houses a programme of temporary exhibits and events. **To find out what's on, visit www.turnercontemporary.org.**

Alternatively, make the most of Margate's simpler charms: paddle in the sea, relax on fantastic beaches, visit the theatre, and enjoy some good food in the town's many cafes and restaurants.

Fact: Entertainers who have performed at the famous Winter Gardens Theatre include Laurel and Hardy, and Dame Vera Lynn.

Quiz of the month

Good books make memorable movies – how many of these have you seen or read? If you get stuck, the answers are below

PIC: REX FEATURES

1 Starring Virginia McKenna, A Town Like Alice was written by which British–born writer and engineer?

2 Which city was the setting for the book and the film, The Prime of Miss Jean Brodie?

3 Who directed the film Women in Love, starring Glenda Jackson, Oliver Reed and Alan Bates?

4 A quest for the Holy Grail is central to the plot of which bestseller that was turned into a film of the same name, starring Tom Hanks?

5 In which year did the romantic drama Atonement win an Oscar for the best original score?

6 An otter was the star of which 1969 film based on the book by Gavin Maxwell?

7 Starring Hugh Grant, which book by Nick Hornby was turned into a film with the same name in 2002?

8 In which Italian city did Helena Bonham Carter and Maggie Smith fail to find A Room With a View?

9 Which Disney box–office success was based on a collection of children's stories by Rudyard Kipling?

10 What was the name of the Second World War fighter pilot played by Kenneth More in the film Reach for the Sky?

11 Whose diary was turned into a romantic comedy starring Renée Zellweger?

12 Julie Christie played Bathsheba Everdene in the 1967 film adaptation of which Thomas Hardy novel?

13 Whose first novel, The World is Full of Married Men, was released as a film in 1979?

14 Sandra Bullock played a law student in A Time to Kill based on the book by which bestselling American thriller writer?

15 Name the character played by Johnny Depp in the 2005 version of Charlie and the Chocolate Factory.

16 Which Shakespeare play inspired the film Kiss Me Kate with music by Cole Porter?

17 Deborah Kerr played a nun in which Powell and Pressburger film based on a novel by Rumer Godden?

18 Starring Jack Nicholson, which 1975 film, based on a novel by Ken Kesey, won five Oscars?

19 Stanley Kubrick's A Clockwork Orange was based on the disturbing book by which author?

20 Which of Graham Greene's books was first made into a film in 1947 and again more recently in 2011?

Answers: 1. Nevil Shute 2. Edinburgh 3. Ken Russell 4. The Da Vinci Code 5. 2008 6. A Ring of Bright Water 7. About a Boy 8. Florence 9. The Jungle Book 10. Douglas Bader 11. Bridget Jones 12. Far from the Madding Crowd 13. Jackie Collins 14. John Grisham 15. Willy Wonka 16. The Taming of the Shrew 17. Black Narcissus 18. One Flew Over the Cuckoo's Nest 19. Anthony Burgess 20. Brighton Rock

Bowled over

BY: LINDA LEWIS

Matt finds the dating game has its pitfalls

The moment I got through the front door, I pulled off my walking boots. My feet were killing me. I'd spent the day hiking with Lorna and I was worn out.

When Lorna phoned the next day to see if I'd like to go ten-pin bowling with her, I put her off. I'll be sixty this year. I've always thought getting older meant slowing down a bit, but Lorna has other ideas.

For the next three evenings, I did little more than read the papers and watch TV. Bliss. There was just one problem – I missed Lorna.

We'd met on the internet. It had been my brother David's idea. "You need to start dating again," he said.

"What for?" I replied. "I'm happy on my own."

He raised his left eyebrow. "In that case, why do you spend every weekend round at our place?" he grinned. "But seriously, Matt, it's three years since Mary died and you're not good on your own."

He found a promising dating site and I'd started filling in the questionnaire when David said: "Don't put a cross there."

"Why not? I can't stand folk music."

"I know, but you need to tick all the boxes. The idea is to meet as many women as possible."

So that's what I did. At first, dating felt strange, but I soon discovered the women were as nervous as I was and I met some very nice ladies. I wasn't looking for romance. All I wanted was company – but then I met Lorna.

As soon as I saw her, I knew she was special. It wasn't love at first sight but being with her made me feel good. Our first date was in the coffee bar next to the bowling alley and when she suggested going bowling, I agreed. I didn't mention that the only time I've played is with my grandchildren on the Wii machine. How could I when I'd ticked bowling as a favourite pastime on the dating site?

As soon as I saw her I knew she was special

And I wasn't even sure then if I'd ever see her again.

Now it was too late. How could I tell her that all the things she loves – ten-pin bowling and seven mile hikes – are things I could do without? In the end I decided there was only one thing I could do – stop seeing her. Once she found out I'd been lying, it would be all over anyway.

I phoned and said I wanted to slow things down a bit.

"I knew you weren't keen when we went bowling the other day. You kept sighing," Lorna said.

"Sorry," I said.

"Well, goodbye then," and she hung up before I could say another word.

For the next few days, I felt lost. I kept making mistakes at work which isn't like me at all. It was only then that I realised I was in love. That was the last thing I expected – I'm fifty-nine years old, for goodness' sake!

I wanted to see Lorna again but it would never have worked. Long hikes and dancing, bowling and jogging – I couldn't have kept up with her for much longer.

That weekend, I went round to David's place. He asked: "What happened? Don't tell me you've broken up with Lorna?"

"We had nothing in common. I like a gentle stroll, she likes a cross-country hike."

He poured me a beer, then nodded towards the kitchen. "Sally loves the theatre. It bores me to tears, but I go with her. She likes Bach, I prefer Take That. We compromise; that's what couples do."

He had a point. I could be miserable on my own, or miserable with Lorna. I smiled. Even with blisters on my feet, I was happy in her company.

"Thanks, David. I'll call her later."

He handed me the phone: "Do it now."

Lorna sounded surprised. "I thought you didn't want to see me any more?"

"I know, and I'm sorry about that. Look, can we meet? There's something I need to tell you."

We met in the coffee bar. The moment I saw her, my spirits soared. I decided I'd do whatever it took to keep her in my life. Rather than beat about the bush, I blurted out the truth. "Lorna, I don't like

PIC: KATE DAVIES

ten-pin bowling. Long walks wear me out and I can't stand line dancing."

"Pardon?"

"All the things you love, I hate them," I explained.

"Why are you telling me this now?"

I reached for her hand, but she pulled it away.

"I think I'm falling for you. If we're to have a future, you need to know the truth."

She looked puzzled. "But on the dating site you said… "

"That was my brother's idea. He told me to tick all the boxes to increase my chances."

For a moment, she sat there staring at me, then she started laughing.

"What are you laughing at?"

"Us," she said. "I hate bowling, too. I only suggested it because I thought you were keen. I prefer a gentle stroll, ending up at a cosy country pub."

"Me, too," I said.

"Really? You're not lying to me again?"

"No." I reached for her hand and this time she let me take it. "I'll never lie to you again."

"Good. Let's drive to a cosy country pub to celebrate!"

Sister act

Barbara (left in both photos) had an idyllic childhood

What's in a word
Apricate
(verb) to bask in the sun. First used in 19th century English literature.

Pet of the month

NAME: Marmalade

AGE: 4 years

OWNERS: Suzette and Roger Mizen, Colchester, Essex

PET LIKES: Having his tummy tickled, his treats of ham and the Go Compare TV adverts!

PET HATES: The sound of the washing machine and the vacuum cleaner

MARMALADE'S STORY: He was an abandoned kitten who visited Suzette and Roger's garden in search of food and a loving family

This picture was taken in our back garden in Middlesex during the 1950s. My sister Jenny, two years older than me, was so happy to be wearing the latest look in swimwear! We had a lovely childhood, with parents who adored each other. Jenny and I both went to ballet and tap lessons, Jenny went horse-riding and I had piano lessons. Christmas was always a special time with wonderful presents. Unknown to us, our dad would make wooden toys for us in his shed. We also loved going to visit our aunt and uncle's farm in Berkshire, travelling in dad's black Austin Seven. Our aunt and uncle had two daughters and we had great fun having midnight feasts with sweets (penny chews, black jacks and sweet cigarettes) bought in the village shop. Jenny was always a trendsetter and looked glamorous in her shirt-waister dress, white stilettos and matching handbag. I would watch her getting ready for a night out, backcombing and lacquering her hair, applying lipstick and then perfume – which was always L'Aimant by Coty. I also remember listening to Radio Luxembourg on her transistor radio, huddled underneath the bedclothes listening to The Hollies or Herman's Hermits. Although we've had our ups and downs in life, I've always loved my big sister.

Barbara Arnot, Walton-on-Naze, Essex

July

Then followed that beautiful season summer.
Filled was the air with a dreamy and magical light;
and the landscape lay as if new created in all the freshness of childhood.
Poet, Henry Wadsworth Longfellow

July 2013

1 Monday

2 Tuesday

3 Wednesday

4 Thursday

American Independence Day

5 Friday

6 Saturday

7 Sunday

If you do one thing

Snack on pistachios. Just a small handful each day and you could see your total cholesterol drop by an average of 6.7 per cent – which could reduce your heart disease risk by 14 per cent. Pistachios are a great source of plant sterols, which are also found in fortified yoghurt drinks and spreads that promise to lower cholesterol.

School days

This is the Ashford Grammar School Music Society performance of 'Pirates of Penzance' in 1955. Pupils and staff always joined in for an annual show – Gilbert and Sullivan were the favourite productions. We rehearsed after school, evenings and weekends, for the event, which was performed daily for a week. On the Sunday afterwards we would have a great party before clearing everything away.

Mrs P Odell, Hampton, Middlesex

Mini Puzzle

Can you unscramble this conundrum to form a nine-letter word?

| G | A | Y | E | R | B | A | L | E |

(answer Agreeably)

Recipe of the week

Steaks on a Tomato and Pepper Bed

Serves: 4
Preparation time: 10 minutes
Cooking time: (on each side) Rare: 3–4 minutes; Medium: 4–5 minutes; Well done: 6–7 minutes

4 x 2–3cm (³/₄–1¹/₄in) lean fillet steaks
2 tsp sunflower oil
1–2 garlic cloves, peeled and finely chopped
200g (7oz) ripe tomatoes, skinned and chopped or
1 x 200g (7oz) can of chopped tomatoes
1 yellow pepper, de-seeded and finely chopped
2 tbsp freshly chopped thyme leaves
2 tbsp Worcestershire sauce
2 tsp capers, drained and rinsed
100g (3_oz) wild rocket leaves, to garnish
Jacket or roast potatoes and 4 tbsp Greek yoghurt, to serve

1 Season the steaks and rub with half the oil. Heat a large, non-stick griddle pan and cook the steaks according to your preference. Transfer to a warm plate and set aside to rest.
2 In the same pan, add the remaining oil to cook the garlic, tomatoes, peppers and thyme for seven to eight minutes, or until soft. Season and add the Worcestershire sauce. Spoon the tomato bed on to four warm plates and scatter with capers.
3 Place the steaks on top and garnish with rocket leaves. Serve with the potatoes and a dollop of Greek yoghurt.

© Simply Beef and Lamb, www.simplybeefandlamb.co.uk

July 2013

8 Monday

9 Tuesday

10 Wednesday

11 Thursday

12 Friday
Battle of the Boyne (Bank Holiday Northern Ireland)

13 Saturday

14 Sunday

If you do one thing

Dry brush your skin using a soft bristle body brush to gently sweep over your skin every morning. Start at your feet and work upwards. It's a great way to remove dead skin cells and brighten your skin – and some experts believe it could help to reduce the appearance of cellulite. Do it before a morning shower and slather on a good moisturiser afterwards.

School days

This photograph, taken in 1938, is of the pupils who attended Cadley School near Marlborough, Wiltshire. I am in the centre of the photograph with the almost toothless smile! Only four of us lived in Cadley – the other pupils either walked or cycled from the outlying farms and cottages. The school closed later that year because of the decreasing numbers of pupils, after which we travelled by bus to Marlborough.

Pamela Hosey, Malaga, Spain

Mini Puzzle

Can you unscramble this conundrum to form a nine-letter word?

| C | R | E | E | P | R | A | N | T |

(answer *Carpenter*)

Recipe of the week

Strawberry Jellies

Serves: 6
Preparation time: 25 minutes, plus 4 hours chilling time
Cooking time: 5 minutes

625g (1lb 4oz) strawberries
50g (2oz) caster sugar
120ml (4½fl oz) water plus 4 tbsp
3 tsp powdered gelatine
Juice of 1 lemon
Red sugar flowers or heart-shaped cake decorations (optional)

1 Slice 400g (14oz) of the strawberries. Gently cook in a lidded saucepan, with the sugar and water, for five minutes – or until the fruit is softened. Meanwhile, dissolve the gelatine in the remaining water.
2 Blend the cooked strawberries and juices, press through a sieve and discard the seeds.
3 Heat the gelatine until it forms a clear liquid. Gradually stir into the fruit purée, then mix in the lemon juice and leave to cool to room temperature.
4 Meanwhile, slice the remaining strawberries, stir into the jelly mixture and pour into six 150ml (¼pint) individual glasses (or one large dish). Stand on a baking tray and chill for four hours, or until set.
5 To serve, dip each mould in hot water and count to ten. Then loosen the edge of the jelly with a wetted finger, turn the mould on to a serving plate, decorate with flowers or hearts and serve – with a little ice cream or custard.
© Seasonal Berries, www.seasonalberries.co.uk

15 Monday

16 Tuesday

17 Wednesday

18 Thursday

19 Friday

20 Saturday

21 Sunday

If you do one thing

Walk for five minutes. Set yourself a target of walking purposefully for just five minutes. Then the next day aim to walk for five minutes more. Set yourself a goal of walking for at least 30 minutes every day. Achieve that and you'll be burning off about 120 extra calories a day – which could lead to you losing 12 pounds in a year.

School days

This is a school photograph of my granddaughter, Alex, taken when she was 11 years old, in her final year at junior school. She is now 13 and is a lovely teenager who helps out at the local British Heart Foundation charity shop after school. She loves English and always has her nose in a book. She would like to be an author or schoolteacher when she grows up.

Jackie Fuell, London

Mini Puzzle

Can you unscramble this conundrum to form a nine-letter word?

| N | E | A | T | E | R | T | I | N |

(answer *Entertain*)

Recipe of the week

Tagliatelle with Salmon, Spinach and Peas

Serves: 4
Preparation time: 5 minutes
Cooking time: 20 minutes

300g (10oz) dried tagliatelli
For the sauce:
2 x 180g (6oz) cans skinless and boneless salmon, drained
25g (1oz) unsalted butter
150g (5oz) peas
100g (3½oz) spinach leaves
200g (7oz) low-fat crème fraîche
Large handful flat-leaf parsley, chopped
25g (1oz) Parmesan, grated
Olive oil, to drizzle

1 Cook the pasta according to packet instructions and drain. Keep warm.
2 In the meantime, melt the butter in a large saucepan over a medium heat. Add the peas and salmon, and cook for one minute. Lower the heat and add the spinach. Allow to cook slowly for one to two minutes.
3 Add the pasta to the salmon sauce, along with the crème fraîche. Gently warm through but do not allow it to boil. Season to taste and serve immediately with a drizzle of olive oil.
© James Martin for John West, www.domorewithfish.co.uk

22 Monday

23 Tuesday

24 Wednesday

25 Thursday

26 Friday

27 Saturday

28 Sunday

If you do one thing

Visit the library. Instead of paying out to read the latest summer blockbuster book see if you can borrow it from your local library. And while you're there, see what else they have on offer. Many allow you to rent films and TV shows on DVD.

School days

Here is my daughter's class photo, taken in 1975. I think this photo is particularly typical of the fashions of the time – look at that wallpaper! My daughter, Heather, is on the front row, fourth from the right. Although she's now in her forties, her hair is as long now as it was then. The children all look so cute, but I wonder how many of their names we could remember now?

Mary Burgin, Sheffield, South Yorkshire

Mini Puzzle

Can you unscramble this conundrum to form a nine-letter word?

| C | O | S | Y | S | C | A | R | E |

(answer Accessory)

Recipe of the week

Raspberry and Vanilla Cambridge Creams

Makes: 6
Preparation time: 20 minutes, plus 4¹/₂ hours chilling time
Cooking time: 25–30 minutes

1 vanilla pod
600ml (1pint) double cream
6 egg yolks
75g (3oz) caster sugar
300g (11oz) raspberries
6 tbsp caster sugar

1. Scrape out the vanilla seeds and place both pod and seeds in a medium saucepan with the cream. Heat gently until it just brings to the boil. Take it off the heat immediately and leave to infuse for 30 minutes.
2. Preheat the oven to 160°C/325°F/Gas Mark 3. Beat the egg yolks and sugar together in a bowl, until creamy. Remove the vanilla pod from the cream and discard, then bring the cream to the boil once more. Gradually mix in the egg yolks, until smooth.
3. Divide the raspberries between six 250ml (8fl.oz), shallow, oven-proof 11¹/₂cm x 2¹/₂cm (4³/₄ x 1in) circular dishes and stand them in a roasting tin.
4. Sieve the vanilla cream over the top. Pour warm water into the roasting tin, to come halfway up the sides of the dishes; then bake the custards, uncovered for 25–30 minutes, or until just set with a slight wobble.
5. Remove from tin and leave to cool before chilling for at least four hours. Sprinkle with sugar and caramelise under a hot grill until just brown. Leave to stand for 30 minutes before serving.

© Valentine Warner for Seasonal Berries, www.seasonalberries.co.uk

29 Monday

30 Tuesday

31 Wednesday

1 Thursday

2 Friday

3 Saturday

4 Sunday

If you do one thing

Check your fridge temperature – it should be between 0-5 °C to prevent harmful bacteria infecting your food. If your fridge is old it might be worth investing in a separate thermometer to check the temperature just to be on the safe side. Your digestion becomes more vulnerable to bugs as you get older so it pays to be vigilant.

School days

Here is a photo of our grandson Troy Harrison. He is nearly seven and had long hair until this cool new style! He loves school and was on the school council last year. He loves all sports and is in the football club, plays badminton and has learnt how to surf, and done an indoor skydive in a wind tunnel! He can play the drums and is going to start electric guitar soon. There is never a quiet moment in his mum and dad's house! He is our only grandchild and the best one in the world.

Pat and Les Tuck, Great Shelford, Cambridge

Mini Puzzle

Can you unscramble this conundrum to form a nine-letter word?

| B | E | S | T | R | A | N | D | Y |

(answer Bystander)

Recipe of the week

Smoked Haddock Breakfast Florentine

Serves: 4
Preparation time: 10 minutes
Cooking time: 20 minutes

2 tbsp vinegar
200g (7oz) dyed smoked haddock
600ml (1pint) milk
4 thick slices of granary bread
1 large bag baby leaf spinach
4 eggs
1 lemon, cut into wedges
For the dressing:
1 small bunch chives, chopped
200g (7oz) Greek yoghurt

1 Get a saucepan ready with nearly boiling water and the vinegar, for poaching the eggs. In a separate pan, place the smoked haddock in the milk. Heat and simmer for ten minutes. Then remove, flake, and set aside. Save the reserved milk.
2 Toast the bread and mix three-quarters of the chives into the yoghurt, along with 75ml (3fl oz) of the milk. Season with plenty of pepper.
3 Then poach the eggs for approximately two-and-a-half minutes – to keep the yolk runny – and wilt the spinach gently in a frying pan.
4 Place the spinach on the toast. Top with the haddock and egg. Then add the dressing and sprinkle over the rest of the chives. Serve immediately with the lemon wedges.
Top tip: Why not replace the haddock with shredded fresh ham? Or, if you're a vegetarian, try sautéed mushrooms.
© Total Greek Yoghurt, www.totalgreekyoghurt.com

Stunning scenery

Head north for breathtaking views in the Scottish Highlands

The Scottish Highlands offer a diverse range of scenery… stunning mountain ranges and wild coastlines that are home to an array of wildlife and little else.

Perhaps, the most popular tourist attraction is Balmoral Castle and it's easy to see why the royals love this part of Great Britain. The fortress is situated within the Cairngorms National Park, which is home to some of Britain's highest mountains. However, the grounds, gardens, and exhibits are only open to the public at certain times of year. **Further information is available by calling 0133 974 2534, or visiting www.balmoralcastle.com.**

For outstanding scenery, head northwest to Kintail and Morvich and you'll experience stunning vistas of rugged and unspoilt countryside. The area is home to the Falls of Glomach (one of the highest waterfalls in Britain) and the Five Sisters of Kintail; a line of peaks that offer great walking and hiking opportunities. To see the highest mountain in Britain, head west – Ben Nevis towers a massive 1,344 metres above the town of Fort William.

Visit Spey Bay's Scottish Dolphin Centre to take part in land-based dolphin watching, learn about the history of salmon fishing, and join wildlife walks. There's an interactive visitor centre and admission is free – so it's great for a day out with the grandchildren if you're on a budget. **Call 0134 382 0339, or visit www.wdcs.org.**

And if you can't resist trying to catch a glimpse of Nessie, head to Inverness-shire and Loch Ness. Whether you see the infamous monster or not, the Highlands still offer the chance to see all sorts of wildlife – including whales, seals, rare sea birds and birds of prey.

Fact: The Queen is said to describe Balmoral as her 'paradise in the Highlands'.

Quiz of the month

Here are a few famous phrases from our favourite novels – how many of these quotes can you recognise?

PIC REX FEATURES

1 "He shall never know how I love him; and that, not because he's handsome, Nelly, but because he's more myself than I am. Whatever our souls are made of, his and mine are the same."

2 "How often have I said to you that when you have eliminated the impossible, whatever remains, however improbable, must be the truth?"

3 "If you live to be 100, I hope I live to be 100 minus 1 day, so I never have to live without you."

4 "It is a truth universally acknowledged that a single man in possession of a good fortune, must be in want of a wife."

5 "No, I don't think I will kiss you, although you need kissing, badly. That's what's wrong with you. You should be kissed and often, and by someone who knows how."

6 "The pain of parting is nothing to the joy of meeting again."

7 "Life appears to me too short to be spent in nursing animosity or registering wrongs."

8 "She generally gave herself very good advice (though she very seldom followed it)."

9 "It was a bright cold day in April and the clocks were striking thirteen."

10 "Faithless is he that says farewell when the road darkens."

11 "You never really understand a person until you consider things from his point of view... Until you climb inside of his skin and walk around in it."

12 "A person is, among all else, a material thing, easily torn and not easily mended."

13 "Love goes towards love as schoolboys from their books. But love from love towards school with heavy looks"

14 "You is getting nosier than a parker."

15 "In my younger and more vulnerable years my father gave me some advice that I've been turning over in my mind ever since."

16 "Love itself is what is left over when being in love has burned away, and this is both an art and a fortunate accident."

17 "Mr and Mrs Dursley of No. 4 Privet Drive were proud to say that they were perfectly normal, thank you very much."

18 "Believe me, my young friend, there is nothing – absolutely nothing – half so much worth doing as simply messing about in boats."

Answers: 1 Wuthering Heights – Emily Brontë, 2 The Sign of the Four – Arthur Conan Doyle, 3 Winnie the Pooh – A A Milne, 4 Pride and Prejudice – Jane Austen, 5 Gone With the Wind – Margaret Mitchell, 6 Nicholas Nickleby – Charles Dickens, 7 Jane Eyre – Charlotte Brontë, 8 Alice's Adventures in Wonderland – Lewis Carroll, 9 1984 – George Orwell, 10 The Fellowship of the Ring – J R R Tolkien, 11 To Kill a Mockingbird – Harper Lee, 12 Atonement – Ian McEwan, 13 Romeo and Juliet – William Shakespeare, 14 The BFG – Roald Dahl, 15 The Great Gatsby – F Scott Fitzgerald, 16 Captain Corelli's Mandolin – Louis de Bernieres, 17 Harry Potter and the Philosopher's Stone – J K Rowling, 18 The Wind in the Willows – Kenneth Grahame

The batting order

BY: KEITH HAVERS

Can George and Finlay bridge the generation gap?

Finlay had never been left alone with his grandfather before. He sat in the tiny lounge with flowery wallpaper and faded photographs in silver frames. The clock on the wall made a strange ticking sound and a shiny ball swung to and fro below the face.

To the seven year old, Granddad's house looked as though it hadn't changed for a hundred years. It didn't even smell like his own house. Instead of the sweet aroma of his mum's air freshener there was a strange odour reminiscent of cabbage.

The old man came out of the kitchen, wiping his hands on a towel. He said: "I've got some job to finish off so you'll have to amuse yourself for a while. Have you got anything to play with?" Finlay looked up at the tall figure and shook his head. He had come away in a bit of a rush as his mum had been asked at the last minute to fill in a shift at the hospital.

George was as uncomfortable as his grandson. It was years since he had looked after young children and he didn't have a clue what they got up to these days.

"Well, what do you normally do in the school holidays? Play football? Trainspotting?"

Finlay didn't even know what trainspotting was. He asked: "Have you got an X-Box, Granddad?"

George scratched his chin. "I've got an old packing crate out the back if you want a box to mess around with. What are you going to do with it? Play castles?"

"No, Granddad. An X-box. It's like a playstation."

"That will be a 'no' then, son."

"What about a Wii?"

"The bathroom is upstairs. Make sure you wash your hands when you've finished."

Finlay sighed. "No, Granddad. It's a sort of computer game."

"Playstations? Computer games? What am I… made of money?" George returned to the kitchen,

'No, Granddad. It's a sort of computer game'

leaving Finlay to flick through the TV channels. The melodic tones of an ice cream van drifted in from the street. The boy trotted in to the kitchen. "Can I have a Magnum, Granddad?"

"I take it that's some sort of ice cream," George said. "It's no wonder kids are overweight these days. You sit in front of the TV all morning then you want to fill your face with saturated fats."

Finlay returned to the lounge. At home, he would be on his trampoline in the garden or his mum might take him swimming. He looked out of the back window but there were no playthings there, only an old shed at the end of the lawn.

Eventually, George finished his chores and realised he should be spending some time with his grandson. "Come on," he said. "Let's go outside and see what we've got."

He led the boy down the garden path and pulled open the door of the shed to peer inside. It was dark and smelled of compost and hadn't been cleared out in years. Finlay knew there would be nothing in there to interest him.

"Hello, what's this?" George hauled an old canvas bag into the daylight and spilled its contents on to the lawn. Half a dozen short wooden poles, a faded red ball and something with a rubber-covered handle.

"What is it?" asked Finlay.

"It's my old cricket set. Surely you know what cricket is?"

The boy looked at him blankly. Having been brought up in the electronic age, the attraction of a leather ball and wooden bat was lost on him.

"Here. I'll show you how to set it up."

Finlay wasn't too keen at first but after ten minutes he had got the hang of batting. George had swapped the hard leather ball for a rubber one and the lad was amused to see him rushing all over the garden to retrieve it. Granddad didn't even seem to mind when it went on to his flower borders or his veg patch.

He explained about runs and boundaries and catches. "How's that!" he'd yell, each time he

PIC: KATE DAVIES

caught the ball.

Eventually, it was the old man's turn to bat. Finlay found he had a natural talent for bowling but his Granddad was no mean batsman. "I used to play for the village, you know. Opening batsman and leg-break bowler."

Finlay thought the leg-break sounded painful but said nothing. He was tickled to hear his Granddad giving his own running commentary as he hit the ball to all corners of the garden. "Oh, and that's a superb drive to covers!" he exclaimed as the ball landed among the cabbages.

"And that one's steered safely through the slips and down to third man for a four!" he grinned as Finlay had to chase down to the greenhouse.

George was beginning to get his own back by getting the boy to run around but then he got carried away. He took a mighty swipe at a short delivery from Finlay that bounced up. The two of them watched the ball sail over the fence into next-door's garden, followed by the sound of breaking glass. Finlay's face fell.

"What do we do now, Granddad?"

"Tell you what," George said, handing the bat to the boy. "You go round and tell them you did it and I'll buy you a Magnum. How's that?"

Sister act

Barbara (left) and Anna were only **18** months apart in age. Inset on holiday in Spain (Anna on right)

My sister, Anna, and I were the eldest of five children. As there is only 18 months between us we have always been very close and, even today, are immediately recognised as sisters. We were born and brought up in London, apart from six months of the war when we were evacuated to Somerset where we spent happy days on a farm. Whatever we did, Anna and I were always together. We made our own enjoyment, walking miles to various parks and playgrounds with our jam sandwiches and drinks of NHS reconstituted orange juice. Luckily, there was no such thing as 'health and safety' as we often played on bombsites and around canals. Mum and Dad taught us both to cook, knit and sew – activities we are still enjoying today. During our teenage years we would often make a dress each in the morning to wear the same evening! We both married and moved away but still kept in touch and spent family Christmases together. Since my husband died in 1996, Anna has been very supportive. We are closer than ever and speak to each other on the phone every evening without fail. For more than 70 years she has been my dear sister and best friend.

Barbara Neal, Maidstone, Kent

What's in a word
Cachinnate
(verb) to laugh loudly. From 19th century Latin.

Pet of the month

NAME: Jasper

AGE: 30 years

OWNER: Norman Hacker, Gosport, Hampshire

PET LIKES: Gem lettuce, vine tomatoes and sleeping in his own little bed in the kitchen

PET HATES: Not getting to do his own thing!

ENDEARING TRAIT: Walking on the pavement alongside Norman in the summer months and enjoying the garden

August

Summer afternoon, summer afternoon;
to me those have always been the two most
beautiful words in the English language.
Author, Henry James

August 2013

5 Monday   Summer Bank Holiday (Scotland)

6 Tuesday

7 Wednesday

8 Thursday

9 Friday

10 Saturday

11 Sunday

If you do one thing

Before you get up and start your day pull back the curtains, open the window a little and get back into bed. People who get a good dose of natural light and a bit of fresh air first thing in the morning tend to feel more positive and get a better night's sleep at the end of the day.

School days

1966 was a year to remember for me, not because England won the World Cup, but because I started nursery school in Bexley, South East London. According to my mother, I hated school for two weeks – perhaps, that's why I look so grumpy in the picture! But after that she says I couldn't wait to get there. It has always taken me a while to settle into things!

Paul Larkins, via email

Mini Puzzle

Can you unscramble this conundrum to form a nine-letter word?

| O | R | G | E | T | C | U | T | E |

(answer Courgette)

Recipe of the week

Speedy Chorizo and Spring Onion Quesadilla

Serves: 4
Preparation time: 10 minutes
Cooking time: 10 minutes

4 large flour tortillas
100g (3¹/₂oz) mature cheddar cheese, grated
3 spring onions, finely chopped
2 tablespoons jalapeño peppers, chopped, (optional)
8 slices of cured chorizo, thinly sliced
Readymade guacamole, sour cream and salsa, to serve

1 Gently heat a large frying pan and lay out two tortillas on a chopping board, ready to fill.
2 In a small bowl, mix together the cheese, spring onions, jalapeño peppers and chorizo.
3 Split the cheese mixture between the two tortillas, leaving a 1cm (¹/₃ in) gap around the edge. Top each tortilla with a remaining tortilla to create a sandwich, then place one 'sandwich' into the frying pan. Gently toast for about two minutes on each side, or until the tortillas are golden brown and the cheese has melted. Keep warm.
4 Repeat with the other quesadilla, before chopping each one into six triangles. Serve immediately with the guacamole, sour cream and salsa.
© Cathedral City, www.cathedralcity.co.uk

12 Monday

13 Tuesday

14 Wednesday

15 Thursday

16 Friday

17 Saturday

18 Sunday

If you do one thing

Pop some popcorn, switch to brown rice, have porridge for breakfast and choose a wholegrain cerea. Regularly eating wholegrain food could help to reduce inflammation in your body and lower your risk of inflammatory conditions such as diabetes and heart disease. Aim to eat three servings a day.

School days

Here are my brothers, Bryn and Gareth, pictured at their primary school in Ashchurch, Gloucestershire in 1965. The comb tucked into Bryn's sock had just been used to give his normally scruffy younger brother a quick tidy-up before the photographer arrived. He has also made sure Gareth's shirt is tucked in and both socks (usually, one was around his ankle) are neatly pulled up.

Marion Reeve, Downham Market, Norfolk

Mini Puzzle

Can you unscramble this conundrum to form a nine-letter word?

B A D S A D L E G

(answer Saddlebag)

Recipe of the week

Red Pepper, Tomato and Cheddar Tartlets (with a kick)

Makes: 8
Preparation time: 15 minutes
Cooking time: 1 hour 45 minutes

2 large onions, peeled and chopped
50g (2oz) olive oil
2 x 400g (12oz) tins chopped tomatoes
1 red chilli, de-seeded and finely diced
A pinch of sugar
2 cloves garlic, peeled and chopped
1 tbsp fresh rosemary, finely chopped
200g (7oz) readymade puff pastry
2 Ramiro red peppers, cut into strips
200g (7oz) vintage cheddar, grated

1 Slowly cook the onions in the olive oil for about 30 minutes, until soft and melting.
2 Add the tomatoes, chilli, sugar, garlic, rosemary, and peppers to the onions, and cook over a gentle heat for about 45 minutes. Stir occasionally, until everything has reduced and become really thick. Season to taste and remove from the heat. Leave to cool.
3 While it cools, preheat the oven to 200°C/400°F/ Gas Mark 6. Roll out the pastry and line eight individual tart tins. Scatter half of the cheese in the bases, then spoon in the tomato filling, and finish with the remaining grated cheese. Bake for about 30 minutes, or until the pastry is crisp and golden. Serve immediately – or leave to cool and pack up for a picnic.

Top tip: This can also be made as one large tart; decorate with rosemary sprigs and serve as a light lunch with salad leaves.
© Pilgrims Choice Cheese, www.pilgrimschoice.com

19 Monday

20 Tuesday

21 Wednesday

22 Thursday

23 Friday

24 Saturday

25 Sunday

If you do one thing

Put your car keys away – and walk or hop on your bike instead. Overweight women who add just 10 minutes of activity to their daily routine a day could dramatically improve your heart health. If your journey is less than a mile try to walk or cycle instead.

School days

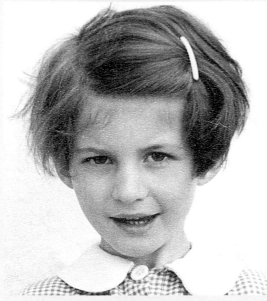

I joined South County Primary School in Gainsborough, Lincolnshire, in 1957 and was six or seven in this photo. My first teacher was Miss Justice, who was handy with a ruler. I went home with red knuckles after showing friends my birthday cards in class. She seemed so tall to a five year old. The school closed in 1993, and had a farewell party which my sister and I went along to.

Joy Harris, Peterborough, Cambridgeshire

Mini Puzzle

Can you unscramble this conundrum to form a nine-letter word?

| B | O | A | S | T | S | A | G | E |

(answer Sabotages)

Recipe of the week

Warm Peri Peri Sardines

Serves: 2
Preparation time: 5 minutes
Cooking time: 15 minutes

2 x 120g (4½oz) sardines in brine, drained
50g (2oz) readymade peri peri sauce
1 x 400g (14oz) can chick peas, drained
1 tsp red wine vinegar
Handful of flat-leaf parsley, chopped
50g (2oz) rocket leaves
Crusty white bread, to serve

1 Preheat the grill to medium and place the sardines on a baking tray. Brush with the peri peri sauce and grill for ten minutes – turning once, until warm through.
2 In the meantime, take a mixing bowl and add the chickpeas, vinegar, and the remaining peri peri sauce. Mix well and season to taste.
3 Just before serving, add the parsley and rocket; toss together. Divide between four serving plates and place two sardines on top of each. Drizzle with any leftover dressing and serve immediately with the bread.

© James Martin for John West, www.domorewithfish.co.uk

August 2013

26 Monday

27 Tuesday

28 Wednesday

29 Thursday

30 Friday

31 Saturday

1 Sunday

If you do one thing

Wear rubber gloves when you're cleaning. Your skin is great at absorbing chemicals – that's why nicotine and HRT patches work. If you don't protect your skin when you're cleaning, the chemicals from your cleaning products could be getting into your bloodstream. More research is needed to discover exactly how harmful this could be to your health, but it's worth protecting yourself in the meantime.

School days

This is me in about 1958, aged six, at Hunningley Lane School in Stairfoot, Yorkshire. At first I thought the badge on my jumper was a Head Boy badge, but then I realised I was much too young for that, and actually held the rather less glamorous position of milk monitor! I moved around to quite a few schools after this, but I have good memories of my time here. **Richard Brooks, via email**

Mini Puzzle

Can you unscramble this conundrum to form a nine-letter word?

N	E	V	E	R	C	R	E	E

(answer Reverence)

Recipe of the week

Chocolate & Tia Maria Fridge Cake

Serves: 10
Preparation time: 30 minutes
Chilling time: At least 12 hours

500g (1lb 2oz) 70% dark chocolate
250g (9oz) Greek yoghurt
250ml (9fl oz) double cream
5 tbsp glucose syrup
75ml (3fl oz) Tia Maria
75ml (3fl oz) strong black coffee
200g (7oz) mixed nuts, dried fruit and broken biscuits of your choice

1 Lightly whip the double cream and fold in the Greek yoghurt. Chill.
2 Mix the coffee and Tia Maria together in a small saucepan, and warm through. Then add the glucose syrup and dissolve. Melt the chocolate in a bowl over a pan of hot water, or in a microwave. Then pour the coffee into the melted chocolate. Fold in the nuts, fruit and biscuits. Gradually fold in the cream, mixing well.
3 Pour the mixture into a 25½cm (10in) round cake tin, and smooth for an even surface. Chill for at least 12 hours, or overnight. To serve, turn the cake out on to a board and cut into ten portions. Serve with a dollop of Greek yoghurt and a sprig of mint.

Top Tip: You could use any fruit and nuts you like. A good combination is amaretto biscuits and almonds, with glacé cherries. And rum or whisky can be substituted for the Tia Maria if you choose.
© Total Greek Yoghurt, www.totalgreekyoghurt.com

Sunshine in the south

Head to Lizard Point and enjoy some picture–postcard charm

Surrounded by sea, the Lizard Peninsula is home to stunning coastlines, sleepy fishing villages and rare plants and flowers. Located southwest of Falmouth and east of Penzance, the Lizard offers the usual Cornish charm, along with a touch of the exotic thanks to its warmer temperatures.

The Lizard Lighthouse marks mainland Britain's southernmost point and the original building dated back to 1619. Before the lighthouse was built the area was notorious for shipwrecks, but it was later demolished after ship owners refused to pay a maintenance toll. Now the replacement, twin-towered lighthouse is open to public tours.

The Lizard is also home to one of the most beautiful beaches in the world – Kynance Cove is owned by the National Trust, and is an Area of Outstanding Natural Beauty. Be sure to sample the delicious homemade cakes at the Kynance Cove Café… and a visit to Cornwall wouldn't be complete without polishing off a Cornish pasty!

Another must-see is the Lizard Marconi Wireless Station. Guglielmo Marconi's wireless experiments took place here in 1901, and the Marconi Company set up a ship-to-shore radio station – the oldest surviving station in the world.

The building is now a museum, but it's almost exactly how it was back then. You can enjoy demonstrations, and there's even a fully operational amateur radio station. Opening times vary, depending on the time of year and the weather, so for more information contact the National Trust.

With thanks to the National Trust, call 0844 800 1895 or visit www.nationaltrust.org.uk.

Fact: It was on the headland cliffs of Rill Point that the Spanish Armada was first spotted in 1588.

Quiz of the month

Families in fiction – how many of these are you familiar with? If you get stuck, the answers are below

PIC REX FEATURES

1 Who wrote a play, called Dear Octopus, about a family reunion?

2 Which book, published in 1812, tells the survival story of a family shipwrecked in the East Indies?

3 What is the name of the family in H E Bates' novel The Darling Buds of May?

4 In the Catherine Cookson trilogy, which family lived at High Banks Hall?

5 Which young rascal has an older brother and sister called Robert and Ethel?

6 Between 1906 and 1921 John Galsworthy wrote five books about several generations of which family?

7 Cider with Rosie recalls the Cotswold childhood of which writer?

8 What is the surname of the four sisters, Meg, Jo, Beth and Amy?

9 My Family and Other Animals by Gerald Durrell is set on which Greek island?

10 The Aged Parent is Wemmick's father in which Charles Dickens novel?

11 Who wrote My Cousin Rachel?

12 Which novel by Rosamunde Pilcher spans several generations of Penelope Keeling's family?

13 The Whiteoak family feature in the Jalna series of books by which American writer?

14 Gertrude is the mother of which Shakespearean character?

15 Which family employed a Newfoundland dog called Nana to look after the three children?

16 Who wrote about Julian, Dick and Anne and their tomboy cousin, Georgina (Georgie)?

17 Cold Comfort Farm is home to which eccentric family?

18 Which best-selling author wrote about twins separated at birth in Sons of Fortune?

19 Which famous literary family lived in the Yorkshire village of Haworth?

20 Which of the Mitford sisters wrote about their childhood in her book Hons and Rebels?

Answers: 1. Dodie Smith 2. Swiss Family Robinson 3. Larkin 4. The Mallens 5. William Brown 6. The Forsyte family 7. Laurie Lee 8. March 9. Corfu 10. Great Expectations 11. Daphne du Maurier 12. The Shell Seekers 13. Mazo de la Roche 14. Hamlet 15. The Darling family 16. Enid Blyton 17. The Starkadders 18. Jeffery Archer 19. The Brontës 20. Jessica

After the storm

BY: LOUISA DE LANGE

Jealousy is ruining Sara and Lisa's holiday...

The lightning illuminated the untidy room – the beach towels, swimsuit hanging on the door knob, sunglasses discarded on the chest of drawers. Then a loud clap of thunder made Sara jump and move closer to her sleeping husband. She could hear the rain drumming on the roof of the beach house.

The day had been oppressive and stifling. And it wasn't only the weather. Sara reflected on her own earlier behaviour. She knew that she had been immature and sulky, but she blamed her sister. Lisa had burst out with her news, destroying the calm and relaxation of their summer holiday.

Next to Sara, her husband, Jeff, snored on, oblivious as usual to any disturbances. She kicked him briefly under the sheet but there was no response. He and Lisa's husband had done nothing to settle the argument, refusing to get involved. They were used to the sisters bickering and took no notice, knowing from experience they would soon be friends again.

But, Sara thought, this was different from their usual quarrels. This was something bigger than a missed birthday or some silly misunderstanding. Gradually the rain abated and she drifted off to sleep.

By the morning, the storm had cleared and Sara woke early. Still groggy from her broken night's sleep, she moved slowly around the kitchen before anyone else stirred. The mug of tea in her hands was hot and comforting.

The house was right next to the beach with wide windows looking out on the waves and clear blue sky. It was small and shabbily decorated with an eclectic mix of furniture, but it was the view that sold it to Sara – uninterrupted shades of blue as far as the eye could see.

They had booked the holiday spontaneously after a conversation on the phone. It was a rare treat for the sisters to spend quality time together

They had booked the holiday spontaneously

and Sara had been looking forward to it for months. But instead of a much-needed break from stress and worry, Lisa's news was ruining it all.

Sara finished her tea, picked up her book and sunglasses, and walked across the rickety boardwalk to the beach.

Even though it was early, the sun was scorching. There were few people about. Only some runners, panting and sweaty, braved the heat. Tiny crabs regarded her from their makeshift holes. Sara flicked a few grains of sand at them and they darted back out of sight.

A figure blocked out the sun. Sara squinted up at the silhouette of her sister. Lisa paused for a second then sat next to her, silently fidgeting with the book on her lap.

Eventually, she said: "I'm sorry."

"What for?"

"You know."

Sara looked at Lisa who was always the peacemaker, always the one to apologise first. She noticed that her sister's body was changing already, showing curves where there had been straight lines. She said: "Well, it's not as though you could have kept it quiet for ever."

"But I shouldn't have blurted it out like that. I was going to sit down with you, be a bit more sensitive."

"Right."

"It's just that we are so excited."

"I can imagine."

And it was true. She could. Sara remembered all those times when she and Jeff had felt the first buzz of anticipation only to discover they were false alarms. All those 'what if' thoughts, the tentative smiles and the planning. But their hopes were invariably shattered a few days later and eventually brought to an end completely when the doctor confirmed that they couldn't have children.

He'd told them that they could keep trying but they shouldn't expect miracles and suggested considering other options. And now here was her younger sister who hadn't even been trying, who'd

PIC: KATE DAVIES

once said she didn't really want children, announcing she was twelve weeks pregnant – and had the fuzzy black-and-white scan photos to prove it.

It was so unfair. Sara wondered whether she was more angry with her sister or with fate itself.

"Do you want to see?" Lisa offered the photos tentatively. Sara took them and held them carefully, knowing how precious they were. Looking closely, she could just about make out a tiny head and hands, and spine curving along the bottom of the picture.

"He's about this big," Lisa said, holding her fingers about six centimetres apart.

"He?"

"Or maybe she," her sister smiled, and shrugged. "We don't know yet, of course, but I can't bear just calling him 'it'. We can't wait, we just want to know!"

"He's going to be beautiful, Lisa," she whispered, handing back the photos. "I know he is."

"Thank you," Lisa said and squeezed her hand. "And you will always be there, won't you? Auntie Sara?"

Sara nodded and looked away, feeling the tears pricking behind her eyes. Auntie. She had never considered that option.

Auntie Sara. Yes, she would always be there, all through his – or her – life. Maybe she and Jeff couldn't have children of their own (although they hadn't ruled out the other options suggested by the doctor) but she would still be Auntie Sara.

She sat back in her chair and raised her face to the sun, feeling its benign warmth. For the first time in months she smiled, her sister's hand still clutched in hers.

'Bottoms Up' Bottle Totes

These make adorable bags to present a bottle of wine for friends. They also make handy carriers for drinks at a picnic. Roll on summer!

You will need:

50x56cm (18x22in) of cotton fabric.
Sewing machine and thread to match your fabric
Scissors
Pins
Measuring tape
Iron and ironing board

Note:

Finished size will fit a standard 750ml (24 fl oz) wine or drinks bottle.
Seam allowance is 1 cm ($\frac{1}{2}$ inch) unless otherwise stated.
Before sewing, fabric should be washed and ironed to prevent fabric shrinkage and dyes running.

1 Cut $\frac{1}{3}$ off the width of the fabric so you have two pieces – one for the main body of the bag 38x50cm (15x19$\frac{1}{2}$in) and one which will make the strap 18x50cm (7x19$\frac{1}{2}$in).

2 For the strap cut the smaller piece in half lengthways to make two pieces 9x50cm (3$\frac{1}{2}$x19$\frac{1}{2}$in). Place the strap pieces together with right-side facing – pin and stitch along one of the short ends (so you have a long thin strip), press the seam open. Fold the strap in half lengthways (right sides facing) and sew along the long edge to form a tube. Turn right side out (using the blunt end of a knitting needle to help you push the fabric through).

3 For the main bag trim the larger piece of material so it measures 34x40cm (13$\frac{1}{2}$x16 in). Fold in half widthways and press a crease. Unfold and bring both raw edges into the centre crease. Measure 25cm (10in) up from the bottom edge of your bag piece and pin the centre of your strap to the pressed-in quarter crease of your bag piece (at the 25cm (10in) mark. Stitch a few times to secure.

4 Sew up the bag by putting the right side facing away from you. Then fold the top edge down 2cm ($\frac{3}{4}$in) and press. Repeat and press. Then pin and top-stitch into place with a 3mm ($\frac{1}{8}$in) allowance from the bottom folded edge. Next, pin the straps to the just-stitched edge, so that they are away from the side and bottom seams. With right sides facing up, fold the bag in half widthways and stitch with a 2$\frac{1}{2}$cm (1in) seam along the bottom of the bag. Stitch once more for extra strength. Now stitch a 1cm ($\frac{1}{2}$ in) seam up the sides, making sure your strap is well away. Turn your bag the right way out and iron to press, and just add bottle.

Variations

Use a different patterned fabric for the strap, either clashing or complementing for a quirky twist. This is a good way to recycle old dresses, curtains and bed sheets.

© Make Hey While the Sun Shines by Pip Lincolne is published by Hardie Grant, £17.99 (Hardback).

Sister act

Only 15 months separated Susan (left) from Jill (right)

I have two sisters and couldn't write about one without the other. Kay is nine years older than I am and Jill is 15 months younger. As children, Jill and I played together but we were very different. While I was quiet and a bit more studious, Jill got into scrapes. My uncle called her Aurora as she always had a lock of hair falling across her eyes like the girl in the 'don't forget the Kia-Ora' advert. In later years Kay told us she felt she was treated differently as Dad always waited for her at the bus stop when she went out but Jill and I were given more freedom and allowed out later. She was also upset because Jill and I shared a Dansette record player but she could never have one. Mother taught us knitting, crocheting and sewing. She would threaten us with a hairbrush if we were naughty but it was a threat that was seldom carried out. Today my sisters are my best friends and we no longer have the age gap that Kay felt we had as children. We all live about five minutes' away from each other and go on outings once a month as well as belonging to the same knitting and patchwork groups.

Susan Green, Scunthorpe, N Lincolnshire

The age gap doesn't matter so much today for sisters (from left) Jill, Kay and Susan

What's in a word

Slubberdegullion

(noun) a dirty, slovenly person. From 17th century English dialect.

Pet of the month

NAME: Oscar

AGE: 4 years

OWNER: Marie and Doug Munro, Arlesey, Bedfordshire

PET LIKES: Red grapes, walkies, sunbathing and all his toys

PET HATES: Having a bath, being told off and being disturbed from his basket

HUMAN TRAITS: He's extremely inquisitive and stubborn, loves a good sulk and is already getting grey whiskers!

September

Autumn, the year's last, loveliest smile.
Poet, William Cullen Bryant

2   Monday

3   Tuesday

4   Wednesday

5   Thursday

6   Friday

7   Saturday

8   Sunday

If you do one thing

Try yoga. Time spent on a yoga mat could be time well spent, especially if you experience back pain. After practising yoga twice a week for six months back pain sufferers said they felt significantly less pain and felt much more positive and optimistic. Yoga is also great for arthritis because it strengthens the muscles around your joints and improves flexibility.

School days

This is me during the end of year school play in 1950 at Tollington Grammar School. I sang 'Temple Bells'. My costume was made from Mum's green silk bedspread, and the make-up was cocoa powder and cold cream, which I can still smell today! I rehearsed at my grandmother's house as she played the piano. The vase on my shoulder is rather small because I dropped the 'best' school flower vase at rehearsals!

**Mrs G Allsop,
Teignmouth, Devon**

Mini Puzzle

Can you unscramble this conundrum to form a nine-letter word?

| P | E | R | B | E | S | T | M | E |

(answer September)

Recipe of the week

Mediterranean Pork Casserole with Fresh Thyme

Serves: 4
Preparation time: 15
Cooking time: 1 hour 15 minutes

2 tsp olive oil
500g (1lb 2oz) pork loin, cubed
1 white onion, chopped
1 garlic clove, finely chopped
1 tsp sweet paprika
2 sprigs fresh thyme, leaves only
1 large green pepper, de-seeded and cut into strips
1 large tomato, de-seeded and cut into strips
200g (7oz) chopped tomatoes with herbs
150g (5oz) green pesto
100ml ($3^{1}/_{2}$fl oz) chicken stock
100g ($3^{1}/_{2}$oz) button mushrooms
Boiled new potatoes and steamed broccoli, or warm granary bread to serve

1 Add the olive oil to a casserole dish, and fry the pork for about five minutes, or until brown. Lower the heat, add the onion and garlic, and cook for another five minutes, or until the onion is soft and translucent.
2 Add the paprika and thyme leaves; season to taste. Stir in the pepper, tomato, chopped tomato, pesto, stock and mushrooms. Bring to the boil, and simmer gently for one hour with the lid on, or until the pork is tender. Stir occasionally.
3 Season to taste. Serve at once with potatoes and broccoli, or warm bread.
© Organic chef Arthur Potts Dawson for Seeds of Change, www.seedsofchange.co.uk

9   Monday

10   Tuesday

11   Wednesday

12   Thursday

13   Friday

14   Saturday

15   Sunday

If you do one thing

Bring the outside in. If you struggle to get out and about, make the most of the view from your windows by hanging large mirrors opposite them. Pick a window that has a scene you like outside it such as your garden or a tree on your street. You'll be able to see the view from more vantage points, which could help you to feel calmer and happier.

School days

The lady in the hat is my grandmother, Mary Price, cutting the cake that she has baked for the school Christmas party. Standing behind her are my brothers, Wyn and Roy. Several generations of our family attended this school in the little village of Glynarthen before it closed last year, having served the local community for more than a century.

Jean Price, Aberystwyth, Ceridigion

Mini Puzzle

Can you unscramble this conundrum to form a nine-letter word?

E	Y	E	D	S	T	R	A	Y

(answer Yesterday)

Recipe of the week

Plum Tray Bake

Serves: 8
Preparation time: 15 minutes
Cooking time: 1 hour 15 minutes,
plus 20 minutes cooling time

110g (4oz) butter, softened
1 tsp vanilla extract
275g (10oz) soft brown sugar
3 medium eggs
110g (4oz) of plain flour and also of self-raising flour, sifted
125ml (4fl oz) milk
50g (2oz) ground hazelnuts
6 small round plums, halved and stoned
50g (2oz) dried cranberries
50g (2oz) hazelnuts, toasted and chopped

1 Preheat the oven 160°C/325°F/Gas Mark 3. Grease a deep 30x20cm (12x8in) baking tin and line with greaseproof paper.
2 Using a wooden spoon, cream the butter and sugar together. Then stir in the eggs, flour, milk, vanilla extract and ground hazelnuts. Gently spread this into the baking tin. Place the plums on top and sprinkle with the cranberries and chopped hazelnuts.
3 Bake for 1 hour 15 minutes, or until cooked through. Leave to cool for at least 20 minutes before lifting out of the tin. Place on a cooling rack or serve immediately with lashings of custard.
© South African Fruit, www.beautifulcountrybeautifulfruit.com

16 Monday

17 Tuesday

18 Wednesday

19 Thursday

20 Friday

21 Saturday

22 Sunday

If you do one thing

See if you can save on your energy bills. Not having to worry about expensive heating bills could make the arrival of the cooler weather a lot less stressful. Speak to your current energy supplier about ways to reduce your costs or have a look at the services of other providers. Visit **yours.co.uk/switching** to compare prices.

School days

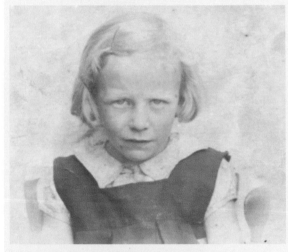

This is me aged nine in 1939, at Carlton School. I came from a large farming family, so we were well-known in the village and I enjoyed school. When it turned out I was left-handed, my Mum made sure that the teachers didn't try and make me write with my right hand, as they had done to my older sister. Both my granddaughters are left-handed, so it obviously runs in the family.

Sheila Manterfield, Carlton, Yorkshire

Mini Puzzle

Can you unscramble this conundrum to form a nine-letter word?

F	E	A	T	S	B	R	A	K

(answer Breakfast)

Recipe of the week

Lamb with Spiced Lentils

Serves: 4
Preparation time: 10 minutes
Cooking time: 20 minutes

4 boneless lamb legs or lamb rump steaks
2 tsp olive oil
1 red onion, peeled and finely chopped
2 tsp ground cumin or garam masala
1 x 400g (14oz) can green or brown lentils, rinsed and drained
1 x 400g (14oz) can of chopped tomatoes
2 tbsp fresh coriander, chopped

1 Heat half the oil in a large, non-stick pan and cook the onion with your chosen spice for two to three minutes, or until soft. Then add the lentils and tomatoes. Season to taste and leave to simmer gently for five to seven minutes, stirring occasionally. Remove from the heat and stir through the coriander.
2 Meanwhile, heat a non-stick griddle pan. Season the steaks, rub with the remaining oil and cook for six to eight minutes on each side.
3 Arrange the lamb slices on top of the lentil mix, spoon any remaining meat juices over the lamb, and serve immediately.

© Simply Beef and Lamb, www.simplybeefandlamb.co.uk

23 Monday

24 Tuesday

25 Wednesday

26 Thursday

27 Friday

28 Saturday

29 Sunday

If you do one thing

Have fish for dinner. Regular fish eaters are much less likely to develop dementia than those who rarely eat fish. Oily fish that are rich in omega-3 fats, such as salmon, mackerel and tuna could help to reduce the inflammation that has been linked to memory decline. Make a simple mackerel paté by mashing cooked mackerel with low-fat cream cheese, a little horseradish and a squeeze of fresh lemon juice.

School days

Here I am with my sister, Pat, in our school blazers. My first school memory is of starting nursery in the year the war ended. The teacher told me to go into the classroom, but instead I went back out into the playground and just kept on walking back towards home! My mum found me sitting on the doorstep, and marched me straight back. Needless to say she made sure I stayed that time!

Margaret Wiltshire, Leicester

Mini Puzzle

Can you unscramble this conundrum to form a nine-letter word?

| T | H | A | T | C | E | E | F | S |

(answer *Factsheet*)

Recipe of the week

Mini Baked Bramble Cheesecakes

Makes: 12
Preparation time: 15 minutes
Cooking time: 20 minutes

200g (7oz) light cream cheese
50g (2oz) caster sugar
2 eggs
1 tsp heaped custard powder
Finely grated rind of 1 lemon
100g ($3^1/_2$oz) fresh or frozen blackberries
25g (1oz) icing sugar

1 Preheat the oven to 180°C/350°F/Gas Mark 4 and grease a 12-hole, non-stick baking tin. In a large mixing bowl, beat together the cream cheese, sugar, eggs, custard powder and lemon rind until just combined. Spoon the cheesecake mixture into the baking tin.

2 Liquidise the blackberries and icing sugar, and swirl a spoonful of the fruit purée into the centre of each cheesecake. You can sieve the purée to remove the pips if you wish.

3 Bake for 20 minutes (or until set) and leave to cool completely before removing from the tin. Serve with a dollop of whipped cream or vanilla ice cream.

© Philadelphia, www.philadelphia.co.uk

September 2013

30 Monday

1 Tuesday

2 Wednesday

3 Thursday

4 Friday

5 Saturday

6 Sunday

If you do one thing

Save money on your prescriptions. A single prescription item costs £7.65 and those bills can soon add up if you have a lot of drugs to take. If you have to pay for more than three prescription items in three months, or more than 13 items in 12 months, you may find it cheaper to buy a Prescription Prepayment Certificate (PPC) from the NHS. A three month PPC will cost you £29.10 and a 12 month PPC £104. Call 0845 850 0030 to find out more.

School days

In this school photo, I am in the third row from the front, right in the middle of the picture. I was very happy at school and liked everything, apart from maths! I was lucky to live just down the street from school so had a very short walk. All the teachers lived around the village, and some went to the same church as me, so I knew them all very well.

Hilda Preene, via email

Mini Puzzle

Can you unscramble this conundrum to form a nine-letter word?

| F | I | E | R | Y | B | O | N | D |

(answer Boyfriend)

Recipe of the week

Minute-Steak Sarnie with Watercress and Horseradish Cream

Serves: 1
Preparation time: 10 minutes
Cooking time: 10 minutes

2 tbsp horseradish sauce
Juice of 1/2 a lemon
25g (1oz) light cream cheese
1 tsp wholegrain mustard
1 tbsp vegetable oil
125g (41/2oz) sirloin minute steak, fat-trimmed
2 slices sourdough bread
25g (1oz) watercress, washed and dried

1 Preheat the grill to high. Add the horseradish, lemon, cheese and mustard to a small bowl and mix well. Season to taste.
2 Add the oil to a frying pan, and heat to smoke. Season the steak on both sides, and cook each side to your personal preference. Leave to rest for the same time as you cooked it.
3 Meanwhile, place the bread under the grill to toast one side. Then smear the sauce over the non-toasted sides and add the watercress leaves. Lay the steak on top, season to taste and serve immediately.

© Philadelphia, www.philadelphia.co.uk

Enjoy the great outdoors

Visit the Lake District, an area that inspired some of our best-loved authors

With its clear lakes, ancient woodlands and wild crags it's no wonder that the Lake District inspired so many of Britain's favourite writers, including William Wordsworth, John Ruskin, Arthur Ransome and Beatrix Potter.

It was Wordsworth's 'Guide through the District of the Lakes' (published in 1820), that helped them become the popular tourist destination they are today. The poet was born very close by, going to school in Hawkshead, and moving to Grasmere later in life. His home, Dove Cottage, is open to the public – as well as a Wordsworth museum and art gallery. **For opening times visit www.wordsworth.org.uk.**

Beatrix Potter also held a deep affection for the National Park, after spending many summer holidays there. She went on to buy Hill Top farm, which helped her create some of her best-loved characters, including Jemima Puddle-Duck. She continued to buy other farms and local land, contributing to the conservation of the Lake District's countryside. Beatrix finally left Hill Top farm and its contents to the National Trust, and they've been duly preserved for visitors. **For more information, call the National Trust on 0844 800 1895, or visit www.nationaltrust.org.uk.**

If you'd prefer to be on and around the lakes themselves, then try a cruise or tackle one of the many guided walks or hikes. Whether you're walking, fishing, cycling or boating, you'll get the chance to see all kinds of wildlife – in and out of the water.

Perhaps, the most popular lake to visit is Windermere: at 10.5 miles long and one mile wide, it's the largest natural lake in England. If you're not sure which lake is for you, head straight to Brockhole – the Lake District Visitor Centre at Windermere. **Find out more by visiting www.brockhole.co.uk.**

Fact: Wordsworth described the Lake District as 'a sort of national property, in which every man has a right and interest who has an eye to perceive and a heart to enjoy.'

Quiz of the month

Sassy, sexy and single-minded – how well do you know your literary heroines? If you get stuck, the answers are below

PIC: REX FEATURES

1 Which Dickens character refused to take off her wedding dress?

2 Name the Austen heroine who can't help but make embarrassing mistakes.

3 Laurie's hot tempered best friend, avid reader, passionate writer and sister to Meg, Beth and Amy.

4 Self-confessed singleton, perpetual dieter and keen diarist – name the star of Helen Fielding's novels.

5 Who said: "I can't think about that right now. If I do, I'll go crazy. I'll think about that tomorrow."

6 Audrey Hepburn played which heroine of a Truman Capote novel?

7 Who heads up The No 1 Ladies Detective Agency?

8 Bird watching and gardening are the hobbies of which cultured female detective?

9 Which orphan heroine has an optimistic philosophy of life called 'The Glad Game'?

10 Who reattaches Peter Pan's shadow?

11 Who said "Reader, I married him"?

12 What was the name of the 18-year-old amateur sleuth created by Edward Stratemeyer?

13 Name the unconventional school-mistress who takes a select group of Scottish school girls under her wing?

14 Which Catherine Cookson heroine is branded as a witch?

15 Which doomed Hardy heroine's life is destroyed by her love for Angel Clare?

16 Name the red haired, freckled heroine who eventually married Gilbert Blythe?

17 Which of Enid Blyton's Famous Five thought domestic duties were dull and just wanted to be 'one of the lads'?

18 Name the real life heroine who was born in the Big Woods?

19 Harry Potter wouldn't have made it through seven novels without his best female friend – what is her name?

20 Who opens a chocolate shop and tempts the pious inhabitants of a French village in a novel by Joanne Harris?

Answers: 1 Miss Haversham, 2 Emma Woodhouse, 3 Josephine 'Jo' March, 4 Bridget Jones, 5 Scarlett O'Hara, 6 Holly Golightly, 7 Mma Precious Ramotswe, 8 Miss Marple, 9 Pollyanna, 10 Wendy Darling, 11 Jane Eyre, 12 Nancy Drew, 13 Miss Jean Brodie, 14 Tilly Trotter, 15 Tess of the d'Urbervilles, 16 Anne of Green Gables, 17 George, 18 Laura Ingalls Wilder, 19 Hermione Granger, 20 Vianne Rocher

A room of her own

BY: JENNY ROMAN

Toby is amazed to learn his Granny's history

The latch clicked behind her. Ruth leaned back against the door and gazed around the room with satisfaction. Yes, it was small, but perfectly adequate for her needs. And it had a few familiar touches; her old dressing table, the rocking chair, the quilted bedspread she'd made when she was expecting Claire. It looked like home already.

It had been kind of Claire to suggest this move. Now there would be three generations under one roof – that didn't happen so often these days.

She heard charging footsteps followed by the thumping of a small fist on the door. "Granny, are you in there?"

For a second, Ruth paused, unwilling to give up her moment of solitude, then pulled open the door.

Toby tumbled into the room. "Mum said you were in here but you were so quiet I didn't believe her!"

Ruth smiled. Toby himself was hardly ever quiet.

"You haven't unpacked yet!" he said, gazing at her suitcases. "Shall I help you?"

Before she had a chance to answer, he started tugging at the zip of the nearest case.

"How about a hug first?" Ruth asked.

Toby clapped his hand over his mouth in a gesture so comical that Ruth found it hard not to laugh. He flew over to her in an instant and gave her a big hug. "Welcome to our house, Granny," he said solemnly.

"Thank you, Toby." Ruth rubbed her hand down his small, warm back.

"Now shall we unpack?" he said.

They started with her clothes. Dresses and skirts in the wardrobe, jumpers folded in a drawer. As they worked, Toby said: "I've told my friends about you coming to live with us. They think it's great."

"Do they?" asked Ruth, surprised.

"Uh-huh. Their grannies live miles away so they don't see them very often, but I'll be able to see you every day."

"You might get bored with that."

Toby considered this possibility for a moment. "I

'When I left home it was to get married'

don't think so. It will be fun."

"My granny lived with us when I was a little girl and it wasn't fun at all." Ruth frowned at the memory of the terrace house with three generations inhabiting four cramped rooms. "Our house was very small so my Nana had to sleep behind a curtain in the sitting room. We always had to go to bed early because Nana needed to get to sleep."

"Did you have to go to bed early every night?" Toby gazed up at her in wonder.

Ruth nodded.

"Even your mum and dad?" Toby looked incredulous.

"Even my mum and dad."

"Why couldn't your gran have slept in your room?"

"Because I shared a big bed with my two sisters."

Toby's eyes widened. "All of you together? Wasn't that annoying?"

"Yes, it was."

When Ruth had been growing up, she had craved privacy. She had prayed for a time when she could be alone and cherished the rare nights when her sisters stayed with friends.

"Did they snore?" Toby wanted to know.

"No. But Joyce used to have vivid dreams and hit out, making me wake in the middle of the night."

"Did you hit her back?"

"Well, no – it wasn't really her fault." Ruth lowered her voice conspiratorially and admitted: "But sometimes I did!"

"I bet you were pleased when you left home and had your own room, Granny."

"Well, it didn't happen like that. You see, when I left home it was to get married to Grandpa so of course I shared a room with him."

Even now, the thought of Donald made her heart contract. He had sprung into her life, full of vitality and mirth. She had never wanted privacy from him but wanted him by her side always.

Toby frowned. "But Grandpa must have been out at work some of the time."

"Yes, he was, but very soon I had your mum and babies need looking after so I was never alone then."

Claire's arrival had turned them into a little

PIC: KATE DAVIES

'Sometimes sharing is better than being alone'

family. Ruth's time was entirely taken up by her husband and daughter.

Toby appeared to be working something out. He squinted thoughtfully and said: "But after Grandpa died last year, you've had your own room since then."

"Yes, except it didn't feel like my room. It still felt like our room, even though Grandpa wasn't there any more."

Little things had haunted her and yet at the same time they were a comfort. His watch lying on the bedside table. An old diary filled with his distinctive handwriting.

Toby's eyes swept round the bedroom in wonder. "So this is your first proper room? The first one all to yourself?"

Ruth nodded.

Toby regarded her for a moment. Very carefully, he put the last jumper in the drawer, then turned to her. "If this is your first proper room, you probably don't want me in it."

Ruth smiled at her grandson. She said: "There will be lots of times when I can be here on my own. Right now, I think it's great that you're here to keep me company."

Toby looked sideways at her as if checking she wasn't just being tactful, then he too broke into a big grin. "You mean sometimes sharing is better than being alone?"

"Indeed it is, Toby."

Sister act

The joy of childhood when dad could rent an apple tree

The black-and-white photo is of me and my sister Jill (on the left) taken in the summer of 1964. That was the year when my father 'rented' an apple tree for a season. There was a bumper crop and we were able to keep the fruit. There were six children in our family (five girls and a boy) and we all went to shake the tree and bring the apples home where they were kept in a set of drawers in the shed. As a treat, we were allowed an apple a day until they were all gone. We sisters shared a bedroom which led to some rivalry and disputes over make-up and tights when we were teenagers. Jill eventually had the room to herself as the others left to get married. Although we are now all scattered we remain a close-knit family. Jill lives only a mile away from me and we see each other several times a week. The colour photo of us both was taken recently, eating apples from the apple tree that I have in my garden.

Helen Jayes, Halesowen, W Midlands

Still delighted to be having an apple a day

What's in a word

Sesquipedalian

(adj) tending to use long or cumbersome words. From 17th century Latin sesquipedalis meaning 'a foot and a half long'.

Pet of the month

NAME: Harry

AGE: 2 years

OWNER: Mary Gall, Mansfield, Nottinghamshire (Mary looks after Harry for her 4-year-old granddaughter Mia)

PET LIKES: Playing football, plenty of sleep, socialising and chocolate digestives for a tasty treat

PET HATES: Loud aeroplane noises as they fly over his hutch, getting his feet wet and, strangely for a rabbit, he doesn't like carrots!

October

Delicious autumn! My very soul is wedded to it,
and if I were a bird I would fly about the earth
seeking the successive autumns.
Novelist, George Eliot

October 2013

7 Monday

8 Tuesday

9 Wednesday

10 Thursday

11 Friday

12 Saturday

13 Sunday

If you do one thing

Have a glass of milk at breakfast. Women who drink skimmed milk in the morning eat, on average 50 calories less at lunch. Milk contains protein which helps you feel fuller for longer so you don't feel the need to snack or over-eat. By making just this one change you could lose five pounds this year.

School days

This photo was taken in 1953 at Buckden Church of England School. I was seven years old. It was taken outside the school, with a grey army blanket covering the wall, and we were given a book with blank pages to pose with! Some of the children in the school were from the Polish Resettlement Camp in Diddington, which was just up the road.

Valerie Milbank, Huntingdon, Cambridgeshire

Mini Puzzle

Can you unscramble this conundrum to form a nine-letter word?

| T | E | P | I | D | F | I | R | E |

(answer Petrified)

Recipe of the week

The Ultimate Black Cherry Rocky Road

Makes: 24
Preparation time: 30 minutes
Chilling time: 2 hours

200g (7oz) Greek yoghurt
500g (1lb 2oz) milk chocolate
250g (9oz) butter
175g (6oz) golden syrup
400g (14oz) rich tea biscuits
100g (3¹/₂oz) mini marshmallows
1 x 400g (14oz) tin of fresh cherries, drained
100g (3¹/₂oz) bag of mini eggs

1. Line a 25¹/₂x30cm (12x10 in) tin with clingfilm. Melt the chocolate, butter and syrup in a bowl over hot water, or in the microwave. Stir in the yoghurt and leave to cool slightly.
2. In the meantime, place the biscuits in a secure bag and roughly crush with a rolling pin.
3. Fold this into the chocolate mixture, with half of the marshmallows and cherries. Mix everything well then pour into the tin. Sprinkle with the remaining marshmallows and mini eggs, and place in the fridge for two hours to chill. Cut into pieces and serve. These are best eaten within two days.

Top tip: To make these a rather grown up snack, use cherries soaked in kirsch or add a good splash of brandy.

© Total Greek Yoghurt, www.totalgreekyoghurt.com

14 Monday

15 Tuesday

16 Wednesday

17 Thursday

18 Friday

19 Saturday

20 Sunday

If you do one thing

Make the most of the things you love. Put a favourite photo, picture, plant, vase of flowers or beloved object in your hallway where you'll see it every time you come home. It's a great way to lift your mood as soon as you enter your house and could help you to feel happier.

School days

This picture is of me at my Primary school in Pilton, Barnstaple, North Devon. I must have been 7 or 8, so it was in the 1950s. My memories of that time centre around free school milk – either gone off in summer because of being left out in the heat or, in winter, the tops risen an inch or two on a neck of frozen milk.

Alison Horton, Lincolnshire

Mini Puzzle

Can you unscramble this conundrum to form a nine-letter word?

M	Y	M	A	S	T	E	R	Y

(answer Asymmetry)

Recipe of the week

Speedy Macaroni Cheese

Serves: 4
Preparation time: 10 minutes
Cooking time: 25 minutes

250g (9oz) dried macaroni
150g (5oz) French beans, trimmed
120g (4^1/$_2$oz) light cream cheese
150ml (5fl oz) semi–skimmed milk
75g (2^1/$_2$oz) Emmental or Gruyère cheese, grated
1 tsp wholegrain mustard
4 rashers lean smoked back bacon, grilled and roughly chopped
12 roasted cherry tomatoes, to serve

1 Cook the macaroni according to the pack instructions, and cut the French beans into thirds. Add to the pasta water for the last three to four minutes of cooking time. Drain, return to the pan, cover and keep warm.
2 Put the cream cheese in a small saucepan with the milk and half the cheese. Heat until the cheeses have just melted. Stir in the mustard and bacon pieces and season to taste.
3 Preheat the grill to high and place the pasta in an ovenproof dish. Pour the cheese sauce over the pasta and beans, and toss lightly. Sprinkle with the remaining cheese and grill for five minutes, or until golden brown. Serve with the roasted cherry tomatoes and some crusty bread.
© Philadelphia, www.philadelphia.co.uk

21 Monday

22 Tuesday

23 Wednesday

24 Thursday

25 Friday

26 Saturday

British Summer Time ends (clocks go back)

27 Sunday

If you do one thing

Do a clothes swap. Get together with your good friends and bring along your unwanted clothes. Not the items that are falling to bits but the things that don't flatter you or no longer fit. Have a trying on session and take home the items you like – for free.

School days

I would have been about 14 in this picture, and the hairstyle is typical of the 1960s, with one side shorter than the other! I hated PE at school, and much preferred cookery lessons. I was also the head of our lunch table. There were eight of us to a table, and I sat at the top and had to make sure the dinner monitors cleared everything away at the end of lunchtime.

Anne Barker, Wakefield, West Yorkshire

Mini Puzzle

Can you unscramble this conundrum to form a nine-letter word?

| S | H | E | R | O | O | R | F | E |

(answer Foreshore)

Recipe of the week

Traditional Pasties

Makes: 8
Preparation time: 15 minutes, plus cooling time
Cooking time: 1 hour

400g (14oz) rump beef steak, chopped
2 tbsp olive oil
1 medium onion, chopped
1 tbsp fresh thyme, chopped
1 tbsp Worcestershire sauce
1 tsp ground coriander
1 tbsp balsamic vinegar
400ml (14fl oz) beef stock
2 large red potatoes, peeled
50g (2oz) frozen peas
500g (1lb 2oz) shortcrust pastry
1 egg, beaten, for brushing

1 Preheat the oven to 200°C/400°F/Gas Mark 6. Season the beef and in a large frying pan with a fitted lid, heat half the oil. Sear the beef on all sides and remove from the pan.
2 Add the onion, thyme and oil, and sauté for five minutes. Now add the beef, coriander, Worcestershire sauce, balsamic vinegar and stock. Simmer for 15 minutes with the lid on, before removing the lid for another 15 minutes, or until reduced.
3 Leave to cool. Cut the potatoes into 2cm cubes and blanch for one minute. Drain before gently mixing with the beef and peas.
4 Divide the pastry into eight and roll out into 5in circles. Divide the filling into the centre of each circle, and brush edges with egg. Bring the pastry together and using your fingers, crimp the edges and seal completely. Brush all over with egg and place on a baking tray. Bake for 30 minutes – or until golden – and serve immediately.
© Bord Bia, www.bordbia.ie

28 Monday

29 Tuesday

30 Wednesday

Hallowe'en

31 Thursday

All Saint's Day

1 Friday

2 Saturday

3 Sunday

If you do one thing

Have a lie in. Make the most of the extra hour in bed when the clocks go back, by staying right there. Catching up on sleep could be great for your waistline. Missing out on sleep upsets the balance of your appetite-regulating hormones making your more likely to over-eat. Stay in bed and you might find you eat less.

School days

This photo was taken when I was six years old at Hackenthorpe Village Infants' School. I am third from the right, in the middle row. My best friends were Debbie Hadwick and Rachael Holyhead, and I still meet up with them for lunch quite often. I remember playtimes well, as there was only one swing, and at lunchtimes you had to queue to be pushed just five times each by the dinner ladies!

Sandy Warne, via email

Mini Puzzle

Can you unscramble this conundrum to form a nine-letter word?

| S | O | B | E | C | A | U | S | E |

(answer Sebaceous)

Recipe of the week

Easy-Peasy Fish Pie

Serves: 4
Preparation time: 10 minutes
Cooking time: 45 minutes

600g (1lb 5oz) potatoes, peeled and cubed
2 tbsp olive oil
1 onion, finely chopped
1 tsp dried mixed herbs
600g (1lb 5oz) fish pie mix, any bones removed
120g (4^1/$_2$oz) cooked frozen prawns, defrosted and drained
200g (7oz) garlic and herb cream cheese
75ml (2^1/$_2$fl oz) semi-skimmed milk
25g (1oz) mature cheddar cheese, finely grated

1 Boil the potatoes in a large saucepan for 15 minutes (or until soft) and drain.
2 Meanwhile, heat the oil in a large, non-stick frying pan. Add the onion and herbs and cook gently for five minutes, or until the onion is soft but not browned.
3 Add the fish (but not the prawns) to the frying pan, and heat until the fish is just cooked through. Add the cream cheese and prawns, and stir until the cheese has melted but not reached boiling point. Gradually add milk until you have a creamy sauce – you may not need all the milk though. Season to taste.
4 Preheat the grill to high and spoon the fish mixture into a pre-warmed, oven-proof dish. Mash the potatoes and use to top the fish mixture. Sprinkle with cheese and grill for 10 minutes; or until the cheese has melted and browned. Serve with peas or a green salad.

© Philadelphia, www.philadelphia.co.uk

Frightfully good fun

Head to Whitby, Bram Stoker's inspiration for the creepy classic, Dracula

Visit the spot that inspired the famous gothic novel, and where author Bram Stoker supposedly put pen to paper in 1890 – his memorial seat is situated on the West Cliff. Bram is thought to have stayed at Whitby's Royal Hotel, which overlooks the harbour and the ruins of Whitby Abbey to the east.

Sink your teeth in even further with The Dracula Experience, a tour that explores the story's many connections with the town; then discover the imposing gothic structure of Whitby Abbey and visit St Mary's Church with its 199 famous steps.

Late October is the best time for horror fans to visit, as the annual Bram Stoker International Film Festival runs from the 25th – 28th October 2012. **To find out more, visit www. bramstokerfilmfestival.com.** For those not taken by terror,

the Captain Cook Memorial Museum and the Whitby Museum are also worth a visit. Captain James Cook was born in nearby Marton, and completed an apprenticeship in Whitby before embarking upon his travels. **Visit www.cookmuseumwhitby. co.uk for further information.**

After all that, there's varied shopping, a great selection of restaurants, and quaint, cobbled streets to explore.

Visitors to nearby Goathland train station will also be pleasantly surprised if they are Heartbeat or Harry Potter fans – they might just recognise it as their beloved Adensfield or Hogsmead station.

And finally, a trip to the seaside wouldn't be complete without a paddle in the sea… Whitby has lovely beaches, where you'll find deckchairs and a traditional seaside atmosphere.

Fact: Author Lewis Carroll frequently stayed in Whitby, and nearby village Sandsend is thought to have inspired his poem 'The Walrus and the Carpenter'.

With thanks to VisitEngland, the national tourist board for England, visit www.visitengland.com.

Quiz of the month

Bold, dashing and debonair – how well do you know your heroes? If you get stuck, the answers are below

PIC REX FEATURES

1 Mitchell Y McDeere is the hero of which 1991 best-selling thriller?

2 How is Sir Percy Blakeney known to readers of Baroness Orczy's historical novel?

3 What is the nickname of the intrepid pilot created by the writer W E Johns?

4 Which actor played Richard Hannay in Hitchcock's film version of The 39 Steps?

5 Christian is the long-suffering hero of which book by John Bunyan?

6 Who created the fictional Royal Navy officer Horatio Hornblower?

7 A martini is the favourite cocktail of which well-known secret agent?

8 Do you know the surname of Sir Walter Scott's Highland hero Rob Roy?

9 Who lived in Puddleby-on-the-Marsh and could talk to animals?

10 In To Kill a Mockingbird who is the lawyer who defends the accused black man, Tom Robinson?

11 Aramis and Porthos are two of Alexander Dumas' musketeers; can you name the third?

12 In The Lord of the Rings, what sort of creature is its hero, Frodo Baggins?

13 Kim is the hero of a novel by which British writer who was born in Bombay in 1865?

14 In the schoolboy story Goodbye, Mr Chips what is the name of the best-loved teacher at Brookfield?

15 Which hero was based on the real-life castaway Alexander Selkirk?

16 Rupert Campbell-Black appears in the Rutshire Chronicles by which best-selling writer?

17 What was the name of the writer and GP who created the character of Dr Finlay?

18 Which of Mark Twain's youthful heroes is mentioned in the song Moon River?

19 Who heroically saves Bertie Wooster from the wrath of his aunts and other disasters?

20 Daniel Deronda is the central character in the last book published by which Victorian novelist?

Answers 1. The Firm 2. The Scarlet Pimpernel 3. Biggles 4. Robert Donat 5. The Pilgrim's Progress 6. C S Forester 7. James Bond 8. MacGregor 9. Dr Dolittle 10. Atticus Finch 11. Athos 12. A hobbit 13. Rudyard Kipling 14. Mr Chipping 15. Robinson Crusoe 16. Jilly Cooper 17. A J Cronin 18. Huckleberry Finn 19. Jeeves 20. George Eliot

Ripe for change

BY: CHRISTINE TENNENT

An apple sets off an unforeseen chain of events

Beth's knuckles whitened on the steering wheel as she drove slowly down the road. 'Why is he being so stubborn about moving?' she asked herself.

A tear trickled down her face. She ought to go back and talk to her father again but there wasn't time; she needed to get home and relieve her husband of the care of their six-month-old twins.

She scrambled in her pocket for a tissue and her fingers encountered instead a smooth, round object. Her dad must have slipped the apple in there when she'd kissed him goodbye. She took a bite, remembering how, when they ripened in October, he always used to slip one in the pocket of her school blazer for lunch.

As she inhaled the aroma of the apple, she could almost feel the wind in her pigtails as her father patiently pushed her backwards and forwards on the swing that hung from the Cox's apple tree. She took another bite – and felt a wriggling sensation on her tongue.

"Oh, no!" Beth shuddered as she caught sight of two pinkish grubs, their tiny black heads bobbing up and down like synchronised swimmers. She threw the apple out of the car window as hard as she could.

"Ouch! Who did that?" yelped the sandy-haired boy cycling along the pavement. The flying apple had smacked him in the eye, dislodging his glasses which fell under the wheel of his bike. His bike toppled over, depositing him in a tangled heap of scrawny freckled arms and legs. The newspapers he'd been delivering fell out on to the pavement.

The lad dabbed at his grazed knee with a tissue as blood trickled down his leg. He placed his bent glasses carefully in his pocket, thinking, 'Mum's going to kill me if they can't be repaired'.

He started stuffing the newspapers back into

'Mum's going to kill me if they can't be repaired'

the bag, trying to smooth them out as best he could. It was his first day as a paper boy. "Just my luck if someone complains," he muttered, blinking back the tears.

"Don't you worry, young man. I saw what happened. I'll tell Mr Garvie at the newsagent's if you get into any trouble." The speaker was a grey-haired lady who'd come out of a nearby house. Her bright blue eyes peered kindly at him as she helped him pick up the remaining papers.

Spotting the offending apple, the boy gave it an almighty kick before proceeding on his way. It fell further along the street where a tired-looking woman in a smart suit was hurrying along, a small dog bouncing along beside her, yapping excitedly. The dog grabbed the apple and tossed it up in the air. As it dropped back on to the pavement the woman's stiletto heel stuck into it and she skidded. Her shoe came off and a ladder appeared in her sheer tights.

She groaned: "Oh, no! Now I'm going to have to change and that will make me really late for work, you daft dog."

The woman was at the end of her tether. No matter how many hours she put in at the office her boss kept dumping more work on her. Skidding on the apple felt like the last straw. 'That is it!' she thought, 'time to look for another job'. One in which her skills were appreciated and she wasn't judged solely on how late she stayed at her desk.

Having pulled the apple off her shoe and tossed it over the crumbling garden wall of an old Victorian house, she returned home to enjoy a leisurely cup of coffee before giving in her notice.

On the other side of the wall an elderly man was inspecting the last of the roses. They weren't a patch on what they used to be when his wife was alive. Even her favourite, the primrose yellow Peace, had developed powdery grey mildew on its leaves. He gave the empty swing hanging from the apple tree a disconsolate push and at that moment an apple came flying over the wall and caught him

PIC: KATE DAVIES

'I know you're missing the old place, Dad'

on the side of his head. Knocked off balance, the old man smacked his temple on the flying swing…

Kneeling on the floor, Beth looked up worriedly at her dad. She said: "That's your books unpacked. They've fitted on there perfectly."

Jack was standing by the window of his new bungalow, his back to his daughter. He was staring out at the small back garden.

Beth went on: "I know you're missing the old place, Dad, but please don't be sad. We're only ten minutes' walk away and it's such a friendly village

– you're going to love it here."

Her father turned towards her, his gentle brown eyes twinkling in a way Beth hadn't seen for ages. "Don't you worry about me, love. I've already found a partner to play dominoes with at the pub. I was just thinking what a relief it is not to have a big garden to tend any more."

"I've been wondering, Dad, what finally persuaded you to sell up?"

"It was when I had that silly little accident with the apple. If I had been concussed, I couldn't help wondering how long it would have been before anyone found me…"

Giving him a hug, Beth asked: "For a house-warming present, how would you like a dwarf apple tree for the patio?"

Sister act

What's in a word

Opsimath

(noun) a person who begins to learn or study later in life. From the late 19th century Greek.

I am the middle sister, sandwiched between Helen (four years older) and Catherine (18 months younger). While Catherine and I were still at school, Helen was setting off each morning to her office job. To us, she lived in a different sphere – grown-up and sophisticated in a tailored suit, nylons and high heels. In 1963, when I left school to go to teachers' training college, Helen surprised me with a present of a little red transistor radio. At home we had all happily shared her Bush radio but it was a treat to have one of my own and it became a treasured possession. I loved listening to Radio Luxembourg in my room in the hostel, with Jimmy Savile or Simon Dee playing all the latest hits. I nursed a broken heart to the strains of Roy Orbison singing It's Over. At the Christmas fancy-dress party, dressed as Cleopatra, I danced to The Beatles' I Feel Fine. I celebrated passing my finals to the sound of The Lovin' Spoonful's album, Daydream. On a sad note, my radio brought me the news of President Kennedy's assassination. I've never forgotten that little radio and the pleasure it gave me, all thanks to a thoughtful gift from my big sister. **Elizabeth Leslie, Blairgowrie, Perthshire**

Pet of the month

NAME: Dinky

AGE: 9 years

OWNER: Jean Cooper, Dunfermline, Scotland

PET LIKES: Watching the animals and birds on TV nature programmes

PET HATES: Drinking water – she often upturns her dish and watches the water spill to the floor!

DINKY'S STORY: Jean bought Dinky as a kitten while on holiday in Edinburgh

November

A wind has blown the rain away and blown the sky away and all the leaves away,
and the trees stand. I think, I too, have known autumn too long.
Poet, E E Cummings

4   Monday

5   Tuesday   Guy Fawkes' Night

6   Wednesday

7   Thursday

8   Friday

9   Saturday

10   Sunday   Remembrance Sunday

If you do one thing

Use a shower puff with your shower gel. Invest in one of those fluffy balls and you'll not only need less shower gel to get clean you'll be putting less detergent on your skin. The ingredients that make bath products foam can actually be quite drying, which in turn could speed up the ageing process.

School days

This photo was taken in about 1969 when I was seven years old and my brother, Mark, was nine (I am on the right). The school was Western Road Infant and Junior, which changed its name while I was there to Westways. Both Mum and Dad also went to the same school. I was captain of the school football team and helped choose the kit we played in (Aston Villa rather than Newcastle!).

Paul Chambers, via email

Mini Puzzle

Can you unscramble this conundrum to form a nine-letter word?

| W | I | S | E | R | F | O | R | K |

(answer Fireworks)

Recipe of the week

Chicken and Mushroom Casserole

Serves: 4
Preparation time: 10 minutes
Cooking time: 35 minutes

1 tbsp olive oil
4 x large chicken breasts,
or 8 x small chicken thighs, skin on
100g (3^1/$_2$oz) mushrooms, halved if large
100g (3^1/$_2$oz) streaky bacon, finely sliced
100g (3^1/$_2$oz) shallots, peeled and halved
1 onion, roughly chopped
1 can cream of chicken condensed soup
100ml (3^1/$_2$fl oz) crème fraîche, or whipping cream
4tbsp fresh tarragon, chopped
100g (3^1/$_2$oz) frozen peas

1 Heat a wide, heatproof casserole pan with the olive oil until hot. Brown the chicken for a few minutes, or until all sides are seared. Add the mushrooms, bacon and shallots and cook for a further five minutes, or until the vegetables have softened slightly.
2 Add the can of soup and the same amount of warm water. Bring to a gentle simmer, cover, and cook for 15 minutes. Then add the crème fraîche, tarragon and peas. Simmer for a further ten minutes, or until the chicken is cooked through and tender. Season to taste, and serve alongside crusty bread, or boiled new potatoes.

© Very Lazy, www.verylazy.co.uk

November 2013

11 Monday

12 Tuesday

13 Wednesday

14 Thursday

15 Friday

16 Saturday

17 Sunday

If you do one thing

Have a glass of pinot noir. Pour yourself a small glass of red wine and you could boost your life-expectancy by half a decade! The antioxidant compounds in red wine are thought to help increase good cholesterol and also minimise blood clots. But you need to go easy – too much alcohol could have the opposite effect.

School days

This is a photo of my brother, Wayne, and myself. I remember we had a long walk to school with Mum pushing our little sister in the pushchair. One very cold winter the path was so icy we just kept slipping over. Eventually we decided to give up walking and just slide along on our bums for a while!

Tracy Munden, Donnington, Lincolnshire

Mini Puzzle

Can you unscramble this conundrum to form a nine-letter word?

| E | N | T | R | Y | A | C | N | E |

(answer Centenary)

Recipe of the week

Traditional Individual Cottage Pies

Serves: 6
Preparation time: 30 minutes
Cooking time: 45 minutes

500g (1lb 2oz) lean beef mince
3 tbsp olive oil
1 large onion, diced
2 carrots, finely diced
2 stalks celery, finely chopped
1 tbsp chopped fresh thyme
1 tbsp flour
2 tbsp tomato purée
360ml (12fl oz) red wine
2 tbsp Worcestershire sauce
For the topping:
900g (2lb) red-skinned potatoes
50g (2oz) butter
3 tbsp milk
6 spring onions, finely chopped
100g (3½oz) mature cheddar cheese

1 Preheat oven to 200°C/400°F/Gas Mark 6. Heat the oil in a large saucepan before adding the onions, carrots, celery, thyme and seasoning. Sauté for ten minutes, or until softened. Add the beef and cook for five more minutes, or until browned.
2 Pour off any excess fat before adding the flour, tomato purée, Worcestershire sauce and red wine. Simmer for 15 minutes, or until the sauce is reduced. Divide between six individual pie tins (or heatproof bowls) and leave to cool slightly.
3 In the meantime, peel the potatoes and cut into 3cm (1in) cubes. Boil in salted water for ten minutes, or until soft. Drain before adding the butter and milk. Mash until smooth, before adding the onions and half the cheese. Divide between the pies and sprinkle the remaining cheese on top. Bake for 30 minutes, or until golden brown.
© Bord Bia, www.bordbia.ie

November 2013

18 Monday

19 Tuesday

20 Wednesday

21 Thursday

22 Friday

23 Saturday

24 Sunday

If you do one thing

Switch to a richer moisturiser. Cold air, central heating and rapid changes of temperature can all impact on your skin. You may find you need a heavier moisturiser than usual to keep your skin looking fresh and feeling supple. If you're worried about looking too shiny during the day you could use a lighter cream during the day and a thicker, more nourishing one at night.

School days

This is my granddaughter, Eloise, aged four. She loves school and is never happier than when she is helping someone. I pick her up from school three days a week while mummy is at work, so we go home to Granddad where there is always a little gift of a sweetie or two hidden under her 'magic pillow'. Ellie also loves coming with me to Zumba classes, so much so that we are trying to get a class sorted out for the children at her school.

Andrea Sleight, Peterborough, Cambridgeshire

Mini Puzzle

Can you unscramble this conundrum to form a nine-letter word?

O	D	D	E	S	T	P	I	E

(answer Deposited)

Recipe of the week

Very Berry Tiramisu

Serves: 6
Preparation time: 25 minutes,
plus at least 2 hours chilling

250g (9oz) mascarpone cheese
4 tbsp icing sugar
150ml (5fl oz) double cream
1 tsp vanilla extract
120ml (4$^{1}/_{2}$fl oz) medium white wine
400g (14oz) strawberries
150g (5oz) raspberries
18 sponge finger biscuits
25g (1oz) milk or dark chocolate, grated

1 Lightly beat the mascarpone cheese and icing sugar in a bowl with a whisk. Gradually whisk in the cream, until smooth. Then mix in the vanilla.
2 Reserve six whole strawberries and three raspberries for decoration. Roughly chop or mash the remaining strawberries and crumble the raspberries, then mix together.
3 Spoon a third of the mascarpone mixture in the base of a 1 litre (1$^{3}/_{4}$ pint) glass serving dish. Cover with half the crushed berries. Pour the wine into a shallow dish and dip half the sponge finger biscuits, one at a time, into the wine. Then arrange in a layer, topping the fruit. Repeat the layers, finally topping with the remaining mascarpone. Chill for two hours, or until needed.
4 Just before serving, add the reserved strawberries (halved), the remaining raspberries and sprinkle on the chocolate.

© Seasonal Berries, www.seasonalberries.co.uk

November 2013

25 Monday

26 Tuesday

27 Wednesday

28 Thursday

29 Friday

St Andrew's Day

30 Saturday

1 Sunday

If you do one thing

Cut the cost of Christmas by suggesting a Secret Santa to your friends or family. Put everyone's name in a hat and pick one each. You buy that person a gift under a specified price limit. You can give them anonymously and try to guess who bought what.

School days

This picture is of my first day at a new school in the mid-eighties – what a smart uniform! One of my main memories of school is that there was always something fun happening – usually involving dancing. Our teachers were always encouraging and I enjoyed my time, although I know it was very different from that of the generations before me.

Natalie Horton, via email

Mini Puzzle

Can you unscramble this conundrum to form a nine-letter word?

E	V	I	L	A	G	E	N	T

(answer Elevating)

Recipe of the week

Spiced Beef, Pumpkin and Carrot Soup

Serves: 4
Preparation time: 15 minutes
Cooking time: 50 minutes,
plus 10 minutes cooling time

225g (8oz) cooked roast beef, shredded
2 tbsp rapeseed or olive oil
1 medium onion, peeled and chopped
2 garlic cloves, peeled and chopped
1 tbsp Madras curry paste, or similar
225g (8oz) carrots, peeled and roughly chopped
450g (1lb) pumpkin or butternut squash,
peeled and cubed
2 celery sticks, chopped
1 litre (1³/₄pints) hot beef or vegetable stock
Splash sweet sherry, optional
4 tsp crème fraîche, to serve
2 tbsp fresh chives or flat-leaf parsley,
chopped, to garnish

1 Heat the oil in a large saucepan, then cook the onion and garlic for two to three minutes. Add the curry paste and cook for a further one or two minutes. Then add the vegetables and stock. Bring to the boil and simmer for 35–40 minutes. Leave to cool for 10 minutes.
2 Blend the soup in batches until you have a fine purée. Return to the pan and add the beef. Bring to the boil, then reduce to a simmer. Add the sherry (if using) and simmer for two to three minutes until piping hot.
3 Season and serve with a dollop of crème fraîche and a sprinkling of fresh herbs.

Top tip: Serve your soup in a small pumpkin! Slice off the top and set aside. Scoop out the seeds and fibres, and hollow out the flesh – leaving 2¹/₂cm (1in) around the inside. When ready, pour the hot soup into the prepared pumpkin and serve immediately.
© Simply Beef and Lamb, www.simplybeefandlamb.co.uk

Beautiful York

This medieval city of variety is a vibrant mix of the old and new

It's the quaint cobbled streets and grand architecture, combined with modern restaurants, shops and bars that keep York unique and fresh. The city is perfect for a long weekend, but has plenty to keep you occupied if you're staying longer.

The Shambles is one of the city's most popular attractions, as one of the best-preserved medieval streets in Europe. It's also thought to be one of the oldest shopping areas and is even mentioned in the Domesday Book. Previously voted Britain's Most Picturesque Street, the overhanging buildings house a range of shops and cafes. If it's retail therapy you're after, York has a lovely mix of well-known high street names alongside unique boutiques and quirky brands. You'll also find Past Images Studios among it all, which offers the chance to have your photograph taken dressed in costume from the medieval, Viking or Victorian era. A great way to remember your trip!

For more information, call 01904 676167, or visit www.past-images.co.uk.

The magnificent York Minster is a real must-see. It's one of the largest – and most impressive – gothic cathedrals in Europe. The building has recently undergone a huge restoration project with work carried out to improve facilities, and also restore a 15th century stained glass window. There are guided tours, and if you're feeling energetic, you can climb the 275 steps to the top of the central tower for an amazing view.

Or you could join one of the many walking tours giving an insight into the history of the city. However, York is supposedly one of the most haunted cities in Europe – so be warned if you choose a ghost walk!

Then (if you've still got the stomach for it) York has a vibrant restaurant scene with a great variety of different cuisines.

Fact: Dame Judi Dench was born in York, and attended The Mount School, an independent, Quaker boarding school.

Quiz of the month

Underhand, scheming and just plain evil – how well do you know your literary villains? If you get stuck the answers are below.

1 What was the name of Sherlock Holmes' nemesis?

2 When Lucy's older brother Edmund discovers the magical world of Narnia for himself he is bewitched by magical Turkish Delight proffered by whom?

3 In Wilkie Collins' The Woman in White who is the unlikely brains behind the plot to deprive Laura Fairlie of her wealth and her sanity?

4 One of Charles Dickens' most vicious creations – a career criminal, child abuser and eventual murderer without a good bone in his body - who is he?

5 He was Dickie Greenleaf's close friend – but Patricia Highsmith's very talented villain wanted to be like him a bit too much.

6 She drives Rebecca to torment and near suicide in Daphne du Maurier's novel

7 'The most powerful dark wizard who ever lived', so feared few dare to speak his name – what is it?

8 She kidnaps Dalmatian puppies for their fur in Dodie Smith's classic – can you name her?

9 A cold, heartless tyrant who demonises the patients of a mental Institution in Ken Kesey's One Flew Over the Cuckoo Nest

10 Captain of the Jolly Roger and arch-enemy of Peter Pan

11 He ceaselessly searched Middle Earth for the Ring, which is eventually brought to destruction by a humble hobbit

PIC: REX FEATURES

12 Dr Jekyll's evil side, a murderous man without a conscience

13 A middle-aged literature professor who becomes obsessed by 12-year-old Dolores 'Lolita' Haze

14 He plots to bring about the downfall of Othello and causes him to kill his beloved Desdemona in one of Shakespeare's Classics

15 A centuries old vampire who has plans for world domination that are eventually thwarted by Bram Stoker's hero Jonathan Harker

16 She wears gloves and pearls and is the most powerful witch in the whole wide world. Roald Dahl's villain is on a quest to rid the world of human children.

17 Huck's alcoholic and abusive father in Mark Twain's adventure story.

18 The villain of Robert Louis Stevenson's Treasure Island – a pirate who seems instantly likeable but turns out to be a mutinous murderer.

Answers: 1 Moriarty, 2 The White Witch (The Lion the Witch and the Wardrobe), 3 Count Fosco, 4 Bill Sykes (Oliver Twist), 5 Tom Ripley (The Talented Mr Ripley), 6 Mrs Danvers (Rebecca), 7 Lord Voldemort (Harry Potter), 8 Cruella de Vil (101 Dalmatians), 9 Nurse Ratched, 10 Captain James Hook (Peter Pan), 11 Sauron (The Lord of the Rings), 12 Mr Hyde (The Strange Case of Dr Jekyll and Mr Hyde), 13 Humbert Humbert, 14 Iago (Othello), 15 Count Dracula (Dracula), 16 The Grand High Witch (The Witches), 17 Pap Finn (The Adventures of Huckleberry Finn), 18 Long John Silver

Only the brave

BY: HELEN HUNT

Henry knows what war can do to a young man...

Henry was adrift in a twilight world of lost comrades. If he closed his eyes he could still hear the marching feet, still feel the cold in his bones and the numbness of fear.

But that was long ago and when he opened his eyes all he saw were the trappings of his life now: the institutional cream walls, the serviceable carpet and the tea trolley with its paper doilies.

"Here's your tea, Harry," said one of the young care assistants.

Henry couldn't be bothered to tell her he wasn't called Harry. What did it matter? It was only a name. He kept his eyes closed and went back through the years.

"Want a cigarette?" Walter said, holding out one from his precious ration. "Keep the mozzies away."

"Thanks," Henry took the proffered cigarette and light.

The tips of the two cigarettes made fire-flies in the dark as they sat on guard duty. Henry was grateful, not just for keeping the mosquitoes at bay, but for the reassuring warm feel of the smoke as it went down into his lungs. He wished it could go right down inside him and melt the icy fear that had lodged in his stomach since the moment he'd arrived in Egypt.

That had been the night before Walter was killed. The night before the pool of ice had crept up into his heart and froze that, too. Despite the pain, Henry struggled not to forget the past. Because if he forgot, who would be left to remember?

As he played his solitary games of patience, the old men around him puzzled over jigsaws or stared with glazed eyes at the communal television set. Henry supposed they all had their own memories of heroism or cowardice to recall or forget...

Graham hitched his rucksack higher on his shoulder and kept walking. His socks had holes in them and his shoes were pinching his feet. The voices

Henry struggled not to forget the past

in his head kept saying: 'Get out. Get away. Run for it'.

Over and over, he replayed the events of the last weeks – the rat-tat-tat of guns, the noise and smoke of war. It was two days since his return from Afghanistan and he still felt the dry tang of fear in his mouth. How could he face going back?

When he'd first arrived in the war zone, he couldn't wait to get stuck in. But he'd had no idea of what to expect. He'd seen it on TV, but that hadn't prepared him for the reality. Now the thought of returning when his leave was over terrified him.

He pushed negative thoughts from his mind and tried to concentrate on something hopeful. Every step took him nearer to the one person he knew who would have some idea of what he was going through. Before he made any decisions, he needed to speak to his grandfather.

The old man had been so proud when Graham had told him he was joining the army. "You're a chip off the old block," he'd laughed, clapping Graham on the back. It was like a secret they could share, a sort of brotherhood.

His grandfather was the bravest man he'd ever known but would Graham be able to face him now, knowing what he did about himself?

One of the care assistants approached. "Harry, you've got a visitor."

"It's not Harry, it's Henry," said a familiar voice.

"Graham! Is it really you, lad?"

Henry strained his eyes to see his grandson, taking in the heavy boots and huge overcoat that seemed to swamp him.

"Tea for my visitor, please," Henry said, speaking in a voice that sounded stronger than it had done for weeks.

Graham sat down and began fiddling with the playing cards, disturbing Henry's neat rows.

"Was it bad, son?" he asked.

Graham didn't answer. He took the cup of tea that the girl had placed in front of him and sipped it. Finally, he said: "You know what it's like, Granddad."

"Aye, I do that."

PIC: KATE DAVIES

'I'm a coward. I don't want to go back'

"I can't go back there," Graham said, his eyes suddenly full of tears. Henry wished he could take him on his knee as he had done when he was a small boy.

"You can't not go back."

"I wish I was as brave as you, Granddad."

Henry rummaged in a drawer for one of his most treasured possessions. "My medal," he said. "And, yes, I'm right proud of it, but it won't bring back Walter, or George, or any of the others."

"After you lost your mates, what kept you going?"

Henry reached in the drawer again and handed Graham a photo. "Your grandmother, and your mother," he said simply.

"But I've let you all down," Graham said. "I'm a coward. I don't want to go back."

"Being afraid doesn't make you a coward. It just makes you not stupid. Back in my day, we didn't have a choice. We were all called up."

"You never thought of running away, though, did you? You carried on and won a medal."

"Yes, but you chose to go. You chose to put yourself in the firing line. That's real courage, however scared you feel inside." To his relief, he saw the younger man proudly straighten his shoulders.

Henry scooped up the cards and dealt them out for a game of rummy. As the two heads bent together, the medal shone on the table between them.

'I Heart You' Necklace

This necklace brings a classic crafting technique bang up to date. Make it for a grandchild, or for yourself!

You will need:

Scraps of colourful 8-ply (DK) wool, or you could buy whole balls, of complementing colours.

2 x 2cm (¾ in) triangular jewellery jump rings

A length of chain to suit, we used 50cm (20in) of nickel chain. (Make sure the links are large enough to thread your jump rings through).

4mm (Size 6) crochet hook

Scissors

Wool needle

Pliers

Note:

Crochet techniques needed:
Chain, slip stitch and double stitches.

1 Firstly, you need to make six heart motifs in different colours of wool.
   Make each one by:
   Making a slip knot, leaving a long tail of 30cm (12in). Put your slip knot on to the crochet hook and pull it firmly (but not too tightly).
   Chain 5 stitches and slip stitch into the very first stitch to form a ring. Now it's time to crochet into this ring.
   Chain 3.
   Now double crochet 10 times into the ring. You should have almost made a round, but not quite. The missing wedge at the top helps to form the heart shape.
   Fasten off to finish the heart and then snip your loose wool, leaving a 30cm (12in) tail. Pull the heart into shape, giving the bottom a tug to make it more pointy.
   Repeat this until you have six hearts in total, making sure you leave the long tails at each end. These will be used to stitch the hearts into formation.

2 Sew your hearts together by arranging your hearts as in the main picture. Taking your first heart in your hand, thread the uppermost wool tail of this heart through your wool needle. Carefully stitch to the next heart with 3-4 well-hidden stitches. Weave in any loose ends, then knot and snip off very close to the work. Repeat with the other hearts using their tails.

3 The final stage! To attach the jump rings to the chain and crocheted piece. Use the pliers to open up the jump rings and carefully hook them evenly on to each side of the crocheted piece. Thread the chain on to each jump ring and use the pliers to close them up again. You have a necklace!

Variations

Once you've mastered the technique, make a matching brooch, bracelets or earrings. Or you could even keep adding hearts and make the most romantic scarf you've ever seen for the cold months ahead!

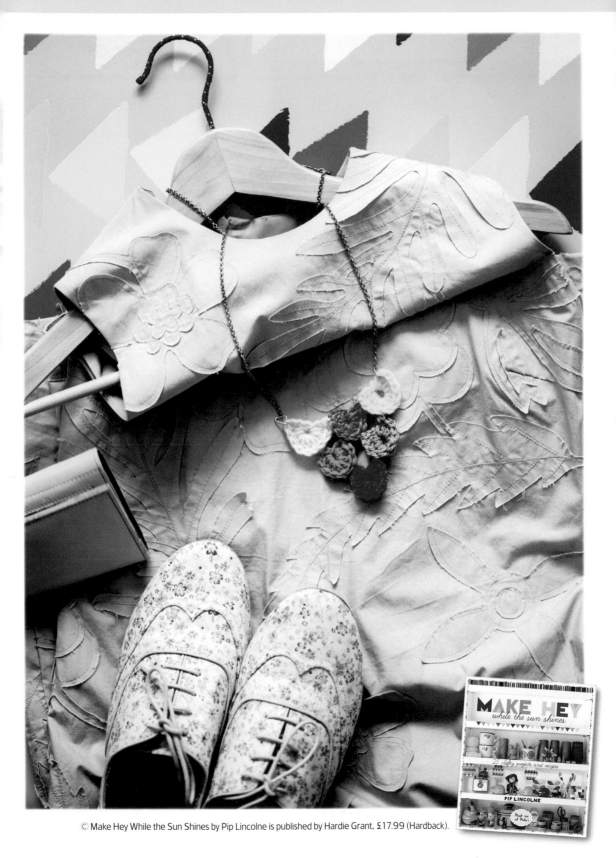

© Make Hey While the Sun Shines by Pip Lincolne is published by Hardie Grant, £17.99 (Hardback).

Sister act

Best of friends and great shoppers!

Pet of the month

NAME: Molly

AGE: 5 years

OWNER: Margaret Gray, Newcastle-upon-Tyne

PET LIKES: A regular half hour of madness with her toy mouse

PET HATES: Other cats that trespass into her garden

ENDEARING TRAIT: Not so endearing, but she does like to use the carpet rather than her many scratch posts to sharpen her claws!

After growing up with two brothers, it was lovely to know that the fourth child in our family was going to be a girl – a sister for me. Jean was born when I was aged six. One of my early memories of her is when a school nature walk took my class past our house and my mum held my new baby sister up to the window for us all to see. I enjoyed Jean when she was at the baby and toddler stages – but oh, how things changed as we grew older! For instance, when I was invited to play with a friend who had a beautiful doll's house, Jean whined to mum that she wanted to come with me. I still remember the smug look of satisfaction on her face as I reluctantly dragged her across the road. As the years went by, the age gap appeared to widen and we had less in common. Then we both met our future husbands and both of us gave birth to sons within five months of each other, so the age gap lessened slightly. A few more years went by and soon we had a daughter each, giving us even more in common. Now that we are in our 50s and 60s the age gap is hardly noticeable. We are the best of friends, enjoying weekends and holidays together and (best of all) shopping at every opportunity!

Sue Thorp, Bradford, W Yorkshire

December

But I am sure that I have always thought of Christmas time,
when it has come round... as a good time; a kind, forgiving, charitable,
pleasant time; the only time I know of, in the long calendar of the year,
when men and women seem by one consent to open their shut-up hearts freely.
Charles Dickens, A Christmas Carol

December 2013

2 Monday   Bank Holiday (Scotland)

3 Tuesday

4 Wednesday

5 Thursday

6 Friday

7 Saturday

8 Sunday

If you do one thing

Start writing your Christmas cards. You can take advantage of second-class post and save a few pennies and you'll have time to write a thoughtful note rather than a stressed-out, hasty scribble.

Recipe of the week

Cumberland Glazed Rolled Shoulder of Lamb with Apple and Pine Nut Stuffing

Serves: 6-8
Preparation time: 20 minutes
Cooking time: Medium: 25 minutes per 450g (1lb) + 25 minutes; Well done: 30 minutes per 450g (1lb) + 30 minutes

1.3kg (3lb) boned and rolled lamb shoulder joint
2 tbsp fresh rosemary leaves, chopped
1 tbsp olive oil
For the stuffing:
50g (2oz) unsalted butter, softened
1 cooking apple, cored and cubed
1 tbsp fresh rosemary leaves, chopped
50g (2oz) pine nuts, toasted
For the glaze:
100g (3^1/$_2$oz) redcurrant jelly
50ml (2fl oz) port, optional
Grated zest and juice of 1 orange

1 Preheat the oven to 180°C/350°F/Gas Mark 4. Unroll the joint (reserving any elasticated meat bands) and coat each side with the rosemary. Leave skin side down and season well.
2 For the stuffing, mix all the ingredients together and spread evenly over the lamb. Roll up and secure with the elasticated meat bands. Place on a metal rack in a large non-stick roasting tin, drizzle with the oil, and roast for the preferred cooking time.
3 Meanwhile, make the glaze by heating all the ingredients in a pan. Bring to the boil before simmering for 15 minutes, or until syrupy, and 10 minutes before the end of cooking, remove the joint from the oven and brush with the glaze, before returning to the oven.
4 Serve immediately with the remaining glaze, alongside roast potatoes and seasonal vegetables.
© Simply Beef and Lamb, www.simplybeefandlamb.co.uk

School days

Here is my school photo. I am on the second row from the front, fourth from the left. Our teacher, Miss Hughes, lived almost opposite us in the village. We used to play skipping and ball on the way to school and, if the rag-and-bone man was outside school at home time, we raced home to get old clothes to trade with him for goldfish or a baby chick.

Mary Rollerson, Tydd, Lincolnshire

Mini Puzzle

Can you unscramble this conundrum to form a nine-letter word?

S	T	E	A	M	I	E	S	T

(answer *Estimates*)

December 2013

9   Monday

10   Tuesday

11   Wednesday

12   Thursday

13   Friday

14   Saturday

15   Sunday

If you do one thing

Have an aromatherapy bath. Put a few drops of frankincense essential oil in your bath. This festive scent is thought to help relieve stress and anxiety, soothe headaches and even ease a persistent cough. If you don't like the smell you could try lavender or sandalwood instead.

School days

When I was five years old I had diphtheria. This my first school photo back at school after I recovered from my stay in hospital. I remember that I had to be pulled along on my three-wheel bicycle, as my legs were still too weak to walk. My brother also had to stay in the isolation hospital for some time, and had a teacher go there to take him work to do.

Pauline Brown, Walsall, West Midlands

Mini Puzzle

Can you unscramble this conundrum to form a nine-letter word?

| T | R | U | E | R | C | E | R | N |

(answer: Recurrent)

Recipe of the week

Cranberry Mince Pies

Makes: 20
Preparation time: 25 minutes
Cooking time: 20 minutes

For the mincemeat:
100g (3^1/$_2$oz) dried cranberries
1 x 400g (14oz) jar of good quality or homemade mincemeat
25g (1 oz) almonds, chopped
For the pastry:
500g (1lb 2oz) plain flour
2 tbsp icing sugar
250g (9oz) butter, diced
Icing sugar for dusting

1 In a small saucepan, cover the cranberries with water and bring to the boil. Simmer for ten minutes and leave to cool.
2 Sift the flour and icing sugar into a large bowl. Then add the butter, and using your fingertips, gently rub in to resemble breadcrumbs. Add six or seven tablespoons of cold water and mix into soft dough. Wrap in clingfilm and chill for ten minutes. Preheat the oven to 180°C/350°F/Gas Mark 4.
3 Drain the cranberries, and mix into the mincemeat and almonds. Roll the pastry to approximately 3mm (^{1}/$_8$ inch) thickness and using an 8cm (3^1/$_2$in) cutter, make 20 rounds. Line a deep bun tin with the rounds, and divide the mincemeat between them. Use the leftover pastry to make a lattice topping. Bake for 15-20 minutes, or until golden brown. Serve warm or cold, with a dollop of cream or brandy butter.
© Ocean Spray Cranberries, www.oceanspray.co.uk

December 2013

16 Monday

17 Tuesday

18 Wednesday

19 Thursday

20 Friday

Shortest Day (Winter Solstice)

21 Saturday

22 Sunday

If you do one thing

Stock up on painkillers and indigestion remedies. Headaches, indigestion and even colds are more common over Christmas, so make sure you have all you need on hand to tackle them if they hit.

School days

This is a picture of my first ever nativity play. I'm in the front row on the right, sitting next to my brother, who was one of the Three Wise Men. I was an angel and had to dance to Tchaikovsky's Dance of the Sugar Plum Fairy. I was a very clumsy child and possibly the most inelegant angel in history – so not a great piece of casting.
Sharon Palmer, Peterborough, Cambridgeshire

Mini Puzzle

Can you unscramble this conundrum to form a nine-letter word?

| P | R | E | S | S | N | S | I | C |

(answer Crispness)

Recipe of the week

Lamb, Feta and Mint-Stuffed Onions

Serves: 4
Preparation time: 20 minutes
Cooking time: 1 hour 15 minutes

225g (8oz) lean lamb mince
4 large onions, weighing about 275g (10oz) each, peeled and left whole
$1/2$ tsp ground cinnamon
50g (2oz) raisins or sultanas
Grated zest of 1 lemon
2 tbsp freshly chopped mint
2 tbsp freshly chopped flat-leaf parsley
50g (2oz) Feta cheese, crumbled
50g (2oz) couscous or small soup pasta shapes, cooked
120ml (4fl oz) hot vegetable stock

1 Slice off the top third from the onions and reserve. Then, using a small spoon or melon baller, remove the centre (until you have approximately two layers left) and finely chop.
2 Carefully trim the root end of each onion and transfer them to a medium, ovenproof dish. Preheat the oven to 180°C/350°F/Gas Mark 4.
3 Heat a large, non-stick pan and dry-fry the mince with half the chopped onion for five to 10 minutes, or until golden. Add the cinnamon and season. Continue to cook for two to three minutes before removing from the heat. Stir in the raisins or sultanas, lemon zest, herbs, feta and couscous.
4 Spoon this into the onion, packing tightly, and put the reserved onion top alongside. Pour the stock around the onions, cover with foil and bake for 40 minutes. Remove foil and cook for a further 20 minutes, or until the onions are tender.
5 Serve immediately with a rocket salad.
© Simply Beef and Lamb, www.simplybeefandlamb.co.uk

23 Monday

24 Tuesday   Christmas Eve

25 Wednesday   Christmas Day

26 Thursday   Boxing Day

27 Friday

28 Saturday

29 Sunday

If you do one thing

Note down the number for NHS Direct – **0845 4647 or log onto the website www.nhsdirect.nhs. uk.** Many doctor's surgeries are closed over the Christmas period but you shouldn't delay getting health advice. There's always a team of doctors and nurses on hand to answer calls and they'll tell you whether you need to see an emergency doctor. Don't forget that your local pharmacist might well be able to help with those niggly health problems too.

School days

Here is my daughter, Laura, dressed as an angel for her school nativity play in the early '90s. She was very pleased to be chosen as she thought only blonde little girls could be angels. Laura is now 26, and a very mature young lady – although I'm sure her Dad would say she hasn't always been an angel since this photo was taken!
Patricia Bradder, Barnsley, South Yorkshire

Mini Puzzle

Can you unscramble this conundrum to form a nine-letter word?

| T | R | I | M | S | C | A | S | H |

(answer Christmas)

Recipe of the week

Baked Ice Cream Sticky Toffee Cupcakes

Makes: 10
Preparation time: 30 minutes
Cooking time: 21 minutes, plus at least 2 hours cooling/chilling time

150g (5oz) pitted dates, finely chopped
2 tsp bicarbonate of soda
150g (5oz) plain flour
1 tsp baking powder
50g (2oz) light brown sugar
75g (3oz) unsalted butter
3 tbsp golden syrup
1 tsp vanilla extract
2 eggs, beaten
10 tsp vanilla ice cream
4 egg whites
200g (7oz) caster sugar

1 Preheat oven to 160°C/325°F/Gas Mark 3 and line a ten-hole muffin tin with paper cases. Cover dates with boiling water, and add half the bicarbonate of soda. Leave for 10 minutes, then drain.
2 Meanwhile, mix the flour, remaining bicarbonate of soda and baking powder. Gently heat the butter and golden syrup until melted. Pour over the brown sugar, adding the dates and vanilla extract. Then add the flour and eggs; stir to combine.
3 Spoon into cases and bake for 18 minutes. Leave to cool for 10-15 minutes, then transfer to a wire rack.
4 Hollow out the top from each cupcake in a cone shape, and add the ice cream. Press down the cut-out lids and freeze for at least an hour, or overnight.
5 20 minutes before serving, preheat oven to 180°C/350°F/Gas Mark 4. Whisk the egg whites until you have soft peaks, then gradually add the caster sugar, whisking to stiff peaks. Remove cakes from the freezer and top with the meringue. Bake for 3 minutes, then serve immediately.
© Fiona Faulkner for Tate & Lyle, www.lylesgoldensyrup.com/kitchen

December 2013

30 Monday

31 Tuesday

New Year's Eve/Hogmanay

1 Wednesday

2 Thursday

3 Friday

4 Saturday

5 Sunday

If you do one thing

Take time to look back over the past year. Reflect on what you've achieved and learned, then sit down and write a list of things you'd like to do next year – whether it's a health goal such as losing weight, or plans to fulfill a dream or to finally take a much longed for holiday.

School days

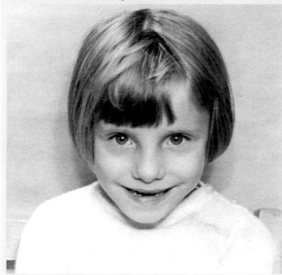

My earliest memory of school was at Willowbrook Infant School in Leicester. There was a houseboat on the brook within the school grounds that we could play on. I also remember the dentist visiting school. We all lined up outside a room and when it was my turn I cried. I was the only child not to get a sticker for being good!

Judith Allen, Leicester

Mini Puzzle

Can you unscramble this conundrum to form a nine-letter word?

I	S	S	U	E	E	C	H	O

(answer Icehouses)

Recipe of the week

Leftover Christmas Pie

Serves: 8
Preparation time: 20-25 minutes
Cooking time: 50-55 minutes

1 tbsp olive oil
25g (1oz) butter
2 large onions, thinly sliced
550g (1lb 4oz) cooked turkey, cut into chunks
1 tbsp fresh thyme leaves, plus extra to garnish
200g (7oz) wholeberry cranberry sauce
500g (1lb 2oz) half-fat crème fraîche
1 tbsp Dijon mustard
1 tbsp cornflour mixed with 1 tbsp water
375g (13oz) packet-ready rolled puff pastry
1 egg, beaten
250g (9oz) leftover stuffing, cut into chunks
450g (1lb) leftover roast vegetables
2 tbsp Parmesan, finely grated

1 Preheat the oven to 180°C/350°F/Gas Mark 4. Heat the oil and butter in a large saucepan, and fry the onions for eight to ten minutes, or until golden and softened. Stir in the cooked turkey, thyme, cranberry sauce, crème fraîche, Dijon mustard and cornflour mixture. Simmer for five minutes, or until thickened, and season to taste.
2 Unroll the pastry and turn a 1.4 litre (2.4pt) oval pie dish on to the pastry. Cut around the rim and then cut another oval around it, about 2cm ($^2/_3$in) away from the rim. Turn the pie dish over and wet the rim of the dish. Arrange the 2cm oval strip over the rim of the dish (cutting to fit if necessary). Brush this with beaten egg.
3 Spoon the pie filling into the dish and scatter the stuffing and vegetables inside. Lift the oval of puff pastry over the pie dish, and press the edges together to seal. Brush with beaten egg. Use any leftover pastry to make a lattice pattern on the pie top. Brush with egg again; scatter with Parmesan and the thyme leaves. Bake for 35-40 minutes, or until golden brown.

© Ocean Spray Cranberries, www.oceanspray.co.uk

Sister act

Tomboy Pat was happiest playing cowboys and indians

What's in a word

Gongoozler

(noun) an idle spectator. First used in the early 20th century. Perhaps, from Lincolnshire dialect gawn and gooze meaning 'to stare and gape'.

Pet of the month

NAME: Roxy

AGE: 3 years

BREED: Jack Russell

OWNER: Jacqueline Littlefield, London

PET LIKES: Sitting on the windowsill watching the world go by, and dressing up for Christmas of course!

PET HATES: The noise of the vacuum cleaner makes her run from room to room

HUMAN TRAITS: Likes nothing more than having a bath, a biscuit and a good old cup of tea!

My sister Pat was born in 1942 when I was five years old. My parents desperately wanted a boy and Pat should indeed have been a boy. While I was happy to be knitting, sewing, colouring pictures or reading, Pat was only happy when playing cowboys and indians with her friend, Alan. She always slept with her gun in her bed and every Christmas she expected to have a new cowboy hat, gun and holster. (One year, someone bought her a doll. With a snort of disgust, she held it by one leg and bashed it against the wall, breaking it to bits!) Pat was afraid of no one. All the kids in our neighbourhood were scared of her and would avoid her when she rode up the street on her bike. Pat always had a bike. She usually had most things she wanted – life was easier that way. While I was a stay-at-home, Pat was always off and away. I hated sporting activities but she revelled in all sports, particularly running, at which she excelled. When she was 18, she joined the army and was soon promoted to sergeant. Although she loved army life, she eventually left, married and had a family. I've always loved her dearly, my sister... our Pat.

Pauline Brown, Walsall, W Midlands

Quiz of the month

Crime thrillers – they're elementary, my dear Watson. If you get stuck, the answers are below

PIC: REX FEATURES

1 In which town does Ruth Rendell's Inspector Wexford live?

2 The Moonstone is said to be the first English detective novel; who wrote it?

3 What nationality was Stieg Larsson, author of The Girl with the Dragon Tattoo?

4 The Big Sleep and The Long Goodbye feature which private investigator created by Raymond Chandler?

5 Which detective wore a deerstalker and smoked a meerschaum pipe?

6 In the TV adaptation of Dalziel and Pascoe, which actor played Detective Superintendent Andy Dalziel?

7 Which of Dorothy L Sayers' detective stories is set in the Galloway region of Scotland?

8 What do P D James' initials stand for?

9 Which country was the birthplace of crime writer Ngaio Marsh in 1895?

10 Who created the crime-solving priest, Father Brown?

11 Which Queen of Crime was married to the archaeologist Sir Max Mallowan?

12 Inspector Morse makes his first appearance in Last Bus to Woodstock by Colin Dexter; in which year was it published?

13 Name the Welsh Benedictine monk who appears in 21 books written by Ellis Peters.

14 Which American crime writer has been dubbed 'The Dickens of Detroit'?

15 Magersfontein Lugg is manservant to which aristocratic detective created by Margery Allingham?

16 In which Dashiell Hammett novel did the crime-solving couple, Nick and Nora Charles appear?

17 In the 1960 TV series, Rupert Davies played which famous Parisian detective?

18 Played by Diana Rigg in the TV series, Mrs Bradley originally appeared in 70 books by which Oxford-born writer?

19 Inspector Alan Grant of Scotland Yard makes his first appearance in The Franchise Affair, written by which Scottish writer?

20 Which TV series is based on the Chief Inspector Barnaby books by Caroline Graham?

Answers: 1. Kingsmarkham 2. Wilkie Collins 3. Swedish 4. Philip Marlowe 5. Sherlock Holmes 6. Warren Clarke 7. Five Red Herrings 8. Phyllis Dorothy 9. New Zealand 10. G K Chesterton 11. Agatha Christie 12. 1975 13. Brother Cadfael 14. Elmore Leonard 15. Albert Campion 16. The Thin Man 17. Maigret 18. Gladys Mitchell 19. Josephine Tey 20. Midsomer Murders

Make mine a sherry

BY: GINETTE POOLEY

Can John and Christine afford Christmas?

John looked down at the bank statement in his hand and frowned. Things were not good. Not good at all.

He would have liked to spend some time juggling the budget to try and make their income match their outgoings better, but Christine was already gathering her shopping bags together and putting on her coat.

"Ready when you are, dear!" she said, brightly.

John mulled over their financial situation as he filled the car up with petrol. Everything had gone up so much lately, that was the trouble. Tapping the last drop of fuel into the tank, he reached for his wallet and wondered what on earth he was going to do.

The pay machine in the car park swallowed up all his loose change. In the supermarket he found himself noting all the prices as Christine strolled around filling their trolley. When had sliced bread shot up to over a pound a loaf, for heaven's sake?

"Are you all right, dear?" Christine asked anxiously as they stacked their groceries on to the check-out counter.

"Hmmm? Oh yes, fine. Fine." John dragged himself back from mentally totting up the items as the girl scanned them. He winced as she announced the final tally. But what could he do? They had to eat.

In the afternoon, Christine surrounded herself with mail order catalogues. She made a list of friends and family and started leafing through for Christmas present ideas.

John sat in his armchair, rubbing his temples. He'd looked at the bank statement again and thought about the bills that remained outstanding. The long and short of it was that they couldn't afford their usual Christmas expenditure, no matter how he added up the figures.

He looked sadly across at his blissfully ignorant wife who was happily jotting down her plans of what to buy whom. Once or twice she jumped up to show him a cardigan that would suit her sister or a board game for the children next-door.

"We could probably do with a new Christmas tree, too," she mused, circling an expensive-looking fibre-optic one. "And port! We must get port this year – we forgot last year and had to make do with a cream sherry."

She frowned suddenly. "Are you okay, darling?"

John nodded, but his heart was heavy. How could he tell her? For all the years they had been married he'd kept them financially secure, even in retirement. But now that his high interest accounts were returning only pennies every month, they were struggling. 'Along with most of the rest of the country, I shouldn't wonder', John reflected silently.

When Christine fetched the phone to place her order, John knew he couldn't delay any longer. With a tremor in his heart, he asked her to wait a moment then placed the bank statement in front of her. As gently as he could, he broke the news that this year they didn't have the funds to run up their usual Christmas bills.

For a moment there was complete silence. Christine stared wordlessly at the bank statement. Then suddenly she jumped up and gave her husband a big bear hug. "Oh, John! Is that all it is? You've been acting so strangely, I thought you were ill or something." Her tears turned to laughter and she kissed the tip of his nose.

John said: "But, darling, I don't think you understand…"

"I understand perfectly," Christine replied firmly. She scrunched up the present list and got a fresh sheet of paper. "We'll just have to economise, like we did when we were first married. Now let's put our thinking caps on and see what we can come up with."

And together they tackled it. John hadn't felt so useful since the day he'd retired, but now he stood humming to himself as he busily bottled chutney and cut slabs of fudge into squares to be wrapped.

They pasted photographs on to hardboard to make jigsaw puzzles for the children and gathered holly and ivy from the hedgerows to decorate the house.

When they went to the supermarket they

They couldn't afford their usual expenditure

PIC: KATE DAVIES

bypassed the boxes of frozen party food and put together an old-fashioned buffet for friends who dropped by on Christmas Eve. Tiny bridge rolls, cheese straws, stuffed eggs and butterfly cakes were eaten with relish and declared delicious. Later, they left the car in the drive and walked across the heath to attend the Christingle service in the church.

In the absence of the computer games they usually bought for the grandchildren, on Christmas Day John took them to play in the park. Was it normal for a 75-year-old gent in his best Sunday trousers to challenge his eight-year-old granddaughter to a skipping race? Probably not,

but John didn't care because suddenly he felt young and free of care.

In the quieter days after Boxing Day, John and Christine sat down and re-jigged their budget to suit their reduced income. They decided to sell their house and move to a smaller property to free up some of their capital.

As they began the process of clearing out cupboards ready for the move, Christine came across an unopened bottle of port in the drinks cabinet. She held it aloft and grinned: "Look, John, we had port all the time and didn't know it."

John smiled back. "Didn't need it though, did we, my love? Sherry did us just as well."